FBI Dan Garrabrandt
Knowledge (M. Thompkins)

Sandy

Somebody's Daughter

Somebody's Daughter

The Hidden Story of
America's Prostituted Children
and the Battle to Save Them

Julian Sher

CHICAGO
REVIEW
PRESS

Library of Congress Cataloging-in-Publication Data

Sher, Julian, 1953–
    Somebody's daughter : the hidden story of America's prostituted
children and the battle to save them / Julian Sher.
        p. cm.
    Includes bibliographical references and index.
    ISBN 978-1-56976-565-4 (hardcover)
    1. Child prostitutes—United States. 2. Child prostitutes—
United States—Prevention. I. Title.
    HQ144.S54 2011
    364.15′34092273—dc22

                            2010030055

Interior design: Monica Baziuk

Published by Chicago Review Press, Incorporated
814 North Franklin Street
Chicago, Illinois 60610
ISBN 978-1-56976-565-4
Printed in the United States of America
5 4 3 2 1

Contents

PART THREE **"Girls Are Not for Sale"**

Author's Note

To protect the young girls and women involved in domestic sex trafficking and to avoid revictimizing them, their names have been changed. No other details of their lives have been altered; there are no composite characters. All the cases described in this book are real, taken from interviews, police files, and court records. The only exceptions where true names are used, sadly, are for those women who have been murdered.

Some quotes have been edited slightly for grammar or clarity.

The terms "child prostitute" and "child prostitution" appear in the book at times because of their wide use in the courts and the media, but they are far from appropriate descriptions. They reduce the victim to an adjective, wrongly implying that the only difference between a minor on the streets and an adult is age. At a minimum, "prostituted child" is more accurate. Child advocates and community workers prefer terms such as "commercially sexually exploited children" or "victims of domestic sex trafficking."

The overwhelming majority of children forced to sell their bodies on the street are girls. Young boys face hardship and abuse as well, but they often fend for themselves to survive. The girls, on the other hand, inevitably fall victim to pimps and organized trafficking networks, which is why they are the focus of this book.

A list of resources for help in the communities and on the Web appears at the back of the book.

Somebody's Daughter

What Happens in Vegas…

"WHEN YOU get to Vegas, you've made it."
Maria could hardly believe her luck. She had been selling her body since she was fourteen on some of the toughest "tracks" in the country—the ghetto corners in Hunts Point in the Bronx, the dark alleys of Philadelphia, the cheap hotels of Boston.

"Do you know how many times I got raped?" she says. "Do you know how many guns I got put to my temples? How many times I had knives to my throat? How many times I got beaten—with hangers, brooms, whips, and belts?"

Now here she was, just seventeen years old, once an aspiring choir-girl from a small town just outside Atlantic City, New Jersey, riding in a white Mercedes-Benz past the dazzling lights on the Las Vegas Strip. She had a pile of money by her side and a snazzy car to drive, and it could not get much better than that.

True, she told herself, the car wasn't hers. The money wasn't hers, either. Like everything else she had, including her body, it all belonged to her pimp. But that didn't matter to the young girl, not then. Nothing was going to diminish the glitter and glamour of this moment. At long last, she had graduated from being a "track ho," working the streets, to a "carpet ho," walking the casino floors.

There was just one refrain running through the teenager's head: *I feel so cool.*

. . .

THE WOMAN stares out from the billboard, wearing a sultry look on her face—and little else.

YOUR PLEASURE IS OUR BUSINESS! is the catchy slogan for a local strip club on the expressway leading to the famous Strip in Las Vegas. But it could just as well be the city's official motto. Everything is for sale here, and nothing sells more than sex.

A big part of what is for sale is illegal sex with minors. The 2009 *National Report on Domestic Minor Sex Trafficking* issued by Shared Hope International put Las Vegas at the top of ten cities it surveyed for the Department of Justice. Shared Hope estimated there were about four hundred young girls being trafficked in Vegas every year thanks in part to what it called a "hyper-sexualized entertainment industry."

On the roofs of taxicabs, big display ads promote "gentlemen's clubs." On street corners, young men hand out flyers to eager tourists announcing toll-free numbers for sexual encounters. The city's Yellow Pages directory boasts eighty-nine pages of listings for "escort services." The section starts with a full-page ad for a "barely legal teen hotline" offering "hundreds of choices" of blonds and brunettes. The next page offers "college teens" and "naughty school girls," and promotions for "teen cheerleaders" and other youthful offerings go on for dozens of pages. Nevada, after all, is a notorious tourist destination because it offers legal prostitution, with close to forty licensed bordellos. It all helps lend what Shared Hope calls a "veneer of legitimacy" to illegal sexual activity with youth.

What many tourists don't realize is that the state still prohibits prostitution in counties with populations of more than four hundred thousand, which includes the largest cities of Las Vegas, nearby Henderson, and Reno. But the geographic niceties of the law don't concern the men who flock here from all over the country and around the world. They are looking for women they can rent by the hour, by the act, or for the night. And they are looking for women of all ages. It is a sad rule of business in the sex trade: wherever women are for sale, the commercial sexual exploitation of young girls is never far away.

"This is the mecca for child prostitution," says Sergeant Detective Gil Shannon. "They all come here."

Shannon should know. He has been a cop in this city for twenty years, most of them with the city's vice unit. And he realizes that his squad's statistics point not so much to success as to the depth of the problem: in the past decade, the Las Vegas police have rescued 1,518 juveniles forced into prostitution from the streets of the city, averaging more than a hundred girls every year. But what happens in Vegas doesn't stay in Vegas. In cities across America, hundreds of thousands of children get caught up in the trade. At least 60 percent of the young children picked up for prostitution-related offenses are not from Vegas.

The number of girls forced to sell their bodies in the streets and in casinos and hotels keeps rising, even as their age keeps dropping. "They are getting younger and younger," Shannon says. Like Maria, they come from all over the country, shipped in by pimps on an underground network that traffics in young flesh. Maria's pimp, a shrewd and ambitious entrepreneur who went by the street name Knowledge, was based in New York and Atlantic City. He had arranged for one of his senior women, nicknamed Lotion, to pick her up at the Las Vegas airport in his Mercedes-Benz. Lotion was tall—Knowledge liked women with height—and pretty, with white-blond hair and a thin body.

"You're going to be a Vegas ho now and that's the best kind of ho to be," Lotion explained as they cruised down the Strip. "This is the best place to be, because Daddy only comes here once every two months to check on us," she said, using the slang term for a pimp. "Daddy" signifies a father figure who requires both submission and affection, someone who professes to love them but will not hesitate to punish them if he thinks they have strayed. "As long as we send him his money all the time," Lotion said, "we can do whatever we want."

Maria's awe turned to anger when they arrived at the comfortable apartment Knowledge kept in Vegas. It came with a two-car garage and a covered parking spot for Knowledge's Mercedes. Inside, it featured wood paneling, expansive carpets, and a wide-screen TV.

"Fuck it! It had to take me this long to work my way out here?" Maria blurted out loud. "We have been living in some shitty-ass place in New York, and this is what you bitches out here have?"

Even as she spoke, she knew the reason. Prejudice is built into the prostitution business. White girls, known as "swans" or "snowflakes" in the trade, are usually a lot more profitable for the pimps than their African American counterparts, called "ducks." It is that simple.

"It's a fact that white women make more money," Knowledge once told the rap music magazine *Ozone*, which called him the most successful pimp in the country. "The average dude that buys pussy is white and they prefer their own kind."

Thanks to her Hispanic background, Maria's light brown skin and straight, dark hair made her somewhat more marketable than the African American girls. But the rules of the game still grated. "If I was white and had blond hair, I'd have been in Las Vegas sooner," she says. "Everybody Knowledge had working there was white except for me." It was her first disappointment with her new life in Vegas. It would not be her last.

That night, dressed in a tight skirt and high heels and carrying a small white purse, Maria set out with Lotion to learn the ropes. "She took me everywhere," Maria recalls. "She wasn't showing me how to be a ho, because I knew how to ho. But she was showing me how to work the Vegas casinos."

Lotion told the teenager where the hottest spots were, where to sit, and where to walk. More important, she gave her tips for staying out of trouble with the law: "Always keep it moving. Never sit for too long. Always move." It was a rule that Maria would soon ignore at her peril.

She had no idea that mistake would help spark a major operation by a new FBI task force that had just been created to rescue children just like her. Maria would find herself at the center of a two-year probe that would shine a light on America's dirty little secret: the exploitation of hundreds of thousands of young girls as prostitutes.

■ ■ ■

"THIS IS my first night out," the skinny teenager said. "So please pray for me."

It was closing on midnight on a hot Phoenix night at the corner of Fifty-first Avenue and McDowell. The girl was talking to a white-haired, soft-spoken grandmother named Kathleen Mitchell. A former prostitute and brothel owner, Mitchell had set up a group called DIGNITY ten years earlier to help women exit the trade. Several evenings a week, the group's members patrol the city's well-known prostitution areas in a white van, offering the young women on the streets some food, water, and a sympathetic ear. They also offer a way out if the women want it.

That night the streets were crowded with garishly dressed pimps, scantily clad women, and prospective clients. Music blared from car radios. One pimp, decked out in green, paraded past on his motorcycle. Another rolled through in his white Cadillac. Still others watched the action from the balconies that lined the hotels near the intersection.

"It was like a carnival," Mitchell says.

She spotted the pretty young girl in the sleeveless top and short skirt and beckoned her over. A pimp, watching her in his rearview mirror, eyed the action suspiciously.

"How are you doing?" Mitchell asked softly, explaining what the DIGNITY program offered. "We just wanted to let you know who we are, and if you need some help, we're here for you," she explained.

"Yeah," was all the nervous teen could say.

"How old are you?" Mitchell asked.

"I'm eighteen," the girl lied.

"Honey, you're not eighteen," Mitchell said, certain the girl was no more than fifteen years old. Mitchell could see the tears in her eyes.

"Do you want to come with us now?"

"I can't," the girl said, trembling as she looked up at the pimp in his car. "I can't right now."

That is when she asked for Mitchell's prayers, and she walked away. "It was so sad," says Mitchell. "I was devastated."

Kathleen Mitchell understood the girl's inability to break free from the bonds of prostitution because she, too, had been trapped, powerless, and trying to delude herself into thinking this was all she deserved. She grew up in Minneapolis, one of five children with two alcoholic parents and little money. Her youngest sister died at eleven months from meningitis. It was her mother, uncharacteristically, who was the more violent parent, prone to throwing things at her father.

What if Daddy leaves? What's going to happen to me? little Kathleen worried. The fear of abandonment marked all her future relationships with men. When she was only nineteen, she married a domineering man who cheated on her constantly. At twenty-six, she left him. Desperate for affection, she fell for an up-and-coming hustler who became a criminal of some renown within the pimping world. "It was horrible and I hated him, but I couldn't leave him." Mitchell says. "I had a fear that if I left, he wouldn't look for me. I was too afraid to find that out."

For twenty years, Mitchell stuck with her abusive pimp partner, through the beatings, arrests, and humiliation. Finally, in 1980, Mitchell decided she was tired of turning tricks for someone else's profit and opened up her own massage parlor and escort service. She became the very successful madam of a very successful brothel. "I had mink coats and fancy cars," she says. "I had all the jewelry you wanted to have. I made a lot of money."

She tried to assuage her guilt about exploiting other women by watching out for the ones she employed. She hid any woman who was running from an abusive pimp, and she would rush out to rescue those who found themselves trapped with dangerous clients. "Kicking down hotel room doors. Throwing hot pots of coffee on people to save the girls," Mitchell says. "I'd even bring guns. Crazy stuff."

Yet she was conflicted; she was sending girls out to do a job she no longer wanted to do herself. "You can't have it both ways," she notes. Mitchell's angst was solved the hard way—she got busted. In 1989, she was indicted on fourteen counts of receiving the earnings of a prostitute, for leading an organized-crime syndicate, and for conducting an illegal enterprise. She pleaded guilty to the felony charge of operating a prostitution enterprise and spent a year in the Durango County Jail. But the short sentence was long enough to be a life-altering experience.

It began with a passage in a book she was reading. She can't remember the book's title but will never forget the words: *We live in a world of lies, and the most degrading ones are the lies we tell ourselves.* Mitchell sat straight up in her jailhouse bunk bed.

"That was my epiphany," she says.

All of a sudden, it was clear that her life was built on falsehoods and fears, on her fear of abandonment by men, her search for validation through prostitution, and her hope for riches through a brothel. She was forty-six years old, and she wanted to change. She needed help.

But in jail, Mitchell found, there was no help for women caught up in prostitution. If you were a drug addict behind bars, there was assistance if you wanted to get clean. If you were an alcoholic, there was a program for you, too. But not for her. And not for all the other women like her.

"I sat in jail and watched women involved in prostitution come and go, a revolving door," she says. "I needed to do something."

She lobbied jail officials to let her set up a support group for prisoners who wanted to get out of the sex trade. She dubbed it DIGNITY, for Developing Individual Growth and New Independence Through Yourself, and she started the weekly meetings with only two or three women. At first it was hard going. Guards teased the women about "going to ho class." Other inmates, no matter how heinous their crimes, looked down on them, too, dismissing them in jailhouse slang as flat-backers. Says Mitchell, "If you're a prostituted person, you are just nothing."

Over time, attendance at the meetings grew, sometimes with as many as twenty women present. Mitchell was committed, even returning once a week after she was released from jail to help lead the group. But outside the prison walls, she discovered the problem was worse, that contempt for women who walked the tracks was greater and the services even more lacking. She would eventually expand DIGNITY into a wide-ranging program that provided outreach services for the women working the streets and a housing and rehab shelter to help those ready to make a break from their pimps.

As a symbol for DIGNITY, Mitchell chose a starfish. The idea came from a story she fondly remembers, in which a man walking along the beach comes upon a child who is picking up starfish that have washed onto the sand and throwing them back into the ocean.

"Why are you doing that?" he asks.

"If I don't, they will die," the child answers.

"But there must be thousands of miles of beaches covered with starfish," the man objects. "You can't possibly make a difference."

And the child says, as she tosses one more starfish into the water, "I made a difference for that one."

...

"I WAS no different than most cops," says Dallas police sergeant Byron Fassett, spitting out chewing tobacco like a big league baseball coach. "I thought, *A whore is a whore is a whore.*"

He wears the uniform of a tough street cop, with a black shirt, blue jeans, and a constantly buzzing cell phone on his belt. He also wears his fifty-plus years well. Only the gray hair shows the strain of what he has seen in the underbelly of his city.

Fassett didn't start off in the tough part of town. He grew up in the wealthy north end of Dallas, a private school football star whose dreams were cut short by a shoulder injury. The early death of his father put a strain on family finances and made a police college grant the only way for Fassett to continue his education. At first he thought he would do the required five years on the force and then quit, but he never did turn in his badge. Indeed, the moment he graduated from the police academy in 1981, he asked to be posted in the rough, crime-ridden southeast section of the city, something few cops—never mind rookies—ever did. Wanting to see action, he found himself in a police station that resembled a fortress, with ten-foot-high fences around the perimeter. "A real eye-opener for a white boy from north Dallas," he says, chuckling at the memory.

By 1986 he had made sergeant, a "blue flamer"—cop slang for someone who shoots through the ranks. Three years after that, he took over the fledging Child Exploitation Unit, which at the time was a small three-officer unit. His first exposure to the problem of prostituted children came in 1992, when a distraught mother, the daughter of a fellow officer, called him for help. Her teenage daughter, Roberta, had gone missing, a runaway.

"I find the kid and she's a prostitute," Fassett recalls. Like many cops, back then he saw prostitution as a victimless crime compared with the mayhem he witnessed in the streets. "Every night I had dead bodies, drug dealers shooting people. I figured if she didn't want to be in this, she would get out of this."

This was, and unfortunately remains, an attitude shared by most people—that these girls are the authors of their own misery. If they don't like the scene, surely they can simply walk away. Besides, they probably enjoy the sex and get paid for it anyway. How is this exploitation?

"I am going after your pimp," Fassett told Roberta with a cop's usual bravado when he first ran into her on the streets.

"I won't testify," she insisted.

"Don't worry, we're going to nail him," the cop assured her.

But Roberta was adamant. "You don't understand. He can do whatever he wants."

She was right; the cop was wrong. Tito "traded off" Roberta to another pimp—a frequent tactic the pimps used to get rid of troublesome girls.

"We lost her," Fassett says.

By seventeen, she was being prostituted across the country. She managed to survive a shooting by a pimp once, but two years later she turned up dead, her body wasted by drugs.

"If I knew then what I know now, I could have saved her. I failed miserably," says Fassett.

That failure gnawed at him. One of Roberta's last police mug shots shows her with pallid skin and sunken eyes, staring listlessly at the camera. "Her eyes haunted me forever," the Dallas cop says. "The life in her eyes was gone."

Shaken by that experience and by other failures to help the teenagers he was spotting on the streets, Fassett tried to get his department to set up something he called the Juvenile Prostitution Diversion Project, pushing it as the right thing to do. But with limited police budgets, the prospect of a new program that would draw money away from other jealous departments was never going to fly. "I got my butt kicked," Fassett admits. "I walked away. No one else gives a crap about these kids. Why should I?"

Except he couldn't walk away. On the street Fassett kept coming upon more girls the system was failing. "It ate me up," he says. "The more we looked, the more we saw."

It would take another decade before Fassett finally succeeded in getting the Dallas police department to set up a pioneering program for prostituted children, one that became a model for police forces across the country. But to do that he had to challenge the very fundamentals of his own law enforcement establishment. The girls he was trying to help didn't see themselves as victims, nor did the cops busting them see them that way. They would be arrested as runaways, petty criminals, drug users, and, often, thanks to fake IDs, adult prostitutes.

Fassett was outraged by what he saw as an egregious double standard. A man who had sex with a minor would be jailed for statutory rape, and she would be treated as the victim she was. But if he left a pile of cash by the bed, she could be locked up as a prostitute, and he might get away with a small fine as a john.

"The justice system knows how to deal with offenders. We know how to deal with victims," Fassett says. "But these kids are both, and they are falling through the cracks."

■ ■ ■

A FRIGHTENED teenager in Vegas, a former brothel madam turned savior in Phoenix, a cop on a mission in Dallas. Three fronts in a battle being waged in the streets of America to save children that most people prefer to ignore.

No one knows precisely how many Marias are out there, forced into prostitution every year in America. These children don't count—and no one is counting them. In a report on what it aptly calls "domestic sex trafficking," the Department of Justice (DOJ) issues this blunt warning: "Among children and teens living on the streets in the United States, involvement in commercial sex activity is a problem of epidemic proportion." Yet it is an epidemic that has gone largely overlooked and untreated.

The most common estimate cited by the DOJ and child protection agencies puts the number of children who are commercially sexually exploited at around three hundred thousand. That figure comes from the only serious study of the problem that has been done—a University of Pennsylvania paper coauthored by Richard J. Estes in 2001 entitled "Commercial Sexual Exploitation of Children in the U.S., Canada and Mexico." For the U.S. portion of the three-year study, researchers chose seventeen cities and then extrapolated their findings for the entire country. They interviewed about a thousand children as well as police and child-care workers, and they gathered statistics from various law enforcement and government agencies.

"Child sexual exploitation is the most hidden form of child abuse in the U.S. and North America today," Estes told reporters when his study was released. "It is the nation's least recognized epidemic."

The irony is that human sex trafficking has become a cause célèbre among many dedicated church and community groups, nongovernmental organizations, and a handful of politicians. But in most cases they focus on the international trade. The U.S. government admirably offers special programs and funding for foreign victims of trafficking but none for domestic victims. The Department of Justice estimates fifteen thousand foreign nationals are trafficked into the country each year for forced labor and sexual slavery. A human tragedy, no doubt, but by all accounts the number of American girls trafficked on American streets is at least ten to twenty times greater.

Yet the United States seems unwilling to recognize that the vast majority of victims of sex trafficking are not foreigners but the girls from next door. It is more comforting to think of prostitution being forced upon children from other countries, not our own. A photo of a sad girl from Mexico sold across the border for sex or the story of a Russian woman tricked into coming to America and trapped in a brothel makes for good fund-raising. But few seem to care about a black girl from the slums of Dallas or a white girl from the wrong side of the tracks in Vegas.

Richard Estes and his colleagues cautioned back in 2001 that their figure of three hundred thousand prostituted children was only an estimate; they called for a more sweeping, better-funded project to "produce an actual headcount of the number of identifiable commercially sexually exploited children in the United States." But such a survey has not happened yet. When Congress looked into the matter six years later, it had to bluntly admit: "No known studies exist that quantify the problem of trafficking in children for the purpose of commercial sexual exploitation in the United States."

There is every reason to believe the "actual headcount" of children forced into prostitution could be much higher than three hundred thousand. Government and police statistics on prostitution, by definition, rely upon official reports of arrests and surveys of children who seek help in shelters and other locations. But many if not most young girls are too frightened, confused, ashamed, or otherwise unable to come forward and be identified as victims of prostitution. In testimony before a special congressional body in 2005, Chris Swecker, the assistant director of the FBI's Criminal Investigative Division, cautioned that relying on crime reports "masks the true prevalence of the problem" since many of the prostituted youth are charged with some other offenses such as substance abuse. "Sex traffickers or pimps debriefed by the FBI indicate approximately 20 to 40 percent of the victims recruited into prostitution are juveniles," he said, indicating that the number of youth sexually trafficked in the United States could be as high as eight hundred thousand.

The real scope of the problem can be gleaned from the number of runaways in America. The DOJ's Office of Juvenile Justice and Delinquency Prevention estimated that about 1.7 million youths between the ages of seven and seventeen flee their homes every year in America. The DOJ classifies more than two-thirds of them as "endangered" because of drugs, criminal activity, and physical or sexual abuse. Those numbers will only increase as the recession and lingering hard times force more children onto the street at the same time as government services are cut back drastically.

How many of those runaways will end up ensnared in prostitution, as Maria did?

Two out of three runaways return home within a week. "However, 33 percent of children who run away are lured into prostitution within 48 hours of leaving home," according to background material prepared for U.S. Senate legislation on runaways in 2009. The Estes study put that number even higher—at more than half. "Approximately 55% of street girls engage in formal prostitution," it reported.

In other words, a significant proportion of the hundreds of thousands of children who run away from home risk falling into some form of sexual exploitation. And make no mistake about it—these are children we are talking about. Not precocious teenagers on the verge of adulthood. A fact sheet about child prostitution on the Justice Department Web site states that the average age at which girls first become victims of prostitution is twelve to fourteen years old.

When these children do get the attention of the system, they are almost always treated as criminals, not victims. And yet the pimps who control them and the johns who purchase sex from minors go largely unpunished. The prostitution of American children is a hidden crime only because we turn our heads and choose not to see. "It's a very dark and quiet crime," says Cynthia Cordes, a federal prosecutor in Kansas City who came up with innovative ways to go after the men who exploit prostituted children. "It happens in areas of town that most people don't go to or don't think about. It happens in the shadows."

This book is about the children whose stories have been in the shadows for too long.

PART ONE

Innocence Lost

1

The Girl from Jersey

LITTLE GIRLS don't dream of growing up to become prostitutes. Maria dreamed of becoming a pastor at her local Methodist church. Dreams are important if you come from a working-class community like Maria's, not far from Atlantic City's casinos, that sees little of the gambling wealth. Simple homes with sparse lawns line the streets. It's a hardscrabble place, but the people make do. On one road leading into the town, a blue welcome sign is adorned with a small rainbow. There are no rainbows on the two signs near the local school that boast the building is not only DRUG FREE but also WEAPONS FREE.

Not far from the school, a stained-glass window and a brown wooden cross dominate a church on Main Street. This was where a young Maria once came to sing every Friday, Saturday, and Sunday with her mother. "I wanted to be in choir," she says.

She was the dutiful youngest daughter of two loving and hard-working parents. She never saw much of her father; he held down two jobs in the service industries. Her mom stayed at home to raise their children. Maria was the baby of the family, with older sisters. "I used to sleep with my mom every night. And I used to hold her every night," Maria says. "I was my mother's little girl."

She was pretty enough to be featured as a model in advertisements for some local stores, wearing cute little dresses and hats. In school, she was attentive and industrious. "I was a great kid," she says. "I was on the honor roll."

But as Maria grew older, the inevitable tensions with her parents set in. She felt a certain unbridgeable distance between her and them. They were traditional and conservative Hispanic; "really old school" is how Maria puts it. And, though loving, they were never very demonstrative. "My parents didn't ever really hug me or kiss me," she says. "It is not like they didn't show me love. The way they showed love was really different."

The differences and distance came into play after Maria, headstrong, tested her boundaries one afternoon to a breaking point. Prostituted children are made, not born, forced onto the streets by myriad circumstances beyond their control, usually some kind of trouble at home and often a trigger event that pushes them over the edge. For Maria, it began in May 1998, when she had just turned twelve. Feeling hemmed in by her parents' rules, she was looking for adventure. "I was never allowed out of the house, ever," she says. "I just wanted to be independent."

She called up her cousin's eighteen-year-old boyfriend, whom she had met a few times at church. "I just wanted to hang out," she recalls. "I wasn't really supposed to go in cars with guys. But he was my cousin's boyfriend. I didn't think he was going to do anything."

He had other things in mind. "He raped and beat me. For two days. Then he kept me in a closet," Maria says. "I pissed on myself and shat on myself. And then he left me on the road." She made it home after two days, but initially she did not tell her parents what had happened, the first of many secrets. They assumed she had just run away briefly. She overcame her shame two weeks later and finally told the truth about the assault. By the time police were called in, scant physical evidence remained. It was her word against that of her assailant. He was not forced to serve any jail time and got off with probation.

Maria was angry and hurt, but then things got worse. At least in the eyes of a troubled twelve-year-old, her family seemed to react to the attack not by showing concern and compassion but by blaming her. They chastised her for misbehaving, for leaving the house without permission, for being wild. The rape never would have happened if she had stayed at home like she was supposed to, they said. Why couldn't she be a good girl?

"They never understood," she says. "My mom never talked to me about it. She was so old-fashioned. It is just the way she was raised. I think that is why she was so sad. I was her little girl and she didn't know what to say."

Deep down, Maria knew that her parents cared about her and that in their own way they were trying their best to cope. They sent her to a psychologist and had doctors pump her with the antidepressants Paxil and Prozac.

For the next year, Maria's turmoil deepened. She turned thirteen, still searching for easy answers to life's complications, in many ways no different from most struggling adolescents. Except the shadow of the rape hung over her. She didn't want drugs to make the pain go away; she wanted acknowledgment of her pain. "What I needed was a hug," she says, "and somebody to tell me that they loved me. That was really all I needed."

She thought maybe she would find that love and acceptance on the street. She ran away from home a few times after the rape but never for more than a day. She first got the idea to leave home when she was watching a movie on the Lifetime Channel, sort of a teenage version of *Pretty Woman*, the Julia Roberts fairy tale about a prostitute who finds romance and riches. Maria sat transfixed as the story of a sixteen-year-old girl played out on the screen before her.

"This little girl was a hooker, and I saw how much money she made," Maria remembers. "Her mom was looking for her. And I think I kind of wanted my mom to look for me. I wanted her to show me more love. You know what I mean?"

Three days shy of her fourteenth birthday, Maria ran away again. This time for good.

Maria was not alone. Every year, more than one and a half million children run away from, or are kicked out of, their homes in the

United States. Thankfully, most return within hours or days. But as many as a third of them, perhaps more, end up selling their bodies to survive.

For Maria, the gambling and tourism haven of Atlantic City was just down the road.

■ ■ ■

THE GAMING capital of the Northeast is a cheesier Las Vegas. In the Nevadan city, the sparkle and glitter goes on for miles; the down-in-the-gutter sleaze is pushed to the extremities. In Atlantic City, the sleaze is in your face. On one side of Atlantic Avenue lies a concert hall for the likes of Barbra Streisand and Neil Diamond. On the other side is a bar that promises "sTopless GoGo," with the *T* capitalized to make it clear the nudity is nonstop as well. GIRLS ON A SWING and OVER 25 GORGEOUS DOLLS, other signs boast.

Although the city's permanent population is only thirty-six thousand, more than thirty million tourists come here each year. The billboard that greets them announces WELCOME TO ATLANTIC CITY. ALWAYS TURNED ON. The sexual allusion is deliberate. Many of the male tourists hope to get "turned on" by paying for sex, and women of all ages seek to satisfy, parading in front of the casinos or behind them on the Boardwalk, which runs between the hotels and the waters of the Atlantic Ocean.

By the summer of 2000, Maria had found a new home.

She had deep, dark eyes and black hair set in braids that ran halfway down her back. She turned heads along the Boardwalk and Atlantic Avenue, and she liked it. One night, outside the Flamingo casino, she met a young woman named Princess. "Skinny and really pretty" is how Maria remembers her.

"How do you keep warm?" Maria asked her, looking at Princess's skimpy outfit.

"Hos never get cold," Princess replied with a laugh. Maria was entranced.

"Oh, yeah," Maria repeated with delight. "Hos don't get cold."

She didn't realize it, but she was being recruited. Although Maria had already started sleeping with men for money, she didn't yet have a regular pimp.

Princess gave the young girl her cell number. "Call me if you want to choose up," she said, using the street slang for choosing a pimp. But Maria, a Boardwalk ingenue, had no idea what Princess meant.

"I thought it was just her way of talking," she says. "I didn't know she had a pimp. I didn't even know what a pimp was."

Maria called Princess the next day, and the older woman sent a cab to bring her to the Red Roof Inn on the outskirts of Atlantic City. They hung out together all day. Princess told Maria how great her "Daddy" was, how generous he was, and how cute. His street name was Tracy, and Princess couldn't wait for her new friend to meet him.

Maria learned her first lesson about pimps right then: they have their own time. It was hours before Tracy showed up, and when he did he had a friend, a business associate named Knowledge, in tow. Partners and sometime rivals, the two men could not have been more different in appearance. Tracy, whose real name was Demetrius Lemus, was "the pretty pimp," as people described him, a handsome Puerto Rican of average height and build with a trim goatee and a pencil-thin moustache. Knowledge, on the other hand, was a hulking presence, a tall African American with a close-cropped beard, deep-set eyes, and a defiant stare. To the impressionable Maria, Tracy was "adorable," while Knowledge was "ugly and fat."

"So, who do you want to be with?" Tracy asked. Maria had already fallen hard for him. "He was Spanish and that kind of reminded me of my dad," she says. "Tracy was sexy and young."

"Let me talk to you real quick in the bathroom," he instructed her.

The pimping world has its own language and laws, and Maria was about to learn both very quickly. In "the life" or "the game," as the prostitution trade is called, the women, known as "bitches," have to submit to a single "Daddy" pimp. They become part of his "stable" and call each other "wives-in-law." A pimp usually chooses his most trusted and experienced woman, called his "bottom girl," to keep the others in line. The golden rule is that when a woman is "in pocket" with one pimp, she is obliged to keep her head bowed in the presence of another pimp and never look at him. "If you got eyes, you got action" is how Knowledge liked to explain it.

In the bathroom, Tracy laid down the law. "This is what you got to do," he said. "When you go out there, you got to put your head down."

Maria was confused. "I got to put my head down?" she asked. "Why?"

"You have to put your head down from now on every time you see any other man 'cause you're in pocket now and you can't disrespect me."

"OK," said the fourteen-year-old.

And she was Tracy's girl. Maria, lonely and shunned by her family, thought she was in love with a man who would shower her with money and affection. Her submission had begun. All the pieces had fallen into place: a traumatic trigger event that tore her from her family, the luring by a "Princess" leading an enchanting and exciting life, a teenage crush on a handsome man.

Maria could not have known then that Tracy was already married with two children. She did not know that he had a vicious, violent streak. She could never have imagined how much Tracy and, especially, Knowledge would soon dominate and eventually threaten her life.

Maria had just joined the underworld of domestic sex trafficking; she had become one of America's prostituted children. "Nobody reports them, nobody is looking for them, and nobody cares about them," says Dan Garrabrant, the FBI agent who would eventually devote two years of his life to rescuing Maria and hunting down her pimps.

"They're the forgotten children."

■ ■ ■

In the beginning, Maria craved the attention, the slinky clothes, and the fast life. Right after their first encounter, Tracy drove his new

recruit to New York City, the center of the operation he and Knowledge ran.

"How old are you?" he asked when they got to his home on
Rochambeau Street in the Bronx.

"Sixteen," Maria said.

Tracy had to know she was lying. By her own admission, Maria
"looked like a baby." Two days later, she told her pimp the truth. "I'm
fourteen," she admitted.

Tracy didn't care. If anything, her youth made her more marketable. The street name he gave her was Baby Girl.

Tracy initiated his new Baby Girl into the business in one of the
toughest prostitution centers in the New York area—Hunts Point, a
warren of dilapidated tenements and dimly lit alleyways in the Bronx.
Maria, still fresh on the scene, got a rush from the excitement and
action on the street. "There were hos everywhere. Pimping and hoing
was the best thing going," she says. She felt sexy and desirable; for
a child of fourteen, it was strangely intoxicating. "I would just walk
around with no bra on, my breasts hanging out, leather boots up to
the middle of my thighs, a thong with my ass cheeks showing."

The pimps packed the corners of Lafayette and Whittier in their
trademark elaborate hats and fancy canes. Tracy and Knowledge were
the exception, opting most of the time for T-shirts and jeans. "It was
just crazy," Maria says. "Just running from the pimps and running
from the cops."

Running from the cops was halfhearted at best, because arrests
were never more than a minor inconvenience. The police considered
adult prostitution a nuisance rather than a crime, while the commercial sexual exploitation of children barely registered on their radar. By
her own count, Maria was arrested around thirty-seven times, at one
point spending as long as seven weeks at Rikers Island, the sprawling,
tough jail between Queens and the Bronx. Whenever she was picked
up by police, she always claimed to be an adult and carried either a
fake ID or none at all. It didn't matter. "They never asked questions,"
she says.

For Maria, jail was never much of a hardship. She was convinced the pimps were bribing the authorities. "Don't worry," said Princess, who was with her the first time she went to jail. "We're golden in this precinct."

"I just sat there with Princess the whole day, and we ate McDonald's and smoked cigarettes," Maria says. "It was like nothing."

As the months wore on, fourteen-year-old Baby Girl fell ever deeper into Tracy's grip. "I thought he was the first guy who cared about me," she says. "I thought he was a man who was actually going to love me."

Maria was not alone. It is not uncommon for victims of abuse to develop a bond with their abusers for a variety of reasons. At a young age, children who are sexually abused by a parent or a person of authority may sense that something is wrong, but they lack the maturity to understand what to do about it. An older woman trapped in a cycle of domestic abuse might struggle to overcome the emotional and physical fears and find the strength to make an escape. Even for an adult woman, complex factors can keep a victim bonded with her abuser unless she gets outside help and intervention. But teenage girls who are pushed into prostitution fall somewhere between because of a unique and potentially dangerous blend of adolescent impetuousness and stubbornness. Too young to recognize they are being manipulated and too old to see themselves as helpless children, they come to endure, if not accept, their own exploitation because, rightly or wrongly, they do not see a better alternative. And all they see in popular culture—from music to movies—is a glorification of the pimping world.

"A bitch's weakness is a pimp's sweetness," says Pimpin' Ken Ivy, a hustler from Milwaukee and Chicago who wrote a bestselling guide to exploiting women called *Pimpology: The 48 Laws of the Game*. One of his most important rules was simple: "Prey on the weak." The women all have a similar story, he says, a history that can be exploited. More often than not, a woman tells him she was "raped as a little girl." "Most hos have low self-esteem for a reason. A pimp looks for that weakness," Pimpin' Ken advises. "Weakness is the best trait a person can find in someone they want to control."

Tracy, like any good pimp, spotted Maria's weakness. She craved the attention she felt she wasn't getting at home. "He showed me love that nobody showed me," she says.

As in all abusive relationships, isolation was central to the pimp's control over the teenager. Tracy did his best to keep Maria cut off from her old way of life. Aside from her clients, she had little contact with anyone but her pimp and the other women in his stable.

"Hos and pimps, we have our own world," she says. "We have own way of talking. Everybody else is 'square.' We are not square, we are 'turned out,' we are turned out to the game."

That insular, isolated existence led to an us-versus-them mentality, a feeling of belonging to her new family and antipathy toward any outsiders who would threaten it. The logic of that world was so twisted that an act that she should have found revolting—a pimp in his midthirties having sex with a fourteen-year-old—she instead saw as a reward. "He let me sleep with him," she says. "And he let the other girls sleep somewhere else in another room."

But there were early signs that Maria was beginning to feel the strain and stress of her life. For one thing, she was exhausted by the long hours, the days running into nights. Then there were the regular, if unpredictable, outbursts of violence. Even Knowledge, Tracy's senior pimping partner, acknowledged that his colleague had a "wicked temper." He once exploded at an airline flight attendant who opened a window shade without asking, and he threatened to kill a waitress who had shown him disrespect. But his worst outbursts were reserved for the women in his stable. "He would be nice and then two minutes later he would be a psycho," Maria says. "He would just snap."

Maria tried to find some comfort in the fact that Tracy beat her less severely than he did the other girls. "If he hit them with a hanger, he would hit me with a belt so the bruises wouldn't be that bad," she says. But she also had enough street smarts to realize that Tracy had good reason to favor the youngest female under his thumb—she was a serious legal liability if she ever squealed to the police.

Slowly and steadily, more signs of her resistance to the pimping game began to emerge. "I used to break the rules," she says with more than a hint of defiance. She would regularly steal glances at rival pimps, breaking the rule about a girl "in pocket."

"I knew exactly what every pimp looked like," she says.

Tracy also wanted Maria, like most of his other girls, to get a tattoo that showed she belonged to him, a common pimp custom that literally brands the women as the pimp's property.

Maria balked. "I didn't do it," she says, "because I never wanted to get branded by his name."

What separated Maria the most from so many of the other girls in Tracy's stable was that, while living in her pimp's world, she still yearned for a return to her normal existence. Indeed, what made her exceptional was that she *had* a normal existence to which she could return. Unlike many of the other young girls on the street, Maria was not fleeing systematic poverty, abuse, or beatings at home.

"There were girls that are just hos. That is all they know. For some of these girls, Tracy was their life," Maria says. "He wasn't my life. I guess it is because I was raised good. Inside, I was never just a ho."

Her family never gave up trying to find her each time she ran away. Her parents had put out posters in the community, and Maria was concerned that even a stranger could recognize her and report back to them.

That tenuous thread to her former life became Maria's lifeline. Over the next few years, an uneasy pattern emerged. Every few months, exhausted by her life on the streets and humiliated by the beatings, Maria would make her way back home, only to find, once back, that reestablishing her life in the "square" world was not as easy as she had hoped.

"Nobody in my family ever understood what I went through," Maria says. Her community was even less forgiving. At the church where she had been a choirgirl, all she heard was a chorus of criticism. "The people in church were hypocrites. They're supposed to talk about love. But no, they talked about me. A lot. I was like *the topic*," she says. "My mom felt bad. She stopped going to church."

School was even worse.

"My boyfriend tells me not to hang out with you," Maria's closest friend told her.

"Why?" Maria asked.

"'Cause everybody is going to think that I am a hooker like you."

Like you. Like she was something dirty to be avoided. Like she had a disease.

"My best friends turned on me," Maria says, her voice cracking. "My girlfriends didn't understand. They just thought I was nasty and I wanted to be a ho."

She suggested they go to the Boardwalk, just to hang out like they used to. "We can't go with you, 'cause everybody is going to know," her friends said.

It became unbearable. The stares, the glares, the whispers. Maria kept switching high schools, trying three different ones in a row, but she couldn't escape the pointing fingers and wagging tongues. For a teenager struggling to find her bearings, it was too much. So she would leave again, go back to Tracy, back to the man she tried desperately to believe really wanted her.

"I thought the only person that cared about me was him," she says. "He never hit me at first when I came back. But then he would find an excuse, and maybe four days later, he would beat the shit out of me."

She would stay a few weeks and then flee once more. A little more time at home, and all Tracy had to do was call her and she'd run back to him. It was a hopeless cycle.

"I knew this life working the tracks wasn't me, but I didn't feel that I fit in at home either," Maria says. In a strange and painful way, people in both worlds saw her with the same disparaging eyes. Maria concluded, "I was just another little whore."

■ ■ ■

PROSTITUTION IS a young woman's game, and Maria, though still a teenager, felt like a veteran. By the time she was seventeen, she had graduated from Baby Girl to a new working name that reflected her seniority: Dynasty.

While never straying far from her pimp Tracy's orbit, she kept shuttling back and forth between the world of prostitution and the "square" world. At one point, she signed up for Job Corps back in New Jersey, a government vocational-training program that allowed young people to learn a trade and earn a high school diploma. A good student before her rape and downward spiral, Maria had never lost her thirst for learning. "I always wanted to know more," she says.

But once again she found that running away from her life on the tracks was never easy. To her dismay, someone recognized her from the street and started a whisper campaign.

"Everyone started looking at me different and I just had to get out of there," she says. She quit and hopped a train to New York, hoping to find Tracy and his stable of women once again. "I knew it was bad to go back to them, but I felt more comfortable with them than I did in my square life," she says.

Back in her old familiar haunts in New York City, Maria made her way to Tracy's home on Rochambeau Avenue. She kept pounding on his door until a neighbor told her the news. "He doesn't live here anymore. I think he went to jail."

It was true; Tracy had been arrested on prostitution-related charges. Alone in New York, Maria decided to walk the dozen or so blocks to the Bronx apartment building on Holland Avenue that she knew was owned by Knowledge, Tracy's fellow pimp. Knowledge had always been the more powerful of the pair. He paid the bills for Tracy's Rochambeau apartment and let Tracy use his cars, even his prized Cadillac Escalade. And when the younger man ended up in jail, Knowledge agreed to run his women and keep their earnings for him until he got out.

Maria knew about Knowledge's clout. She could not forget the time Tracy sent her and several of his other women on a rare trip to Miami to earn some extra cash. They ran into a bevy of Knowledge's girls, all of them better dressed, better fed, and better treated. Or so it seemed to an impressionable girl just starting out in "the life."

"Damn, I wanted to go with them," she says. Knowledge was treating his women to a Caribbean vacation while she and Tracy's other women were packing to return to the cold and dreary streets of the Bronx.

Maria, mindful of becoming what pimps call a Choosy Suzie, a prostitute who switches pimps often, had stuck it out with Tracy back then. But now, with her first pimp in jail, moving up to Knowledge's stable seemed like an attractive option. "I figured it was time for me to be a bigger, better ho—and Knowledge was going to teach me how to do it better," she says.

She knocked on Knowledge's door. The women inside told her the pimp was not home yet, but they called to tell him about the new arrival. It was another four hours before Knowledge showed up, but when he did, it was in his usual style. The brand-new white Mercedes-Benz pulled up to the curb. From the driver's side, out stepped a statuesque woman with long, thick brown hair. Her name was Goddess.

Wow! She is allowed to drive that Benz? Maria thought, suitably impressed and jealous.

Then Knowledge stepped out. While he would never be described as handsome, his immense build—he packed 380 pounds onto a six-foot, four-inch frame—did convey an unmistakable sense of power. Where once she had seen him as overweight, now his size and girth seemed to offer safety and security.

He approached the awestruck teen and asked, "Tracy is in jail, so what are you going to do?"

Maria blurted out that she wasn't sure. Knowledge suggested she stay with him and make money that he would bank for his incarcerated partner. "Tracy is my man, and he has been my man ever since you were a little kid." Knowledge promised, "I will take care of you."

Knowledge called his new girl Suprema, and she did her best to live up to the name even if she was one of the youngest in his stable. "When I was with Tracy I was just a track ho," Maria says. "But I wanted to be a carpet ho like everybody else. I wanted to walk the carpet in the casinos, too."

The pimp started his new acquisition at the bottom. "Don't think you are going to get all the privileges my hos get," he warned her. "Don't think you will be riding in my car or driving my car."

Maria was bitter. "He kind of fucked me with that," she says. "I had to work myself up."

She started by working the New York tracks for Knowledge. The sex as always was perfunctory—a chore, never a pleasure.

"You don't even like the sex," Maria says. "It has never been anything to me, because I got raped. I got it taken away from me and I tried to turn it around and change it into something that benefited me, to make money."

She learned early how tightly Knowledge controlled the money and his women. One day, Maria stepped outside for a smoke on the front stoop of the Holland Avenue home. "What the fuck are you doing?" Knowledge scolded her when he found her. "You're not allowed to sit out here."

"What?" asked a startled Maria. Her pimp told her bluntly he didn't want the women in his stable interacting with the neighbors.

"It was like a prison," Maria later recalled. "Because you can't leave."

Except on Knowledge's orders. He dispatched her to an infamous track on Kensington Avenue in the tough northeast end of Philadelphia. As seedy and rundown as Hunts Point back in the Bronx, it was much more frightening, with constant beatings and stabbings. Murders were not uncommon. It was risky enough for the older women who walked that track; Maria was all of four feet, eleven inches. "I got hit and beaten up there so many times," Maria says. "It was really scary at nighttime."

She called her "daddy" to beg him to let her come back to New York, but he made her tough it out. And for the first time ever, she broke a thousand dollars in earnings in a single night. She was so excited she could not wait to tell him. "I felt with the more money I made, the more he liked me," she says.

She lost weight and let her hair grow long. She was getting older and prettier, and Knowledge now had someone more valuable he could market upscale. "It is time for you to learn how to work in a casino," he told her.

He sent two of his older women, Goddess and Madonna, to teach Maria the basics of operating out of the gambling joints in Atlantic City. At the start, they also collected her earnings to make sure Knowledge got his full take. Nonetheless, Maria was thrilled. She was on her way to becoming a carpet ho.

But for a girl from New Jersey, being so close to her home came with risks, because her family was always on the lookout for her. One night as she looked for clients in the casinos, a friend of the family did spot her and called the police. The officers had to tie up a furious Maria's hands and feet to get her into their cruiser, but not before she managed to break her cell phone. A wise precaution, because the phone had Knowledge's frequently dialed number stored in it. At the station, she was released into her parents' custody, only to bolt from home soon afterward.

"You broke your phone?" Knowledge said with a mixture of pride and amazement when his Suprema returned to the fold. "You are such a smart bitch!"

He decided it was safer for Maria to move back to New York. But keeping her away from her concerned family—and the lucrative tracks of Atlantic City—cut into her earning potential. By Thanksgiving weekend, nearly two months later, Knowledge had had enough. "Damn, you haven't been my bitch for that long for me not to work you somewhere," he complained.

That's when he hit on the idea of shipping her to Vegas. Knowledge bought Maria a new wardrobe and sent her to get her hair and nails done. It was December 2003. After three years of walking the streets of New Jersey, New York, Boston, and Philadelphia, this was Maria's big chance.

■ ■ ■

LAS VEGAS was big time, with big money and even bigger dreams. She had no illusions. She knew this was an investment on Knowledge's part, not a sign of his affection. Still, Maria could barely contain her excitement. She was certain she would love Las Vegas and Vegas would love her back. She was young, pretty, and selling what many there wanted to buy: sex.

But the girl who had done so well for Knowledge in Atlantic City, New York, and Philadelphia couldn't seem to find her stride on the tracks of Vegas. She was nervous, out of her league, and overwhelmed.

"I felt like I was this tiny little person in this huge place. It was too much pressure," she says. "You are supposed to make a thousand dollars a night out there, and I am like, how the fuck do you make that?'"

After three days, the glitter of the desert gambling-and-sex capital was wearing thin. Maria grew increasingly frustrated. "I wasn't making a dollar. I wasn't making nothing at all," she says. "And I thought, *Knowledge is going to hate me.*"

Indeed, Knowledge vented his anger with her over the phone from New York. "I don't know what I am going to do with you," he told her. "I am probably going to have to bring you back here."

Things got worse when Lotion, the woman who had given Maria the basic lessons for surviving on the Vegas Strip, was herself arrested on a simple prostitution charge. Knowledge ordered Maria to drive downtown to the police station to bail Lotion out. He wired her the money to post the bond.

That's how Maria found herself driving through the streets of Vegas in the white Benz, a tempting pile of money at her side. Feeling "so cool" because she had made it. If ever there was a moment in her life when she felt on top of the world, this was it—the heat of the Vegas action, the fancy car, the cash, the illusion of power and freedom.

And yet maybe it was the sense of being at the peak of her game that also brought out in Maria the depth of her despair. As happened so many times during her years of working the tracks, Maria found herself torn between her two worlds. For a brief moment, she entertained the prospect of making a break, running away from it all.

I could just leave right now, she thought. *With this Benz and all this money.*

She called one of her older sisters back in Jersey. "I just really want to come home," she told her.

"Come back," her sister urged.

Maria was teetering on the edge again, caught between her life on the streets and the one she had fled. Home may have been humiliating, with everyone looking at her and judging her, but it was safe. She wavered. As much as she wanted out of "the life," she also had an overriding fear of Knowledge's wrath if she attempted to leave.

Her pimp, a keen reader of people who liked to credit his success to his "pimptuition," sensed her unease. He talked to her on the phone that day for several hours. He was understandably nervous; his seventeen-year-old Suprema had become his lifeline in Vegas. "He called me because I knew where all the money was, I had the car, and Lotion was in jail," she says.

Knowledge tried to sweet-talk Maria, as he always did. He promised to make her a star at his recording studio in New York, aptly named Hoodlum Records. "We are going to be rich together," he told her. And once again Maria was swayed by his entreaties of love and affection. She decided to stick around—"only for a few more days," she told herself.

But since the age of fourteen she had been telling herself the same story. *Just a few more days, a few more weeks, and I am out of this life.*

To please Knowledge, Maria had even written the lyrics to a rap song, hoping his Hoodlum studios would make it a hit:

I wasn't raised in the hood with roaches and rats
I told you I'm from the 'burbs with welcome door mats

Life is a hustle so I'll gets me mine
Yeah I was paying a pimp, breaking myself for every dime
From Hummers to Benzs, Pimp of the Year
I was down for his crown

You like the way he touches you
You don't have a clue

Every bitch got hope, potential
Running to some pimp, you don't need no credentials

The words capture Maria's anguish, her independent spirit as a girl who had hope and potential, yet at the same time they express loyalty, almost love, to her "Pimp of the Year."

"You get brainwashed," says Maria. "I got addicted to a lifestyle. I was going to be a hooker for the rest of my life."

2

High-Risk Victims

HELPING MARIA and the tens of thousands of girls like her was never going to be easy. It would take not just people who cared enough to do something but people who understood how to help, not alienate, the girls trapped in the life. Understood what pushed a child into prostitution. Understood it was not by choice but because of a collision of circumstances beyond a girl's control. Understood the grip a pimp could wield over an impressionable teenager.

Slowly, painfully, by the late 1990s and into the early decade of the new century, the landscape in the battle against prostituted children began to change on two important fronts. In the communities, former prostitutes, women who once were in the same position as Maria and were now trying to help those still out there, began to set up shelters and rehab programs. At the same time, a few farsighted and caring cops also began to shake things up, taking on the misconceptions and the prejudices within the police bureaucracy and the entire justice system. The change began with several local police forces and eventually spread to the upper reaches of the FBI.

The cops and the community workers would not always see eye to eye. They would clash over whether detention or voluntary treatment was the best way to help these girls. They would disagree over how much pressure should be brought to bear on the young girls to get them to testify against their pimps. But everyone agreed that to stand any chance of changing the lives of prostituted children, they first had to change the very way the system looked at them.

...

As FAR back as the early 1980s, a handful of organizations on the
East and West coasts dedicated themselves to helping children forced
into prostitution.* In Connecticut, the Paul and Lisa Program, started
with a grant from a local church, reached out to thousands of children
at risk through education in schools, detention centers, and on the
streets. In California, Dr. Lois Lee, a scholar turned activist, set up a
drop-in center for street children who had come to Hollywood with
dreams of stardom only to face the nightmares of drugs and prostitution. Her Children of the Night organization grew into a well-funded
live-in shelter and recovery center that became one of the preferred
placement centers for girls picked up by law enforcement across the
country.

But in the late 1990s, a new type of community group emerged,
with a more political and social edge, built by women who understood
the ravages of prostitution because they had lived it, survived, and
now determined to help other women. In Phoenix, former brothel
operator Kathleen Mitchell was bringing DIGNITY to women on the
streets and behind bars with a strong focus on treating prostitution
as an addiction. In Minneapolis-St. Paul, Vednita Carter, an African
American stripper turned activist, looked to the past and the vestiges
of slavery in modern-day prostitution to help young girls break free.
And in New York, a onetime prison missionary named Rachel Lloyd,
who as a teenager was nearly killed by her pimp, wanted to empower
young girls to become survivors with the strength to change the very
laws that oppressed them.

For Kathleen Mitchell, her arrest on prostitution charges in 1989
ended her career as a brothel owner and launched her calling as an
advocate for women of all ages forced into prostitution. Her time in
prison opened her eyes to the plight of the young women behind bars
who were trying to leave the sex trade, but once she left prison she

---

* For a list of groups helping sexually exploited children, see the Resources for Help section
at the end of this book.

discovered an even greater need for her DIGNITY program on the streets. It struck home as she watched a young woman named Kathy, whom she had befriended in the Durango jail, try to survive on the outside.

Authorities released Kathy from jail in the dark of night, around 2:00 A.M., a common practice back then, Mitchell says, and one that often caused the newly released prisoner to step right back into prostitution. Ordinary people didn't care much about prostitutes; why should people who run prisons care any more? Kathy was picked up by a man who took her to a hotel and got her high. "Then he beat her badly, burned her with cigarettes, and told her to go out and make some money," Mitchell says.

Kathy was rearrested soon after, and her pimp promptly bailed her out. The sorry cycle continued—drugs, beatings, arrests. "I'm afraid to leave," Kathy complained to Mitchell the last time she was incarcerated. "But I'm not going to jail for him again."

Not long after, police found her body in the desert outside of Phoenix, her throat cut from one ear to the other. "If there was a place she could have gone when she walked out that door, then maybe she could have lived," says Mitchell.

The seed was planted: young women trying to get out of the life needed a safe place to recover and rebuild. That conviction was reinforced when Mitchell got a job at a shelter for women fleeing domestic violence, only to discover that disdain for sex trade victims was rampant even among battered women. She befriended Karen, who was just nineteen when she came to the shelter with two infants, trying to escape the pimp who had fathered them.

"The women would look differently at her," Mitchell says. "They started pulling their kids away from her."

When Mitchell came back to work after one weekend, she found a note from Karen. *I'm sorry, I could not stay*, the teenager wrote. *I don't think anybody knows what it feels like to be a disposable person.*

Mitchell was heartbroken and enraged. "That was one of the saddest things I had ever heard in my life," she says.

She decided that no more women in Phoenix should be made to feel they are disposable, not if she could help it. With assistance from the local Catholic Charities Community Services, she got a small grant in 1995 from the city to fund a street outreach project. The program tried to teach women basic life skills and provided transportation for women released from jail to a safe place. Mitchell also put out a small newsletter called *We're Closed*, adapting the name from a common expression women would use when they could not stand the thought of turning another trick after a long night: "Sorry, I'm closed."

"It's empowering to say no," says Mitchell.

DIGNITY had moved from the jail cells to the streets. By the next year, Mitchell had secured enough funding to go one step further, with a residential house providing shelter and a rehabilitation program for women who had left prostitution. They began with five women, eventually expanding to fifteen beds. From the start, Mitchell found that getting the women off drugs and keeping them straight were integral to having them think differently about themselves.

"You either prostitute to get money for drugs or you start prostitution and you use drugs to forget about what you're doing," she says. "They pretty much go hand in hand."

Kathleen Mitchell had come a long way since her days as a brothel madam in the 1980s. But the prostitution scene had also changed dramatically. Over the years Mitchell watched as the women on the tracks became younger and younger. And that meant DIGNITY had to chart new programs for young girls forced into prostitution if Mitchell wanted to make a difference and save more "starfish."

• • •

VEDNITA CARTER had started the summer of 1972 with the best of intentions. A bright young African American woman, she was attending college in St. Paul, Minnesota, and thought she would make some money over the summer. Instead, she ended up with a very different kind of education.

Carter saw an ad in the newspaper for "dancers who wanted to make big money." A thousand dollars a week—a lot of money for a young woman trying to pay for college. Carter soon found herself caught up in the stripping industry. She began using cocaine and got involved with a man who encouraged her to start making more money by selling sex.

Carter was struck by the prejudices built into the prostitution world, the ever-present discrimination between swans and ducks. "The black and Hispanic women got sent to all the dangerous dives, and the white women would always get the high-class clubs," Carter says. "I was treated differently because of my color."

Fortunately, Carter's brush with the sex trade lasted less than a year. "I had support systems, friends, and family," she says.

She managed to get out with her health and hopes intact, but that exposure to the raw side of life changed her. Although she returned to school, she never managed to get her degree. Instead, like Mitchell, she began counseling incarcerated women. For six years, she directed the women's services program for an activist group called WHISPER (Women Hurt in Systems of Prostitution Engaged in Revolt), though the name did not do justice to the group's militancy. The women roared their anger against the violence visited upon women of the streets and against what they saw as misguided attempts by predominantly white middle-class feminists who sought to paint prostitution as "a form of sexual liberation." One of WHISPER's best-known campaigns was a bitterly sarcastic help-wanted ad that played on the limited opportunities for poor minority women.

> Are you tired of mindless, low skilled, low-paying jobs? Would you like a career with flexible hours? Working with people? Offering a professional service?
>
> ▪ No experience required. No high school diploma needed. No minimum age requirement. On-the-job training provided.
>
> ▪ Special opportunities for poor women—single mothers—women of color.

The WHISPER ad ended with the warning:

- Injuries sustained through performance of services include but
are not limited to cuts, bruises, lacerations, internal hemorrhaging,
broken bones, suffocation, mutilation, disfigurement, dismember-
ment, and death.

NOTE: Accusations of rape will be treated as a breach of contract by
employee.

With limited funding, WHISPER tried to offer some women a shelter from the vicissitudes of that kind of life, but the group fell apart in
the early 1990s. Carter was devastated by its demise. "Women were
breaking down, they were on their knees crying," she says. "This was
their place of refuge. Now they had nowhere to go."

Carter wanted to be sure the forgotten women of the Twin Cities
had somewhere to go. In October 1996, she founded Breaking Free
in one of the toughest, poorest neighborhoods on the east side of St.
Paul. From the start, it would have a strong, angry voice.

"We understand prostitution as a vicious cycle of violence, incarceration, and addiction," says its statement of principles, drawing
inspiration from WHISPER.

Carter scrounged together what funds she could from government
and private donors. Breaking Free was able to offer transitional housing where young women could leave their pimps and learn the basic
skills required to live independently. A special youth program targeted
girls between the ages of fourteen and eighteen who had been referred
by the courts or came from the overcrowded homeless shelters.

But Carter wanted to do more than provide the young women and
girls with a roof over their heads. The overwhelming majority of the
victims she was helping were black women, trapped in poverty that
made them especially vulnerable to prostitution. African American
women, including prostituted underage girls, are pushed to the most
dangerous areas of the industry, the deserted streets and the seediest
strip clubs and motels.

In what little spare time she had, Carter began studying the history
of slavery and came to an important conclusion. "The legacy of physi-

cal, sexual, and psychological abuse continues to have lasting, scar-
ring effects on the lives of many African American women," she says.
"Prostitution is an extension of slavery."

In the coming years, Carter would expand her analysis in articles in
academic and legal journals. She sharpened her criticism of the racism
that contributes to pushing minority women into prostitution. But she
was also forced to challenge the pimp culture within a community still
shackled by what Carter saw as the invisible chains of slavery's legacy.

· · ·

IT TOOK seventeen stitches to close the cut across the palm of Rachel
Lloyd's right hand. The scar is a permanent testimony to how close
her pimp came to killing her.

"It's a reminder of how many emotional scars abuse can leave and a
reminder of why I do what I do," she wrote in her online biography.

Lloyd strides through the streets of Harlem on her way to the
offices of Girls Educational and Mentoring Services (GEMS), the
groundbreaking organization that she built and heads, with the same
purposeful intensity that marks all her work. She has long dark hair
and deep, intense eyes, and as she answers yet-another cell phone call,
there's more than a little trace of the accent that reflects her British
roots. GEMS is located in one of the reclaimed neighborhoods of
Harlem. There's a Starbucks a couple of blocks away, and renovated
homes dot the tree-lined streets. But the gentrification only goes so far:
a poster outside the police station just around the corner from GEMS
offers a hundred dollars for stolen guns, "no questions asked."

There is no sign identifying GEMS on the outside of the building
that serves as its headquarters; for safety reasons, the group does not
want to advertise that this is a refuge for hurt and vulnerable young
girls. But there is one indication that this is no ordinary building in
the corner of the glass front door, where a small picture of a smiling
girl with long, frizzy hair is taped to the glass. Underneath her face are
the dates of her birth and death at just twenty-three years of age. One
of the girls who didn't make it. "You are a diamond that will always
sparkle in our lives," the poster says.

Lloyd's own sparkle was nearly snuffed out when she was a teenager struggling to survive in England. At thirteen, she left school to support an alcoholic mother, and after stints in factories and restaurants she drifted into petty crime. She drank and did drugs. A rape and three failed suicide attempts put her in the hospital. "I continued to slip through the cracks of a system that would eventually give up on me," Lloyd wrote. At seventeen, she tried to make a new start in Europe and ended up in Germany, only to find herself hopeless and broke, turning her first trick in a Munich strip club as a way to survive. She was a prostituted youth for two years, until a crack-crazed pimp tried to kill her. Ironically, that attack also gave her chance to take her life back.

She found refuge in a church where what she calls "some good folks" took her in and gave her much-needed care—and a new calling. "I realized God didn't put me on this earth for this," she says. "I needed to find out what God intended for my life." It didn't take her long. In 1997, she came to the United States to work as a missionary in prisons with women trying to leave prostitution, much like Kathleen Mitchell and Vednita Carter had done. She was dismayed to discover there were even fewer services for the young girls who were around the same age she was when she got into the life. "I was seeing girls being cycled in and out of prison," Lloyd says. "I felt compelled to start something."

Two years later, at age twenty-three, with little more than idealism to guide her, Lloyd created GEMS as a kitchen table project in her home. In the next decade, it grew to become one of the country's most active organizations fighting commercial sexual exploitation. Like its sister groups that were beginning to take shape in other cities, GEMS offered shelter and a strict tough-love approach to rehabilitation. But with a twist.

"We're the only one committed to survivor leadership," says Lloyd. "There is something very empowering and very healing in helping other people as part of your own recovery."

The GEMS girls who had made the break from their pimps went back out into the streets at night and into the juvenile detention centers as part of an organized outreach program to speak to other teens still caught up in that world. That commitment to empowerment even-tually led Lloyd and her girls to do a lot more than outreach. They took on the politicians and power brokers in New York, setting their sights on not just changing their lives but changing the very laws of the country.

Perhaps not coincidentally, Lloyd, Carter, and Mitchell all started their work with women behind bars. They had seen the worst of what prostitution had to offer women, the women society had discarded and abandoned. They knew that they were fighting against something that the public—much less the police and politicians—did not want to know about. And they knew that rescuing girls like Maria is not like saving damsels in distress, charging in like white knights and carrying them off to a happily-ever-after. It is about respecting them, offering them hope, and nourishing the inner strength they need in order to break the very strong bonds of prostitution.

It was a lesson that law enforcement had to learn as well.

■ ■ ■

FOR YEARS, Byron Fassett struggled to bring that same insight to an institution not always known for its sensitivity—the police. As head of the Child Exploitation Unit, the Dallas sergeant had his hands full with murders, kidnappings, and online child predators. But he and his officers started investigating child prostitution cases informally, above and beyond their normal duties. In 1995, Fassett approached an aggressive prosecutor in the district attorney's office, Tim Gallagher, with evidence that the number of prostituted children was growing in the Dallas area.

"Let's tackle it," Gallagher said.

Police busted a ring that was moving young girls between Memphis and Dallas; one of the pimps in charge got thirty years behind bars. But that was the exception. For the next several years, successful pros-ecutions were few and far between. "The pimps were better at dealing with us than we were at dealing with them," says Gallagher.

Fassett was not prepared to give up. Like the community activists, Fassett realized that cops have to understand what drives young girls into prostitution if they stand any chance of helping them. Like any good detective, he began to investigate the problem. He felt sure he was missing something, that he was not seeing the wider picture—and if he could not, then how could the justice system?

All through 2003 and 2004, Fassett patiently reviewed the cases of children arrested for prostitution in the Dallas police system. He discovered an overwhelming and largely overlooked trend: they were almost all runaways. Three out of four of them had fled their homes for one reason or another; almost half of them were repeat offenders, having run away more than four times. Girls like Nancy, first spotted as a runaway in September 2003 when she was fourteen. A police photo shows her as a cute young teen in a red top. Within a year, police had picked her up at least eight more times as a runaway. Her face had turned angry and pale, her hair was a mess, and her arms shook with the involuntary tremors of a crack addict. Eventually she was locked up in prison as an adult on charges of aggravated robbery. Another child lost.

It is a disturbing pattern: they start as runaways, then become prostituted children, and when they become adults under the law they are "just" prostitutes—punished, processed, and penalized by the system.

Fassett discovered that the police and the courts were spending countless hours and money finding children like Nancy and returning them to their parents or foster homes, only to have the girls bolt again. He calculated that each runaway cost the city several hundred dollars every time the child was picked up and returned home. Multiply the numbers of repeat runaways, and the situation added up to a pile of wasted taxpayer dollars. Now Fassett had something he could bring to his police chief besides a conviction that the right thing had to be done. He promised he could turn the situation around with only a small budget and a handful of investigators.

At the end of 2004, the chief gave him two patrol officers to run a test program over six months. Fassett never looked back. He dubbed his team the High Risk Victims and Trafficking (HRVT) unit, a deliberate choice of words that made child prostitution neither a vice nor a moral issue but a crime of abuse. The officers set up shop in a corner of the third floor at police headquarters, but it would be some time before they would feel at home.

Prejudices against prostitution die hard, and from the start the team had to battle indifference, even outright hostility, within its ranks. There was grumbling when the HRVT unit officers began interviewing arrested girls in the more comfortable surroundings of their offices instead of keeping them in the holding cells on the first floor. That violated the juvenile code, Fassett was told. So he went before the Juvenile Board and got his interview rooms designated as a "certified juvenile holding facility."

The contempt toward the girls was always there, however. Once, when an HRVT member was walking out of a police station with a victim she had just rescued, one of the officers shouted out derisively, "Why you bothering? She going to be back soon anyways—she's a ho."

But slowly the HRVT squad began to gain support in the rank and file. Members of the unit made up small laminated cards and handed them out to every officer on patrol, announcing a new protocol:

When a juvenile is found involved in or connected with prostitution or a juvenile is found violating curfew in a high prostitution area, contact a High Risk Victims Squad detective.

The card also listed a twenty-four-hour cell phone number. The result was that the endangered children on the street started getting flagged—and getting help. The street cops were pleased with the arrangement; Fassett's team did all the work but was more than glad to let the beat cops get the credit for it.

Every time a child's case file came across their desks, they put a large red stamp that read HRVT on it. In a bureaucratic system that shuffles paper and often forgets the children whose names are written on the sheets, the stamp was like planting a red flag. "Once you label a kid, they can't turn their heads," Fassett explains. "We were going to be a thorn in their sides until people listened."

The new system of flagging runaways soon produced results. Patty was the first girl the HRVT team found—although "found" is perhaps not the right word, since she had long been in the system, just ignored. She had thirteen runaway incidents, beginning at age twelve. Her mother had had a series of boyfriends traipsing through her home; Patty alleged one of them sexually abused her, but no one believed her. She attempted suicide, ran away several more times, and fell into prostitution. All of her sorry history was dutifully logged in the police and court system, but no one had paid much heed.

But in November 2004, she was finally identified as a high-risk victim. Fassett's unit stepped in and brought charges against the man who had assaulted her, and Patty was eventually placed in a decent foster home. "She thrived after that," says Fassett, noting with almost fatherly pride that she made straight A's in school. A first real success story for the new unit.

The High Risk Victims Unit started showing up in court to urge the judges and prosecutors to take these cases more seriously. In one case, the team intervened to stop the courts from releasing a girl into the hands of a pimp who claimed to be her father. In another, they stopped the courts from returning a runaway to her mother, who was beating her with a board. "By documenting these cases, by showing up in court, the judges started asking questions and people started paying attention," says Fassett.

It worked. Judges who previously had taken fifteen minutes to dispose of a case now spent a couple of hours deliberating. The district attorney's office devoted new resources to the problem. Tim Gallagher had taken over as head of the DA's Organized Crime Bureau; he assigned two prosecutors to handle prostituted-child cases and develop an expertise in a legal arena fraught with difficulties. "The public's attitude generally was that these kids were criminals," Gallagher says. "In the process of the trials, we had to educate the jurors and sometimes the judges."

Byron Fassett aimed for nothing less than revolutionizing the way the entire justice system, from the cops on the street to the judges and prosecutors, looked at juvenile prostitution.

"There was absolutely no one who advocates for these kids. Our goal from the onset was to get them viewed as their own class of victims. These girls weren't running to something, they were running from something," Fassett concludes. "We didn't have a prostitution problem, we had a runaway problem. And we were ignoring both."

. . .

IN OTHER cities, the same pattern emerged. Once they started looking, police found a problem they had been ignoring on the very streets they were supposed to be patrolling. In California, Oakland police identified 293 teens under eighteen being prostituted by at least 155 pimps between the end of 2001 and the middle of 2003.

"In hard times, police become the safety net of last resort," says Sergeant William Finnie. He surveys his beat in Midtown Manhattan—two city blocks of jammed escalators, packed hallways, and rushing commuters at the world's busiest bus terminal, the Port Authority. Each day, nearly two hundred thousand people pass through here, and Finnie leads a special police squad of youth officers on the lookout for runaways. They watch for the stragglers, for the young, nervous teens who get off the bus, often with no luggage and nowhere to go.

Tacked to the wall in the terminal's small police station is a poster of a Norman Rockwell painting called *The Runaway* that is reminiscent of a more innocent time, with a little boy carrying a red hobo bundle at the end of a stick, sitting next to a cop and a clerk at a soda fountain. Today's reality is less idyllic; the bulletin boards at the cop shop are covered with dozens of "Missing Kids" notices, and one dark poster warns LIFE ON THE STREET IS A DEAD END.

The Port Authority police pick up about three thousand runaways, or DOEs, as they call them—"danger of being exploited"—every year. Sometimes a pimp has paid for the child's bus ticket; sometimes the child is coming at the request of someone she or he met on the Internet. One of Finnie's cops stopped a sixteen-year-old from Illinois when he noticed she had worn-out clothes but on her feet were shiny red stilettos her pimp had given her. There was a baby-faced twelve-year-old who stonewalled Finnie's team for hours until she broke down and admitted she had come to New York to prostitute herself. Another time, it was a thirteen-year-old whose confession of being part of a human-trafficking ring led to the arrests of twenty people.

"This is where they come—the children with big dreams in the Big Apple," says Finnie. "If we can stop them before they head out that door into the city, maybe we can save them."

In Boston, detective Kelly O'Connell, a twenty-two-year veteran of the force who cut her teeth fighting the tough street gangs in the city, pulled all the police records of teen runaways and found four hundred girls between the ages of eleven and seventeen caught up in prostitution. She also discovered that, in most of the cases, the pimps were not just random criminals but senior members of some of Boston's most sophisticated and violent street gangs.

"Gangs used to make their money selling drugs and through other illegal means," she says. Prostitution wasn't incidental to the city's burgeoning gang violence. It was one of its causes.

O'Connell began compiling intelligence on gang members she suspected were involved in pimping. She put together mug shots of them and collated them into a book she titled *Street Predators*, which she updates and sends out regularly to all the stations. Each page has two or three photos, with the names and other identifying details kept on a separate sheet so witnesses can be shown the faces as part of a photo lineup. By integrating child prostitution into daily police antigang procedures, she began to change the way it was handled. And she started going after the pimp gang leaders, one after another.

But as awareness of the problem grew, local investigators across the country began to realize that they could not solve a national crime problem in one city alone. Since the pimps were well connected, organized, and networking across state lines, from one coast to the other, law enforcement was going to have to do the same. And that meant the FBI had to enter the battle.

The initiative to prod the federal agency into action came from a Florida probation officer turned FBI agent with a passion for helping children. After graduating from the FBI Academy in 1992, Eileen Jacob got assigned to the Crimes Against Children unit in the Bureau's

San Francisco office, where she opened up a few cases on child prostitution. Or, as the FBI quaintly called it at the time, the "white slave trade."

The term was a holdover from the nation's first major antiprostitution law introduced in 1910, which was officially called the White Slave Traffic Act, though it was more commonly known as the Mann Act after its main congressional proponent, Representative James Mann. Enacted during a period of social upheaval and moral panic, the law talked about "prostitution or debauchery" and over the years had been used with dubious merit against such celebrities as Chuck Berry, Charlie Chaplin, and Jack Johnson, America's first African American heavyweight champion.

The FBI's use of the anachronistic label "white slave trade" nine decades later was symptomatic of how the Bureau, like much of law enforcement, was out of touch with the changing face of prostituted children in America. The colors of those faces were changing, literally, from the start of the century when the White Slave Traffic Act got its name; there were a lot more black and Hispanic girls being recruited into the trafficking networks. The same kind of black and Latino victims who had historically been overlooked by law enforcement and the media—a missing white girl from a middle-class suburb would often get a lot more attention than yet another runaway from the inner city.

Nevertheless, to its credit, the FBI had a strong tradition of going after criminals who harmed children, from murderers to interstate kidnappers, and had already proven itself quick to adapt to the evolving trends of crimes against children. As far back as 1996, the FBI had set up the Innocent Images initiative to tackle the new threats of Internet predators and child abuse images online.* But, like most police agencies, it still had a blind spot when it came to prostituted children. On the Internet, the victim could be a cute, blue-eyed six-year-old with curly blond hair. On the street, the police were just as

---

* For a full account of the success of the Innocent Images program, see my book *Caught in the Web: Inside the Police Hunt to Rescue Children from Online Predators.*

likely to pick up a teenager in a skimpy halter top who punctuated every outburst against them with enough swearwords to make even a cop blush.

"They didn't look all that innocent, compared with the kids whose photos we were finding on the Web," Jacob admits.

Jacob herself had been inspired to take up the cause when she heard a young survivor of prostitution speak at a training conference for child abuse investigators. The girl told her story of life on the streets and gave an impassioned plea for understanding. "It just hit me like a ton of bricks," says Jacob. But she still had a hard time convincing her colleagues that the girls on the street were just like the children whose images of abuse were being captured on the Web, that they, too, did not have a "choice" in their abuse. "People just didn't understand it," Jacob says, "so there was almost no funding for fighting child prostitution."

She got a chance to do something about it in 2001 when she was promoted to a job as a supervisory special agent (SSA) at FBI headquarters in Washington. Every SSA is assigned an area to oversee, and Jacob got responsibility for the "white slave trade." She knew the FBI bureaucracy thrives on statistics and reports, so Jacob began crunching the numbers on a national scale—looking at all cases of prostituted children, regardless of race, just as Byron Fassett and Kelly O'Connell had done locally.

The bad news was that the FBI's statistics on domestic sex trafficking were not easily accessible. Every time the FBI opened a case, part of the assigned file number gave an indication what kind of crime it was—there were special codes for child abductions, missing children, and child pornography. But, children forced into prostitution did not have their own designation; there was only a code for "white slave trade," which, though inclusive of all races, could include everything from prostituted adults to foreign trafficking. "It was difficult to say how many real cases of child prostitution we were handling," Jacob says.

The good news was that Jacob soon became the FBI's point person at the National Center for Missing and Exploited Children (NCMEC), the clearinghouse for all police and public reports about child abuse.

At NCMEC's headquarters in Arlington, Virginia, she had access to one of the largest databases in the country of crimes against children, and she kept digging—through FBI files, NCMEC's collection of millions of archives, even newspaper stories and court records. She reviewed the Estes study and other surveys.

The FBI's own fieldwork revealed the extent of the overlooked crime wave. "Sex traffickers or pimps debriefed by the FBI indicate approximately 20–40 percent of the victims recruited into prostitution are juveniles," one report noted. Like her police colleagues in Dallas and Boston, Jacob found that a large number of the girls classified by the justice and social welfare systems as runaways were in fact sexually exploited youth trapped in prostitution networks.

"Here was a crime that wasn't getting solved. It wasn't even being seen as a crime," says Jacob. "These kids were being sold, branded, and trafficked."

With her statistics and analysis in hand, by early 2003 she had drawn up an eighteen-page proposal for a countrywide FBI initiative to tackle the problem of commercially sexually exploited children. She argued that for the FBI to take violence against children seriously, it had to consider the beatings and brutality suffered by prostituted children. If the Bureau was so devoted to saving children whose images of repeated rapes were being posted on the Web, then what about the children being victimized by pimps and johns nine or ten times a night?

Jacob's report went all the way up the chain to the director's office. In June 2003, the Innocence Lost program was born, "designed to address," as the FBI put it, "the growing problem of children forced into prostitution." The name of the initiative was significant, sending a clear message that the young victims caught up in domestic sex trafficking were just as innocent as the children whose images of abuse were flooding the Web.

The new program brought together three powerful branches of the law enforcement and child safety network. From the FBI's Violent Crimes and Major Offenders Section came special agents and analysts. The National Center for Missing and Exploited Children began training hundreds of state and federal law enforcement officers, prosecutors, and social service workers across the country. And the Child Exploitation and Obscenity Section (CEOS) of the Department of Justice brought in the legal firepower.

"For the longest time, the justice system really just didn't recognize child prostitution as a problem," says CEOS chief Drew Oosterbaan. "If someone didn't go after this as a separate problem, it was never going to be dealt with."

As the nation's top child abuse prosecutor, Oosterbaan had seen more than his share of young victims. He had played an instrumental role in making sure the DOJ was more robust in going after Internet predators by working closely with the FBI's Innocent Images team. Now he wanted to do the same with the Innocence Lost initiative. He knew that in most cases the girls arrested or brought in as witnesses didn't tell authorities they were under eighteen.

"And even if people found out, there was no way to deal with that girl in the system," says Oosterbaan. "There were no services, no places to put them. This was completely off the radar."

Oosterbaan began lobbying for more funds and more attention to prostituted children within the DOJ and in Congress. He dispatched prosecutors from his D.C. office to assist in complex cases, not just at the federal level but also with state attorneys. In the often fractious and competitive world of prosecuting crime, that cooperation was rare and welcome. CEOS was quite willing to stay in the background and let state prosecutors take the glory for convicting pimps.

The FBI set up Innocence Lost task forces—federal agents working with local and state police—in fourteen cities across the country, including Chicago, Detroit, Miami, Newark, New York, Philadelphia, San Francisco, and Washington, D.C. Eventually that number would grow to more than thirty. In cities where police were already active in the local battle, the FBI offered extra resources and money for more complicated investigations that required wiretaps. In Dallas, Byron Fassett's HRVT unit began working with the FBI to probe pimping operations that crossed state lines. In Boston, Detective O'Connell teamed up with the FBI to investigate an escort service that advertised on the Web and in various local publications, shipping girls as young as thirteen between New York and Boston. The two entrepreneurs behind the trafficking scheme eventually were sentenced to between five and nine years.

That was just the start. Rather than just the small-time pimps, the FBI wanted to target big-time criminal conspiracies, the trafficking networks that moved hundreds of girls across the nation and made millions of dollars from that trade.

Law enforcement was beginning to get the manpower, the teamwork, and the legal clout needed to crack down on trafficking. What would be harder to secure was a change in attitude toward the girls the crackdown was supposed to help.

■ ■ ■

WHO ARE these girls? Where do they come from? How do they end up on the street? Outsiders—and that includes most police officers, judges, the general public, and politicians—mistakenly believe that if these girls don't like what they are doing they can just walk away.

What a growing number of dedicated cops and community activists began to realize is that the illusion of choice is the biggest obstacle to getting people to see these girls as the victims they are. "In order to have a choice you need to have two viable options to choose from," says DIGNITY's Kathleen Mitchell. "The choice for these girls is not 'Do you want to turn a trick or do you want a wonderful life?' That's not even on the table."

Most girls on the tracks are running from something worse they faced at home. In survey after survey, in one city after another, statistics show that prostituted children suffer prior abuse at a staggeringly high rate:

> In Las Vegas, the police STOP program found that two-thirds of the youth they arrested between 2004 and 2006 for prostitution-related offenses had been victims of sexual assault or family molestation.

> In Minneapolis–St. Paul, Vednita Carter and her Breaking Free group found that 75 percent of the women serving jail time there had been

sexually or physically abused before the age of eighteen. Two-thirds were women of color, and three-quarters were single and unemployed, living in poverty. Ninety percent abused drugs or alcohol.

In New York, the Office of Children and Family Services determined that about 85 percent of prostituted girls had been investigated for abuse or neglect as part of an open child welfare case; 75 percent had been in foster care.

In Dallas, Byron Fassett worked closely with the staff at Letot, an emergency shelter and long-term treatment and counseling center for runaways in Dallas. Letot had helped over seventy thousand since opening its doors in 1979; the staff found that 93 percent of the runaways suffered from some kind of sexual abuse.

On a national level, the numbers are similar. The Estes study of 2001 estimated that 40 percent of the girls who engaged in prostitution were sexually abused at home. A study by the National Institute of Justice found that sexual abuse victims were twenty-eight times more likely than the general population to end up in prostitution.

The conclusion was inescapable: "Prostitution is just a symptom, often of an unresolved prior abuse," says Fassett. "Something happened to that child along the line to send her off in a different direction."

Indeed, many of the minors who end up under the thumbs of pimps didn't even "choose" to flee from abuse at home—they were not runaways but throwaways. About half of the youths in homeless shelters had been kicked out of their home at least once. The Estes study found that more than fifty-one thousand of the estimated three hundred thousand children sexually exploited in the United States every year— about one in six—"were thrown out of their homes by a parent or guardian."

And more often than not, someone the girl knows or trusts lures her into the life. A 2008 DePaul University College of Law study— "Domestic Sex Trafficking in Chicago"—interviewed one hundred women involved in prostitution, one-third of whom had started when they were between twelve and fifteen years old. Eleven percent said they were recruited by family members; 19 percent by friends or girlfriends; and another 29 percent by boyfriends.

Once a desperate teenager finds herself under the spell of a pimp, once she is drawn in by the lure of fancy clothes, money, and undying love, she clings to the promise of emotional and economic security, things every child needs—and every neglected child craves. Abusive relationships at any age involve control, dependence, and elements of brainwashing. The FBI's Eileen Jacob sees parallels between a prostituted girl's slow ride into entrapment and the predicament of a woman who finds herself in an abusive relationship with her husband. "You don't have a wonderful marriage, then wake up one morning and suddenly he starts beating on you and you leave," she says. "It's a gradual process. There is mental abuse and many women feel trapped and unable to escape."

Even if a young girl on the street could summon up the courage to make a break for it, leaving is not easy. Fear and shame keep many girls in "the life." Pimps often find out where the girls used to live, then threaten to harm or kill their families if they quit or go to the cops. If the girls do manage to make it off the streets, the disgrace and humiliation attached to prostitution can drive them back, as Maria found out.

And even when girls do exercise a measure of bad judgment and engage in risky behavior, that surely does not justify blaming them for their predicament. "Sometimes you make bad choices, but does that mean you have to pay for the rest of your life?" asks Byron Fassett. Why, he wonders, does no one blame a child who keeps silent for years about sexual abuse at the hands of a priest or a family member? "No one suggests they had a 'choice,'" he notes. Yet when it comes to children trapped in the sex trade, "No one is mad at the pimp or the john, but we're mad at the kids." What infuriates Fassett even more is that the johns who create the demand for sex with underage victims and the pimps who feed and profit from the demand were getting away with it.

This search by the cops for a deeper understanding of the factors at play with prostituted children is not an academic sociological exercise. It has concrete policy implications. From a policing point of view, it means that these are not children who are going to step forward and report their abuse. Nor, in most cases, will their families. For traditional crimes against children, police more often than not rely on parental or public outcry or self-reporting by the victim.

"No one was going to scream for these children," says Fassett. "Our traditional investigative models were not going to work."

■ ■ ■

DAN GARRABRANT was never one to stick to traditional investigative models that do not work. He was one of ten FBI agents in the Atlantic City area assigned to what the bureau called "violent crime"—from the Mafia to Russian gangs to murders for hire. But his passion was going after pimps.

He does not look like your typically bland, suited-and-tied federal agent, not with his occasional goatee and penchant for plaid short-sleeved shirts. He also holds two undergraduate degrees, one in criminal justice and the other in psychology. To work his way through college, he spent five years in hospitals and group homes helping adolescent sex offenders, many of whom had been sexually victimized themselves before turning on other children. After graduation, he got a job as a probation and parole officer, with a heavy caseload of sex offenders. Law enforcement runs in his family—his father and several uncles were cops—and he jumped at the chance to become a police officer when a job opened up in Delaware. After eight years with the local violent crimes task force, he applied to the FBI.

Garrabrant's experience with troubled teens sparked his early interest in the commercial sexual exploitation of young girls. "Today's pimps are drug lords who got smart," he says. "They've realized they can make a lot more money pushing girls rather than dope and if they get caught, the penalties are a lot less severe."

"The sex trade," he continues, "is the new drug trade."

So Garrabrant was thrilled to be named the FBI's point man for the new Innocence Lost initiative in the high-prostitution nexus of Atlantic City. The FBI wanted to target the entrepreneurs who were operating below the radar, the sophisticated businessmen who were laundering their profits from the trafficking of children. That suited Garrabrant just fine. He began compiling a list of the biggest pimps in the well-traveled Atlantic City–New York corridor. And the same questions kept bothering him: *Who are the men whose names keep coming up in one interview after another with the women being arrested? Who are the guys driving around in jacked-up Escalades and Navigators who've been in the game for fifteen or twenty years because no one has been able to make cases against them?*

One name Garrabrant kept hearing was Knowledge. Other pimps talked about him. The women on the street would mention him. But the police had no real identity or location. "Everyone knew Knowledge, but no one ever knew who Knowledge was," says the FBI man.

Within weeks of arriving in Atlantic City, Garrabrant got the break he was waiting for. A chance arrest in Vegas, an anonymous tip from New York about a pimp, and a new sense of cooperation between the FBI and local police thrust Garrabrant into a complex criminal conspiracy investigation that would span several states.

It all came about thanks to a tough, foulmouthed, and seemingly unrepentant girl from Jersey who once wanted nothing more than to sing in the church choir.

3

Maria's Dilemma

As Maria boarded the JetBlue flight from JFK airport early in December 2003, her pimp's words kept ringing in her head. "You better not say who your pimp is if you get arrested," he had told her. "They are going to drill you and drill you and drill you to try to get it out of you."

Knowledge was wise to warn Maria about the police in Las Vegas. As Knowledge dispatched his young Suprema to the Nevada gaming resort, the FBI and police in a handful of cities across the country were finally beginning to figure out effective ways to tackle the problem of prostituted children. And Las Vegas was the one city in the country where the police had been on the offensive for some time.

Child prostitution hit Vegas early and hit it hard. The sheer size of the sex trade in the state and the subsequent flood of children into the city had forced the police to react. As far back as 1994, the Las Vegas Metropolitan Police Department set up Operation STOP, for Stop Turning Out Child Prostitutes. It started with four officers. By the time Sergeant Gil Shannon was running it in 2003, the STOP group had expanded to eight full-time investigators. It remains to this day the largest city police team in the country devoted exclusively to prostituted children.

"There's one," Shannon says as he points to a girl in a skimpy black dress, clutching a small white purse. He's driving an unmarked police vehicle along Tropicana Boulevard, just west of the Strip. The busy road is one of the main tracks where young girls hang out. "A few years ago, these girls believed in Santa Claus," the vice cop says. "Now their pimp is selling them another dream. He's convinced them it's him and her against the world; he loves her and he's her best friend."

To help stem the flood, Shannon made sure there were plenty of other people to be "our eyes and ears," as he puts it. Every patrol officer in the department is required to notify Shannon's squad if they come across an under-eighteen-year-old suspected of engaging in prostitution, and they face disciplinary action if they fail to do so. The hotels and casinos—as Maria would soon discover—have a network of security personnel who work undercover, pretending to be tourists but watching out for illegal activity. The vice unit also calls upon civilians, from hotel and casino workers to cab drivers, to pass on information about any suspected underage victims.

But the cops found they have to be careful about some civilians. In the gambling establishments, crooked staff members are more interested in fueling the sex trade than fighting it. Jill, a beautiful blond teenager who would eventually be rescued from prostitution by the Vegas vice cops, relied on a casino "host" to steer business her way. His job was to take care of the "high rollers," usually out-of-town businessmen. "So I would get the guys who could afford to pay a lot," she says, "and I'd give him 20 percent."

At another large casino, one bartender had an elaborate set of signals—a coaster left on top of a drink, a napkin folded a certain way—to warn women working the floor whenever he spotted an undercover officer. Shannon's vice squad had to run a sting, using an undercover female cop pretending to ask the bartender for help, to flush him out and bust him.

The Vegas STOP unit learned one important lesson early on: it had to separate its policing from its protection. The same cops who arrested the girls would not then try to break them away from their pimps. "If I arrest a girl, how am I going to establish a rapport with her?" asks Shannon. "She's going to say, 'You're the same guy who brought me down here and you're trying to tell me you're going to help me out?'"

They worked out a strict division of tasks. The vice officers assigned to enforcement spot the minors and bring them to the juvenile detention center. Then a separate team of specially trained vice officers moves into action. They are cops like Aaron Stanton, a young father with a hint of a beard and hair that curls over his ears. Stanton is one of those police officers who thrive on the grit and glitter of crime in Las Vegas. "It's a great city to be a cop," he says.

At any hour of the day or night, Stanton will get a call about the latest underage victim who was picked up in a prostitution bust or an undercover operation, and he makes his way down to the detention center. He is always struck by how the girls change. When he first sees them in their "work outfits," they do not seem much like children, with skimpy dresses, daring hairdos, heavy makeup, and flashy nails. After they shower, clean up, and put on the detention center's sweatpants and tops, they lose their street-worn years. "Then it hits you, these are really just kids," Stanton says.

Invariably, the girls are not receptive to him, at least not at first. They are tough, and they are angry, and Stanton knows he has to be straight with them. "I never try to bullshit them," Stanton explains. "These kids are sharp. They have radar. Their lives depend on reading a man, be it a pimp or a trick, so they know when someone is lying to them. You really have to be genuine to earn their trust."

It is a lesson he put to good use one night when he found himself face-to-face in a detention center with an angry girl from New Jersey.

■ ■ ■

IT WAS close to midnight on December 5, 2003, when Maria plopped herself down on a corner stool near one of the slot machines at Bellagio, one of the more ostentatious casinos even by Vegas standards. Outside, multicolored fountains spurt giant plumes of water to a musical score. Inside, stores like Chanel, Tiffany, and Armani line the "Via Bellagio." Cocktail waitresses clad in black miniskirts and lace tops cruise the rows of slot machines.

Maria hardly looked out of place in a black halter top and a tight jean skirt. The patrons at the upscale casino on the Las Vegas Strip were the usual mix of blue-rinse seniors, young couples on their honeymoons, and balding men on the make. No clocks were anywhere to be seen, of course. In Vegas, the casino owners want the tourists to lose track of time. For Maria, the night seemed endless. She had gone another evening without a client.

Her years on the street had earned Maria a reputation for being smart, sassy, and strong. But in the overwhelming hustle and bustle of Vegas, the seventeen-year-old had a bad feeling. "This shit, it was too big for me," she says. "I couldn't take it."

It had been a rough week for the teenager. Knowledge was growing impatient with her lack of income. Earlier in the week she had posted bail for Lotion, the more seasoned woman who had been her guide in Vegas, and that evening, both women were back in the casinos. But Maria felt her older partner, rather than being the guide and mentor she needed, was ungrateful and unhelpful. "The snotty bitch didn't really want to teach me anything," Maria complains. "I didn't know what the fuck I was doing. She missed out telling me a lot."

Like the need to watch out for the undercover security guards at the casinos. The hotels in Atlantic City, of course, had them. But in Atlantic City, they didn't scare Maria. "I know who they are," she says with an almost professional pride, "and you can spot them from a mile away." Vegas, she was discovering, was different. Although she didn't stand out among the waitresses and some patrons, by staying on the same slot machine stool for hours, Maria was breaking one of the cardinal rules for a carpet ho—keep moving so the undercover cops and the casino security agents don't spot you. "I wasn't supposed to be sitting there for two hours," she says. "But I just gave up. I couldn't do it anymore."

By the time a handsome young Hispanic man approached, she was desperate. The two of them began a light banter and then started negotiating the price. That's when the man pulled out his badge, identifying himself as a security officer for the casino. "I couldn't believe he was a fucking cop," Maria says. "So stupid."

The agent led Maria downstairs to a holding room. Maria was nervous but also strangely relieved. "Vegas was too tough for me. It was too hard," she says.

Maria had been arrested plenty of times before, at least three dozen times in New York City alone. She knew the routine, how to play the game, how to lie. And Knowledge provided all his underage girls with fake IDs. Usually Maria fudged her age by only a few years, claiming to be twenty or twenty-one, which was a stretch though not implausible given her looks. But for the first time in her street career Maria was flustered, and in the security room in the basement of Bellagio she mistakenly gave her date of birth as 1981, making her an unconvincing twenty-three-year-old. She told the police she was a local girl from Vegas, but her purse was filled with out-of-state receipts. She invented a tale of her parents being crack users.

"I was always on the game, every time I got arrested. I had always been cool before, but for some reason this one time I didn't feel right," Maria says. "My heart was racing. I was freaked out."

The cops booked her on charges of loitering for the purpose of prostitution and giving false information to a police officer. It was 1:30 A.M.

• • •

FROM THE outside, pink stucco walls make the Clark County Detention Center look vaguely like a suburban high school, except for the barbed wire that runs along the high fences. Inside, more than two hundred juvenile inmates, arrested for everything from drugs and assault to loitering, cram the hallways. At any given time, about thirty of them are female. And they all want out, fast.

Usually jail time was no more than an inconvenience for Knowledge's women. But as the hours and then the days slipped by, it wasn't working out that way for Maria. Why, she wondered, had Lotion not shown up to bail her out? Instead her only visitors were two officers— "two damned cops," as Maria calls them—from the Las Vegas vice squad. Maria was used to cops being either indifferent or insensitive. During her many arrests, none of them had ever bothered to find out her real age. "Cops treat us like shit," she says. "They say horrible things to you. I can't tell you how many times a cop made me cry. They just treated me like crap."

But she soon found out the Vegas cops were different. "Most cops will just push you through the system," she says. "These guys wanted to know everything about you."

Aaron Stanton was one of the two "damned cops" who came to see Maria in the early morning hours after her arrest. He was impressed by the cagey seventeen-year-old who sat across from him in the interview room. "She was well versed in the game," he says. "She had been incarcerated in quite a few places as an adult, and you could tell she was pretty tough."

Stanton was following the well-established division of labor within the Vegas police—stepping in as part of Gil Shannon's youth squad whenever street cops, casino security personnel, or undercover vice cops arrested any underage girls. His goal was to use those precious hours when a vulnerable girl was away from her pimp to try to break her free from his grasp. But Maria did not budge. She wasn't like a lot of the other girls Stanton had dealt with, girls who were resolute at first but then opened up after a few hours or days.

Stanton had time and patience. "These girls have an excellent bs meter," he says. "They're not going to give you their trust right away. They are rough around the edges and you have to get inside them, deprogram them, and find out that they truly are a child. That's really all they are on the inside—a frightened, angry child."

Maria may have been frightened and angry, but she was also stubborn; her stonewalling went on for another month. From jail, Maria got in touch with her mother. Her parents knew little about the law or what her daughter was really caught up in. Maria had spun a story about how Knowledge ran a recording studio and had promised to launch the former choirgirl's singing career. They had no money to hire a lawyer, so Maria's mother asked for Knowledge's number. But Maria was too scared to give it up. She assumed the phone calls at the detention center were monitored. Suprema did not want to betray her pimp.

She was driven in part by an intense, if misplaced, sense of loyalty, not just to Knowledge but to the women around him whom she had come to see as family—even Lotion, the "snotty bitch." "He was not just like some small-time pimp," Maria says. "I knew that if I told on him, I had thirty-five other people to worry about. Thirty-five bitches that are going to fucking hate me after this. Thirty-five people's lives."

But as the days and weeks wore on, Maria grew impatient. Where was Lotion with that damn bail money? Knowledge always took care of his girls' legal hassles promptly, like when he had asked Maria to get Lotion out of jail. And just that previous summer, when Maria was arrested in Boston, he ordered one of his other women to drive from New York in his Cadillac Escalade to bail her out. This time in Las Vegas, things were different. Knowledge and his women were nowhere to be seen.

What Maria did not know but what the cops had surmised was that this was not neglect or distraction on the part of her pimp. This was a calculated move for survival. Before, Maria had been booked, processed, and promptly bailed out as an adult. This time, she had been clearly identified as a minor, and her pimp had no doubt decided he would be safer staying as far away from her as possible. For the usually shrewd Knowledge, it was a miscalculation that proved catastrophic. Because after a month of stewing behind bars, Maria found her fear turning to anger.

Couldn't Knowledge come down and pass himself off as her uncle, an old pimp trick to get underage charges out of jail? Couldn't Lotion, Goddess, or any one of Knowledge's women at least make an appearance during one of Maria's court dates? Maria was furious. Not once did Lotion or any of Knowledge's other women come by as a show of support. "Like just so I could see that they cared," Maria said. Here she was putting her ass on the line for Knowledge, and he dropped her cold. "Not even a goddamn letter," Maria complained.

In the end, she cracked over cigarettes. "Give me some cigarettes and I will tell you what you want to know," she told Stanton. He brought her a whole pack and took her out for some fresh air in the detention center's parking lot where they sat on the curb and talked. As she smoked, she began talking about her pimp.

"Listen," she began. "This is who he is."

True to form, she lied. She made up a fake street name for Knowledge, calling him Finesse, the nickname of one of his associates. She gave the cops a colorful but wildly inaccurate description. "He's tall, dark, and he's got a scar underneath his eye," she told them. "He's got hair down to his shoulders in cornrows."

But she did let slip some useful pieces of information, including her own street names and the names of some of the women with her in Vegas. Maria did not know the address of Knowledge's comfortable home in Vegas, so Stanton got her a temporary release, and they drove to Silverado Ranch Boulevard in south Vegas, where she pointed out the location of a housing complex known as the Savannah Apartments. It may not have been enough to get an arrest warrant—they still had no real identity for her pimp—but there was enough information to conduct a search.

Police records indicate they completed their last debrief with Maria at 6:15 P.M. on December 30. Nine days later, the Vegas cops carried out their raid. It was 6:45 P.M. on January 8, 2004. Two women were on the premises, but neither of them would give up the name of their pimp. There was plenty of evidence, such as business records, documents, and Western Union money order receipts, that pointed to an extensive pimping operation. Scattered around the home were photographs of some of the women posing on what looked like a first-class cruise ship. Stanton had come across such "trophy" photos before on police raids, but he was struck by the apparent luxury vacations to which Maria's pimp had treated his women. "Not too many pimps take their girls on cruises," he says. "It was then that we realized we were dealing with someone different."

It wasn't just the wealth that impressed Stanton but also the sophisticated way it was managed. He found envelopes for each of the women working for the pimp, with receipts for food, taxis, cigarettes, and condoms. Two ledgers carefully documented the earnings of the women by day, week, and year. "The records were meticulous," Stanton recalls. "Groceries, bills, everything, all in a filing cabinet, kept very clean and organized. I had never seen this before."

But who was this mysterious pimp Maria had called Finesse? There were several names in the various business records the police found; the rental application had been filled out by a man who claimed he earned one hundred thousand dollars a year as the CEO of an entertainment company. Officers ran the man's name through their criminal databases but found nothing. Nor did a match appear even among state drivers' license records. They were stumped.

"We couldn't find his name anywhere in our records, so at the time it didn't mean much to us," says Stanton. They'd gone as far as they could, at least for the moment.

Maria had shown them the way to the apartment, and now she was getting ready to fly back home to New Jersey to her family, to what she thought was a safe haven. In her mind she was making as clean an escape as possible. She didn't think she had betrayed Knowledge's trust, not really.

"I told, but only enough to get home," she rationalizes even now.

■ ■ ■

BACK HOME in New Jersey, the FBI's Innocence Lost agent in the Atlantic City area was immersing himself in the sordid and sad world of prostituted children.

When Dan Garrabrant came across underage girls caught up in the trade—either on the street or in custody—he dispensed with the usual law enforcement code of dispassion and distance. "You can stand there and say 'name, date of birth, roll your hands for fingerprints, look ahead at the camera, look right,' but then there is no connection," he says. "It's just a number, and you're processing them until they get out." He found that if he took the time to talk to the young girls, to listen to them, to prove that he really cared about them, the interviews could be cathartic. And not just for the girls. "That's the hardest part about it," says the FBI man. "As they are talking and disclosing more about themselves you become more a part of their lives. You start to understand more about how they got to where they are, and you genuinely begin to care more about them. It exposes you a little bit more."

Garrabrant wanted that raw exposure. He wanted to understand what drove these girls to something he considered nothing more than a modern-day slave trade. And he wanted to go after the men running the networks. As luck would have it, within his first week on the job Garrabrant received an anonymous handwritten letter from a disgruntled pimp in New York who was one of Knowledge's rivals. The pimp claimed that Knowledge was recruiting minors into a prostitution ring "which has netted him over $1,000,000," a network that stretched from the East Coast to Las Vegas. He also alleged that Knowledge's real name was Matthew Thompkins. It was a good lead, but it was just innuendo, not proof. Garrabrant ran that name through the criminal databases but again came up empty. Whoever Thompkins was, he had no criminal record. The agent was undeterred and phoned some cops he knew on the Vegas vice squad.

"Have you ever heard about this guy Knowledge?" he asked.

"Yeah," one of the vice cops told the federal agent. "He's a huge pimp down here. He's got all these girls working for him." Beyond that, they had nothing. They had no reason to connect Knowledge with the pimp in the Savannah Apartments that Maria had told them about.

"Hey, while you're on the phone," the Vegas cop added. "We just sent a girl who was working for a pimp named Finesse out here back to Jersey."

He gave Garrabrant Maria's name and what few other details they had on her. The Vegas investigators did not connect her to Knowledge, and Garrabrant didn't either. There was no reason to. She was just another girl, caught in just another pimp's grasp. But Garrabrant figured it would be worth paying her a visit just the same. Nothing to lose, he figured.

"OK," he told the Vegas cops. "Let me try and go talk to her."

■ ■ ■

IN EARLY January 2004, Maria was living temporarily with her parents, torn by guilt and fear. She was loyal enough to her pimp and especially the other women in his stable to be wracked by indecision. "I snitched on them," she says. "I just felt so bad." But she also had a strong enough sense of survival to know that she had to keep her mouth shut about what had happened in the Las Vegas detention center. Knowledge didn't know where she was living, but he did have her cell phone number. Within two weeks of her return from Vegas, he gave her a call.

"I am such a tough girl, I didn't say anything," she assured him.

"That is why you are my fucking supreme bitch," he said, playing on her nickname Suprema. "I knew you could be strong."

Keeping Knowledge in the dark about what she had told the Vegas cops was one thing. Maria had a much bigger problem when the FBI came knocking on her door. The Nevada cops had given FBI agent Dan Garrabrant Maria's full name and her parents' address, and he dropped by one February afternoon to see if she was there. She wasn't, but her mom called her at a friend's place.

Like most encounters between a man with a badge and a streetwise girl with an attitude, the meeting between Garrabrant and Maria did not start well.

"Tell that motherfucker to get the fuck out of my house and to never fucking come back," Maria exploded over the phone. "The police fucked my life up already."

She was used to brushing off cops who didn't care about, much less understand, prostituted children. But Garrabrant had a good read on her—he knew she was scared that her pimp was going to find her and punish her for talking to the cops. He also knew if he didn't take care of girls like her, no one else would, not other cops, not social workers, not schools. "Closing our eyes doesn't make these children disappear," he says. "The pimps are devoting a lot of time and energy to wooing these girls. And we're not."

A week later, Garrabrant returned to see if Maria had had a change of heart. Maria's mother let him in the house; Maria had just gotten out of bed and had dressed provocatively in a deliberate attempt to shock him, Garrabrant thought. He'd seen that before with young women forced into the trade, using sex to appear tough and hide their anger and guilt.

"Hey, it's me again," he said. "Did you miss me?"

His low-key manner disarmed the girl, though she tried to keep up her cool demeanor.

"We have a lot to talk about," Garrabrant continued. "And I'm not going to push you."

"I am not cooperating," Maria retorted. Just to make sure he got the point, she added, "And I am not telling you shit."

OK, Garrabrant realized, he was going to have to take this slowly. "I know you're mad right now," he said. "I am not going to make you say anything else, but I'll come back in a week."

Maria barely grunted a reply. But she sensed there was something different about this man. Not just different from most of the other cops she'd met but also different from most of the adults she knew. "He didn't judge me," she says. "He seemed like he genuinely cared."

Garrabrant kept his word. He kept coming back over the next couple of months. He met her sisters and spent time with her parents. Her mother took out the pictures she had saved of Maria when she was a little girl, modeling clothes for local stores. "Look at what she used to be," she said. "My little Maria, she was so cute." *Before she turned into a prostitute* were the words that went unsaid.

Garrabrant knew that parents had a hard time dealing with daughters who had turned to the streets. He also knew that girls like Maria hated the condescension and contempt most people directed toward them. "They're thinking *I'm a whore and that's how they're going to view me, as a whore*," he says. "It's not really until you allow them to talk about what they've gone through, who they are, and what they dream about that the kids start to open up."

"But that's what takes time—the one thing most police officers working these cases just don't have," the FBI agent continues. "I think for Maria and for a lot of girls there aren't many people besides their pimp who ever took the time to be with them."

Garrabrant understood that the only sure way to get through to Maria was to give her something no one else was offering her: respect. Slowly, he began to break down her hostility and build up her trust. She was impressed in spite of herself. "He listened to every single story I ever had to say. And half of them were lies. I lied my ass off to him, too. I just tried to lie to everybody," she says.

For his part, Garrabrant sensed that fear was a big part of what was driving her, fear of rejection, of retribution, of finally having to face consequences. "She had been doing it since she was thirteen years old," he says. "She was out there, she was tired, and she was just afraid. She just wanted someone she could talk to and trust and try to work it out for her."

His patience paid off. Haltingly at first, then in a rush, Maria opened up. She spoke about her days and nights in New York, Atlantic City, and Philadelphia, about being arrested in Vegas and feeling betrayed by her pimp. Then she dropped the bombshell: she revealed that her pimp's street name was not Finesse as she had claimed in Vegas but, rather, Knowledge. His real name, she said, was Matthew Thompkins.

Here was the breakthrough the FBI needed. Maria had given Garrabrant the same name the anonymous letter writer had supplied a few months earlier. What's more, when Garrabrant contacted the Vegas cops with this new information, he learned that one of the names that had turned up in the documents they found at the Savannah Apartments was spelled Tompkins. It had to be same man.

Maria's disclosures connected the raids in Vegas with the mysterious Knowledge whom Garrabrant had been tracking in the Northeast. By March, the FBI agent was on a plane to Las Vegas to find out more about Maria's pimp.

"We'll give you anything you want," local investigators told him. Garrabrant was grateful, because relations between local police agencies and the Bureau were often strained. Police by definition are territorial, protective of their jurisdiction. Not the Vegas cops. They knew better. The problem of prostituted children did not stop at the city limits; the police could not, either.

"Pimps like Knowledge were always flooding girls like Maria into the city," says Aaron Stanton of the vice squad. As he soon discovered, the flood went both ways. Knowledge was also trafficking local girls back to New York.

"The Vegas cops basically opened up everything," Garrabrant says. The search of Knowledge's Vegas apartments turned up plenty of paper, photographs, and business documents. Now that investigators knew that it all belonged to one Matthew Thompkins, the stash took on new significance.

"Once we got to Vegas, we knew we had something big," says Garrabrant.

■ ■ ■

IT DIDN'T take long for Maria, back in Jersey, to find herself on the streets again. For most of her teen years, this was the only life she knew.

She tried to move away from Knowledge's grasp and began "renegading"—operating on her own without the protection of a pimp. It was a risky venture.

Knowledge ruled much of the action on the streets in Atlantic City. Maria had to assure Knowledge that she had protected his empire during her arrest in Vegas. And now she had a new secret she had to keep from Knowledge: her cooperation with the FBI. But Maria, ever the wily street survivor, felt confident she could pull it off.

So she was not unduly alarmed when in April 2004, four months after her return from Vegas, she got a call from Knowledge.

"Drive your ass here now," Knowledge yelled, ordering her to New York. Maria was more intrigued than frightened. As a bonus, Knowledge let her take his much-prized Escalade to make the trip.

Oh shit, Maria thought, *he wants me that bad?* She assumed that he just wanted to have sex with her, a frequent occurrence between Knowledge and the women around him. Maybe, just maybe, that was why he was so insistent. Unable and somewhat afraid to say no, she got on the turnpike that was just a few minutes from Knowledge's Galloway home and headed toward New York.

What Maria didn't know was that Knowledge had already learned many of the details of the police raids on his Vegas apartments. He hadn't broken the law to get the police reports but instead had used it, because it was common practice for courts to unseal search warrants after police completed a raid. Knowledge was smart enough to get a copy of the warrants, albeit with some sensitive information edited out. But it was enough for him to figure out what the teenager had told the cops.

When Maria arrived in New York she faced an enraged pimp. A huge, heavyset, angry pimp, towering over a teenage girl who was under five feet tall.

"What did you say to the cops?" he yelled.

"I didn't tell them anything," Maria said, and added that she just gave them a general location of his apartments, which was largely true. She realized her voice was quavering.

"You stupid bitch, that was enough!"

"You don't understand," she pleaded. "I was in jail for a month, and they told me that if I didn't tell them anything they would never let me go."

Knowledge was not assuaged. He dragged her over to one of his many New York apartments, the one that Maria always thought was so hot because it had a flat-screen TV that came down from the ceiling in the bedroom and a home movie theater downstairs. But there would be no entertainment that night. Maria and the other girls were put to work shredding papers, destroying their receipts and any other evidence they could find of his operations. "Papers, pictures, journals—we just started throwing stuff away," Maria recalls.

Throughout, Maria endured glares and outbursts from the women under Knowledge.

"I can't believe you did this to us," one of them said.

"You fucked up everyone's life, bitch," shouted another.

"Guys, I didn't really say anything." Maria tried again to defend her actions. "I don't understand how the police got all the information."

Knowledge's temper was growing. "Bitch, I even gave you a phone in my name, my real fucking name."

That's your stupid fault, Maria thought, but she wisely kept her mouth shut. As the tension mounted in the apartment, she decided she had to get out of there. Fast.

Later that night, she sneaked out and turned a trick for five hundred dollars. This time she didn't have to fork over any of her earnings to a pimp.

Maria was a month shy of her eighteenth birthday, but in many ways she was still a child. She had no concept of the dangers she faced. All she cared about was the thick wad of cash in her pocket. "That was a lot of money to me," she says. *I'm rich!* she thought.

She hopped on a Greyhound bus back home. And to a whole mess of trouble.

· 4 ·

The Wealth of Knowledge

Just a few miles from Maria's home outside Atlantic City, at the FBI's office in Northfield, special agent Dan Garrabrant worked late into the night. Documents were piling up. Even as Knowledge was busy shredding some of his business records, Garrabrant was just as busy collecting a mountain of paperwork on his target.

Patiently, he began to reach out to police from Las Vegas, New York City, and Boston, probing into the extent of Knowledge's operations. This was not going to be an ordinary street bust of a local pimp. He wanted to conduct what he called an intelligence-driven operation against a major domestic child-sex-trafficking scheme. That was the tough mandate of the FBI's Innocence Lost project, one year old at that time, in late spring 2004.

The Bureau had just scored its first major success against a large-scale pimping operation in May 2004, when nine federal arrest warrants were issued in the Oklahoma City area. Called Stormy Nights, the yearlong probe had targeted the interstate prostitution of children at truck stops and call services nationwide. Bobby Prince Jr., a nineteen-year-old football and track star in Wichita, Kansas, had lured girls from the local high school who thought they were going on day trips to Oklahoma. Instead he and his father held them in hotels and sent them to sell sex at various truck stops, shipping the girls as far as Denver, Miami, Houston, and Dallas.

"The guys have so much control over your mind. They scare you," one fifteen-year-old told *People* magazine after the FBI case was wrapped up. "They say things like, 'If you leave, I'll kill you and your family.'"

The FBI probe identified forty-eight pimps using the truck stop network, half of them trafficking juveniles. Eventually, the older Prince got twelve and a half years in prison; his son was sentenced to almost six years. Seven other pimps went to jail, some for even longer terms. Sixteen underage girls were recovered, and several of them had begun to rebuild their lives.

Dan Garrabrant wanted to do the same thing for Maria and the other girls caught up in Knowledge's web. But to succeed he needed to find out everything he could about his target. Stormy Nights had taught the FBI that busting a major pimping operation took time, planning, and long-term surveillance. Garrabrant set about to prove to his FBI superiors and the Department of Justice prosecutors that Knowledge was running a massive criminal enterprise worthy of a federal judicial assault. It would take close to a year—until spring 2005—for Garrabrant to build enough of a case to convince Washington to investigate and prosecute the pimp.

He began to gather financial records and tax files and conducted property and title searches. He got pen registers on Knowledge's phones—endless lists that showed every incoming and outgoing call. Not as sophisticated as wiretaps, these devices don't monitor the content of the calls, just who makes and receives them. Knowledge had at least a dozen phones for his women, but few were in his name. "It was an insane amount of material," says Garrabrant.

Knowledge went by several names over the years: Seymore Benjamin, Craig Williams, and Brandon Williams. Even as Matthew Thompkins his middle name was reported as Devon and Leon. But slowly, Garrabrant pieced together a picture of man who combined his shrewd business sense with a penchant for brutality to build a lucrative pimping enterprise that stretched from the shore of Atlantic City to Boston, Philadelphia, New York, and out west to the Strip in Vegas.

. . .

PERHAPS TO embellish his image as a tough guy from the 'hood, Thompkins put out the story that he hailed from Compton, southeast of Los Angeles, a city rife with gangs and drug wars. In fact, his roots were more prosaic, though perhaps just as grim. Born three days after Christmas in 1968, Thompkins grew up in the Edenwald Projects, the largest housing development in the Bronx with more than five thousand people crammed into forty buildings. He never really strayed far from his New York roots, though his pimping profits would allow him to move into classier homes.

A pimp by night, Thompkins was also, as implausible as it sounds, a mailman by day. For ten years, starting in 1994, he worked regularly for the U.S. Postal Service in Manhattanville, a neighborhood squeezed between Harlem and the Hudson River. He stopped showing up for work from September 2004 onward, under the guise of sick leave, holidays, and eventually leave without pay. It was a sweet job made even sweeter because it gave him a legitimate cover for his pimping income, and, as investigators would later learn, it also gave him insider information on how to use postal money orders to launder ill-gotten cash.

Thompkins was also a member of an obscure group called the Five Percenters. A breakaway faction of the Nation of Islam, the group takes its name from its belief that only 5 percent of the world's population is "righteous," speaking the truth. Each member has to master both a Supreme Alphabet and Supreme Mathematics, a complicated theory of numerology, after which the individual becomes a self-proclaimed god. Through the Five Percenters Thompkins earned his street name, Knowledge Born Allah, or Knowledge for short.

Mailman. Member of a fringe group. Pimp. Knowledge had many faces, but above all he was a ruthless and relentless manager of money.

"This is serious business," he told *Ozone*, the rap music magazine that ran a portrait of him as "the most successful pimp in the country." He added, "Sex isn't the focal point, money is."

While Knowledge refused to disclose to the magazine exactly how much money he had—"suffice to say that he makes a lot of money,"

the article said—the FBI managed to nail down a pretty good estimate. By the age of thirty-five, the pimp had eight luxury cars, including Hummers and various BMWs, and he owned almost as many
homes. Two New York bank accounts contained over seven hundred
thousand dollars. And that's the money he had in the bank. How
much more was he making from his pimping business? Just one of the
women under him, Slim Shady, later told authorities she alone pulled
in more than $222,000 in one year. Garrabrant, who in his years
of policing had seen plenty of profitable crime operations, found the
numbers staggering. "You can work big drug cases, and some of the
guys don't even clear a quarter of a million dollars," he says. "Knowledge was making that from just one girl."

And Thompkins was shrewd enough to do all that without attract-
ing the heat that dogged his competitors, whom he dismissed as "celebrity pimps." Except for the tattoo on his right forearm that read PIMP
OR DIE, Knowledge eschewed the glitz and gaudiness of the pimping
world. He dressed down, favoring a polo shirt, blue jeans, and black
boots.

"Not many people know what he looks like," *Ozone* reported,
because he "prefers... not to draw too much attention." Even for the
Ozone portrait he was careful to use an alias and not allow any pictures of him or the women in his stable.

Ironically, that lack of traditional pimp pizzazz drew some of the
women to him. Goddess, the tall brunette who would one day so
impress Maria, told the magazine that, after a stint in prison on a
drug charge, she gave up waitressing to earn more money as a stripper.
Then she started working the track and hooked up with Knowledge
because he had a "humble demeanor."

"Rich people don't put on all their jewelry," she said. "He's not
flashy."

But if he lacked flash, he thought big. What set Thompkins apart
from most other pimps were his finely honed management skills,
some of which he may have learned in an earlier stint as a manager
at a McDonald's, during which he attended the chain's well-regarded
administration school, affectionately known as Hamburger Univer-

sity. "I'm like the CEO of a Fortune 500 company," he once boasted. "I run one of the best Ho-grams in the country."

He was a creative manager even when it came to running something as traditional as a brothel. Early on in his career, after renting a house at the corner of Sixty-second and Lexington in Manhattan to run as a brothel, he advertised the women available for sex in publications such as the *Village Voice* and the *New York Sex Guide*, then had Goddess track which ads drew more customers. Never one to miss a business opportunity or a chance to save money, he made some of the women in the stable sleep with the photographer who took the pictures for the ads instead of paying for his services.

In Vegas, he saw another opportunity. To cater to customers who felt nervous about being seen picking up women on the street or in casinos, he set up a phone escort service called Upscale Exotics in a seedy second-floor office just off the Vegas Strip. Customers could simply book appointments with his women by giving their credit card numbers over the phone.

"He was a very bright guy," admits Garrabrant. "But the guy was just completely full of himself. It was all about him."

"Pimps are born, hos are made," Knowledge liked to say, and he kept his women on a tight leash financially and psychologically. All of his women knew one another only by their nicknames—as Suprema, Fortune, Madonna, Goddess, and Lotion. At one point, Knowledge simultaneously ran a mother and daughter out of different houses with neither of them knowing the other was in his stable.

He would front each woman twenty dollars a day to pay for expenses. It was never enough. Maria remembers that after buying her cigarettes she had about thirteen dollars left for everything from food to cab fare. The women were required to provide receipts for everything they bought, no matter if it was a Baby Ruth candy bar or a bottle of water. And they had to keep a "trap book" with records of how much money they made for him each night. Down to the last penny. Literally. Once when she was in Philadelphia with a woman named Reflection, Maria tossed some pennies she had received as change on the floor.

"Pick them up, those are Daddy's pennies," Reflection said.

"Are you serious?" asked Maria, still new to Knowledge's stable. "He wants the pennies, too?"

"Yes, he wants everything," came the answer.

Maria kept her retort to herself. *That's ridiculous*, she thought. *This guy's got a million dollars and he wants pennies.* But she picked them up.

To manage the constant flow of money, Knowledge called on Meredith, perhaps the most educated woman in his stable and one of his first recruits. With dark hair that fell over her shoulders, large gold earrings, and a beaming smile, she looked very much like the confident, college-educated woman she was. They had first met in New York in 1990, when she was fourteen years old, and she wanted to be with him so badly that she tried running away from home by tying bedsheets together and lowering them out her tenth-floor apartment window. But as she made her way to the ground the sheets ripped, and she plummeted several stories, fracturing both legs and several vertebrae. As she lay in the hospital, Knowledge came to visit, continuing his plan to win her over.

And it worked. After she recuperated, she started working for him. By the time she was fifteen he'd taken her to Hunts Point, taught her what to watch out for, how to negotiate prices for "dates," and just how far she should let tricks go with her. She gave birth to two of his children, a boy and, four years later, a girl. Eventually she would discover that those were not his only offspring.

Meredith stood by Knowledge almost to the end, when the FBI probe pushed her to question her allegiance to the man who had seduced her as a child. Until that point, she blinkered her eyes as she managed his increasingly complex financial operation. Even when she left—first in 1994 to take some college courses, then again in 2000, this time to study in England—something kept pulling her back, maybe loyalty, love, or the sense that her children needed their father, and what he did for a living simply didn't matter, at least not then. "I was still part of his life," she later explained.

To protect his profits, Knowledge created an elaborate money-laundering scheme, and Meredith juggled the books to hide his true wealth. The deeds for several of his properties in Yonkers, in the Bronx, and near Atlantic City were in her name, as were his 2003 Land Rover and 2000 Mercedes-Benz 500. And she placed a 2002 Cadillac Escalade in her mother's name so she could get a loan to purchase another vehicle for the pimp.

In the Bronx, the women in Knowledge's stable lived in a four-apartment building he owned on Holland Avenue. If they were assigned to the casinos and Boardwalk in Atlantic City, he had a spacious three-story home in the nearby suburb of Galloway. In Vegas, the women had access to two additional homes. For good measure, Knowledge also had a condo in Yonkers as well as Tracy's apartment on Rochambeau Avenue. Meredith used the "trap money"—slang for prostitution revenue—to pay the bills and utilities at Knowledge's various homes, but she also created fake leases and log books showing rent payments by members of the stable. By claiming to have several tenants paying thousands of dollars, Knowledge created a cover for the real source of his income.

When Knowledge's women were out of town, in Vegas or Atlantic City or Boston, they wired their earnings back to his New York headquarters, often with postal service money orders. To protect himself further, he had the women occasionally use other money transfer points, such as Western Union. (The money-wire service requires a test question to ensure safe pickup at the other end. His was *What is it for?* The answer was *All 4 love.*)

To keep all that cash coming in from his pimping business, Knowledge combined finesse with fear. "He was just smooth. Very cool, calm, and collected," Garrabrant says. "He could talk the pants off anybody."

One of his favorite baits for luring girls was Hoodlum Records, the recording studio in the basement of his Holland Avenue home in the Bronx. Just as he had promised Maria during her troubled days in Vegas, Knowledge told nearly every woman he was trying to bring into his stable that she had a big music career ahead of her if she would only stick by him. (The Hoodlum front had another advantage for Knowledge—Meredith could write letters to various probation departments and claim that the women had legitimate employment with the company, with the goal of getting them back on the streets faster.)

When lies didn't work, there were always fists. If his girls stepped out of line, Knowledge gave them beatings—he called them "headcuts"—with everything from cords and belts to dog chains dipped in alcohol. "He could be the sweetest talker one minute," says Maria. "And then the next he would beat the crap out of a girl if she misbehaved."

The beatings were legion at the New York apartments, at his home in Atlantic City, in hotels and cheap motels. Once Knowledge battered Lotion so badly with a pole that she lost control of her bladder. He used whatever items he had on hand. In New York, he came over to Tracy's apartment on Rochambeau Avenue to beat a teenage girl named Armani with a frozen chicken and a gun. Slim Shady got her first headcut after she allegedly pocketed $420 in trap money one night instead of turning it over to her boss. In 2003, after she used some of her front money to buy marijuana, Knowledge beat Slim Shady so forcefully with a metal chain she was left with a permanent scar on her right thigh. Another time, Knowledge drove her and Fortune to the Crown Motel in the Bronx, where he forced them to undress, then beat them with a belt.

Fortune and Madonna, two of the white "swans" in his stable, faced some of Knowledge's harshest treatment. "He treated the white girls like even more shit," says Maria. "He said it was reverse slavery." Fortune later testified that, between 1998 and 2005, Thompkins beat her with belts, chairs, fans, and lamps for "not following his rules, for talking back, or for looking at the wrong man." In one incident, Thompkins threatened her while holding a razor to her face.

But the razors, the whips, and the belts were the private face of the pimp. To the public, to his friends, his fellow postal workers, and his family, he was the garrulous gentleman.

"People loved him," says Garrabrant. "His family didn't see him as the guy who was beating the hell out of an underaged girl and pimping prostitutes. If you were Matthew's friend, Matthew could treat you really well, he could lend you money, he could take you out to a concert, he could take you out to Vegas, he would treat you right. Everyone got treated great, except for the people that were out there making him all of the money. They got the shit beat out of them."

■ ■ ■

BEYOND ITS sophistication, what struck FBI investigators about Knowledge's operation was its sheer scale. The Bureau calculated that over the course of his career he had more than seventy-five women working for him, sometimes up to a dozen all at once. "That's a lot of women to manage and run and make profit from," says Garrabrant. "Your average pimp has got maybe two or three girls. Talking to them every day, maintaining them, keeping them 'in pocket,' that's a full-time job."

Besides New York, Atlantic City, and Las Vegas, Knowledge dispatched his women to several hot spots across the country. Fortune went to Washington, D.C., Boston, and Seattle. Slim Shady was trafficked to Philadelphia and Youngstown, Ohio. Once he sent Lotion and White Diamond to Atlanta to sell themselves at an NBA All-Star game.

The hours were grueling—twelve hours each weeknight and up to fourteen hours on weekend nights. For Knowledge's black women, the situation was even worse because they tended to make less for each encounter.

"In order to come up, you have to stay down," Knowledge told Slim Shady. For her that meant putting in twenty-hour days, at the Hunts Point track from noon to 5:00 P.M., the Bronx track in the Baychester neighborhood from 5:00 P.M. to midnight, and then on the streets of Manhattan until 8:00 the following morning.

Ever the expert manipulator, Knowledge at one point had the women keep a bar chart, complete with sparkles and glitter, to tally who made the most money each night. He was following rule 29 from

Pimpology by Pimpin' Ken Ivy: "Play one ho against the next." "Competition breeds excellence," Pimpin' Ken wrote. "If you can get your workers going at one another, you will always win."

More important, Knowledge expected each of his women to bring in yet more profit by recruiting new girls into the fold. Slim Shady, for example, claimed that she alone brought about forty women into the stable over a period of several years; Knowledge wanted "all of the women working for him to bring home potential girls," she said.

The prize, at least in Knowledge's eyes, was the recruitment of underage girls. "Over the course of our investigation, we identified thirty-six minors who had worked for him in the past six or seven years," Garrabrant says. Three dozen real children. The FBI didn't just have tips, suspicions, or nicknames of girls who may or may not have existed but rather a long list of minors whom investigators were able to pinpoint with full names and dates of birth.

In addition, almost all of the older women in his stable—"older" being a relative term, since most of the women who were of legal age were in their early twenties—had been recruited when they were minors. Fortune was just seventeen when she met Knowledge in the Bronx in July 1998, a strikingly beautiful white "swan" with an easy smile and long blond hair. Slim Shady was a sixteen-year-old when she joined the stable in 1999. And Princess, who had first lured then fourteen-year-old Maria into the game back in Atlantic City, was also only sixteen when she began to make money for Knowledge.

Sometimes Knowledge's girls targeted their own siblings—even smart Meredith, who in spring 2002 brought her seventeen-year-old sister into the fold. Knowledge called her White Diamond. Fortune proved to be aptly named, too, for she was a relentless recruiter, bringing at least ten new members to Knowledge's stable, including her own sister, who at seventeen was given the street name Madonna by Knowledge. With dyed blond hair, blue eyes, and a friendly smile, Madonna in turn became what *Ozone* magazine shamelessly described as "one of his most reliable and profitable whores." Madonna told the magazine she'd been "ambitious but bored with no direction" as a psychology student at a college in Atlanta when her big sister brought her to Vegas for a summer vacation and introduced her to her pimp.

"This is my new life," she said. "I feel fulfilled now."

She certainly did a good job of keeping Knowledge's pockets full. One night, she boasted to the magazine, she earned fifty-six thousand dollars when a wealthy, drunk client agreed to give her that amount if she would quit her job and come live with him. When the client passed out, she left in a hurry and just as quickly delivered the cash to Knowledge. "All my money goes to him," she explained.

Knowledge was also aware that the penalties for trafficking in children were much more severe than those meted out for adult prostitution charges, so he forbade his girls from revealing not just their actual names but their real ages to one another. They were punished fast and hard if they ever broke that rule. In the summer of 1999, when Slim Shady was still only sixteen, she made the mistake of telling another young woman her true age. Knowledge slapped her in the face for her indiscretion.

For her part, Maria says she never realized there were so many other underage girls in Knowledge's grip. "I had always thought that I was pretty much the only one," she says.

Maria had no inkling that Knowledge's network was busy recruiting another minor in Las Vegas only a few months after she been arrested there.

■ ■ ■

HER NAME was Sandy. Only fourteen, she had lived most of her life in the historic West Side of Las Vegas, though its history was not necessarily something to be proud of. It was here that black entertainers were forced to stay when they were barred from living on or near the Strip as late as the 1960s. Four decades later, it had become one of the poorest, most crime ridden neighborhoods in the city.

Sandy lived with her mother and grandmother in a small house that had been built in the 1940s. Her mother worked long hours; Sandy's tough but caring grandmother ruled the roost. The home was filled with religious icons and paintings, but all the teenager had to do was walk outside the door to see what people were worshiping on the street—lots of money, fast, easy money from drugs and prostitution. Sandy later told police she was introduced to her first pimp by a next-door neighbor.

Don "Woody" Fieselman, one of the Vegas cops who eventually took on Sandy's case, could never put his finger on a single event that would have pushed her into the game. "The more I talked to these girls, the less I could figure out why they ended up in it," he says. "But one thing always stands out: the lack of a father figure. They are looking for love."

By June 2005, Sandy was walking the tracks of Tropicana Avenue and Paradise Boulevard for a hustler named Sack Money. That was when she bumped into two of Knowledge's women, Madonna and Slim Shady, both eager to enhance their status with their pimp by recruiting more young girls into the fold. Slim Shady convinced Sandy to come with her to the Aladdin Casino on the Strip where the young girl made a quick $450, which was immediately confiscated for Knowledge.

Sandy claimed she was seventeen, which still would have made her entry into the prostitution trade illegal, but Slim suspected she was at least three years younger than that. Much as Princess had entrapped Maria a couple of years earlier in Atlantic City, she easily swayed the Vegas girl with talk about the attractions of "the life" with Knowledge back in New York. It was ironic—while the glitter of Vegas had seemed so appealing to Maria after the grime of New York and New Jersey, for Sandy, the East Coast sounded like a grand escape from the slums of the West Side of Vegas. Both girls were chasing a dream, not a destination.

Slim called Knowledge with news of her latest catch. At McCarran International Airport, she paid cash for both their tickets on JetBlue (the discount carrier was always Knowledge's favorite airline). She traveled under her real name while Sandy assumed the identity of Tamika Davis. Once they landed at JFK, Slim took the child directly to Knowledge's home on Holland Avenue so he could inspect her.

Meredith chided Slim for bringing home someone so young, and she raised her concerns to Knowledge, but, as she'd later testify, he didn't seem worried a bit. It is not clear why Meredith, who had recruited her own seventeen-year-old sister, would suddenly develop qualms about the ages of girls working for Knowledge. Maybe Sandy's extreme vulnerability pricked at her conscience. Or maybe it was just that she was finally growing tired of Knowledge's interest in young girls. Whatever the reason, she later told FBI agent Dan Garrabrant the incident with Sandy was the beginning of her disenchantment with the pimp and her recognition that all he was interested in was money.

Knowledge certainly had no misgivings. When Sandy confirmed she was only fourteen, the pimp brushed it off. "A lot of girls started working for me when they were young," he said.

Knowledge promptly sent Slim and Goddess out shopping for one hundred dollars' worth of clothes for the new recruit and returned to another of Knowledge's apartments, this one on Tall Tulip Lane in Yonkers. The next day Goddess, Madonna, and Reflection drove Sandy to Atlantic City to work the track there. Knowledge promised what must have seemed like the world to a poor girl from the rough streets of Vegas. "I'll get a car, go shopping, and live by myself," she later recounted her dreams to the police.

By July 5, four days after flying to New York, Sandy was working the casinos for Knowledge. Goddess taught her how to act and how much to charge. "Just don't price yourself cheap," she told the girl.

Goddess also instructed the minor that if she was ever picked up by police, she should claim she was Sherry Brown, born on August 12, 1986, which would make her nineteen years old. At the end of her shift, Sandy joined the other women back at Knowledge's home in the Atlantic City suburb of Galloway, where they stuffed their cash in an envelope and wrote their name, the date, their earnings, and their expenses. Sandy slipped three hundred dollars into her envelope for her first night's work.

But the glamour must have worn off quickly for the young teen from Vegas, because when Knowledge showed up to collect his money "she started screaming and crying because she wanted to go home," according to later court filings.

Knowledge gave her a swift backhand slap across the face. "Shut up and don't disrespect me," he bellowed. Not long after, Knowledge took the fourteen-year-old to a New Jersey motel and had sex with her.

Barely six days had passed since Sandy had left Las Vegas.

• • •

As SANDY was trying to survive inside Knowledge's "stable," Maria was struggling to make it on the outside.

For several months now, she had tried to eke out a living by renegading, fending for herself on the tough-as-nails tracks of Atlantic City. One night Knowledge pulled up in his Hummer and beckoned to her, and she climbed inside. At first it was the friendly, charming Knowledge on display that evening. He popped a CD into his car's sound system, claiming he had recorded it at his Hoodlum Records operation. "This could have been me and you," he said, dangling the prospect of rap fame and fortune that Maria was supposedly missing. "We could have been everything."

Although Maria wasn't buying the pimp's song and dance, she did feel a pang of regret over leaving the stability and protection that Knowledge—as a powerful pimp—had provided. She spent an hour in the car with the pimp. By the end, Knowledge was back to business. He warned her that in "his" town, if she wanted to sell sex, she could not do so on his streets.

"Listen to me," Knowledge said, his face turning cold. "You cannot work Atlantic City. You can only work in the strip clubs."

Maria got out of the car and walked away, shaken but still confident she could make it on her own. *Nobody can touch me*, she told herself.

It was an odd duel of nerves. A streetwise girl was convinced her former pimp couldn't harm her, and her pimp was sure the police couldn't touch him. They would both be proven wrong.

PART TWO

Confronting the Pimps

Taking on Pimp Culture

Knowledge cherished the trophy. Perhaps more than his Mercedes-Benz, his Hummer, his flat-screen TV, and his Caribbean cruises.

It stood about four feet tall: four ornately carved wooden columns, topped by a golden statue of a pimp in a cape, wearing a crown on his head and holding a royal scepter in his hands. A sort of Oscar for a hustler. Matthew Thompkins won it as the International Pimp of the Year at the annual Players Ball held in Washington, D.C., in 2003, the same year Maria got arrested for selling her body for him. The Players Ball was like the Academy Awards night for pimps, a self-congratulatory PR festival. The myth of the ostentatious yet cool pimp was so deeply ingrained in society that a song heralding the bling-bang lifestyle would win an award at the real Oscar ceremonies a few years later.

How do you fight that kind of social acceptance, if not outright promotion, of the pimping world? The police and community activists soon realized that, to help young women forced into prostitution, they would have to confront not just the pimps but the culture in the news media, books, movies, and music that promoted them as cool and hip.

As Maria notes, "How come we're treated like dirt and the pimps are treated like celebrities and stars?"

■ ■ ■

THE PLAYERS Ball got its start in Chicago in November 1974 as a birthday celebration for one of the granddaddies of pimping, a self-styled king of the hustlers who called himself Bishop Don "Magic" Juan. His Web site boasts that what he calls his "pimpilicious style" put him "into the international spotlight, making him the envy of hip-hop moguls, Hollywood celebrities, sports figures, and stalwarts of business alike." He was not exaggerating much: his exploits had been featured on HBO and on Comedy Central's *The Daily Show* and in various rap music videos and documentaries. With his matching lime green jacket, pants, and hat, eyeglasses with star-shaped frames, and diamond rings the size of baseballs on his fingers that spell out "Magic" and "Juan," he was a natural as the prototypical pimp and swaggering spokesman.

"The Players Ball brings people together to recognize that pimpin' is hard work, despite what the public thinks," Don Juan once told Salon. com, no doubt with a straight face. "The Ball appreciates the blood, sweat, and tears it takes for a guy with a third-grade education to be driving a Rolls and wearing diamonds."

Choosing the winner isn't hard. Prior to each Ball, Don Juan and his pals sit around and debate over drinks which hustler has made the biggest pile of money and the biggest name for himself. Not surprisingly, Don Juan won the coveted award as the best pimp for thirteen years in a row. When he finally retired in the mid-1980s, other hustlers like Knowledge got a chance at winning the big prize. And the stakes got bigger, with imitations of the Players Ball cropping up in Miami, Atlanta, and Las Vegas.

The celebrity pimps often get fawning portraits in the media, which is all the more disturbing considering that just beneath the surface bling, the real-life grime and gore of pimping are not hard to find. Don Juan himself admitted that he was not above giving women "a whoopin'" with a hanger or whip, then pouring alcohol on the cuts and literally rubbing salt in their wounds. "You got to have a woman that no matter what, she want to see you on top, whether she has to spend 150 years in jail," he boasted to Salon.

Not everyone was fooled. In Atlanta in 2003, the hundreds of "players" who wanted to attend the pimp ball had to make it past

protesters carrying signs that read SHAME and PIMPIN AIN'T POPU-
LAR. State court judge Janis Gordon decried the event, telling the local
newspaper that "having a pimp convention is totally inappropriate."
As a former federal prosecutor she had helped jail fourteen Atlanta
pimps for trafficking underage girls, and she used video from previous
Players Balls attended by some of the accused to make the case under
federal racketeering laws that they were operating criminal enterprises
much as organized crime does.

Next, the pimps ran into trouble in Illinois. Three decades after Don
Juan first brought his Players Ball to Chicago, his reception in his hometown finally turned sour. It was December 3, 2005; only the day before,
the world had marked the fifty-fifth anniversary of the UN passing its
antitrafficking and antiprostitution treaty. A wide array of community
activists and local politicians turned out in the suburb of Maywood
where the pimps had rented a local banquet hall for their event. The
mayor, state representatives, and religious leaders denounced the event
during a news conference and noisy street protest.

"Stop glamorizing pain. Stop glamorizing abuse. Stop glamorizing the slavery of women," said Brenda Myers-Powell, a survivor of
prostitution who had been shot five times and stabbed on numerous
occasions. "If we allow stuff like this to continue and go on in our
community, it gives out messages to our young that it is cool."

Tina Fundt, at the time an outreach organizer for the Polaris Project, a group formed to prevent human trafficking, noted that she herself had been trafficked right there in Chicago when she was only
fourteen years old. "It's a ball for child molesters. It's a ball for rapists,
because that's what pimps do."

It was bitter cold that night, but that didn't stop dozens of protesters from marching across the street from the banquet hall, chanting
"Hey, hey, ho, ho, all the pimps have got to go." But it also didn't stop
the pimp partygoers from packing the standing-room-only celebration,
which was right across the street from local police headquarters. And
it didn't stop police from helping the organizers out, including setting
up barricades to prevent the protesters from blocking the entrance to
the hall and having off-duty officers provide extra security inside.

Moonlighting by off-duty cops at private affairs did not violate the letter of police department rules, but in an angry editorial the *Chicago Sun-Times* noted that it surely violated the spirit of what law enforcement was all about. "It would be absurd for off-duty police officers to provide security for alleged gang leaders and drug dealers," the paper pointed out. "Why then is it proper for them to provide security for a bash thrown to celebrate pimps?"

• • •

PIMPS ARE celebrated in all forms of popular culture, from books to Hollywood movies to music videos.

Mainstream publishers have no qualms about putting out pimping guides. Books like *Pimpin Ain't Easy: An Education on the Life* and *The Pimp Game: Instructional Guide* are steady sellers on Amazon. Simon and Schuster reportedly gave "Pimpin Ken" Ivy, who made his name plying the trade on the streets of Chicago and Milwaukee, a six-figure deal to peddle his street smarts into his how-to book for wannabe pimps. In *Pimpology*, Ivy shows off pictures of himself with the likes of boxing champion Evander Holyfield and actor Jamie Foxx, and he offers advice on how to exploit women for the money they can make and then discard them when they are used up. "She gave some real good head, but he still preferred the bread," he writes. "A burnout is a ho that has expired—her time is up, like a cigarette with no butt."

Substitute the word "pimp" for the synonymous "domestic sex trafficker," and it is hard to imagine publishers putting out such how-to books. Yet pimps, arguably, are just like the much-decried international human traffickers, except they usually keep their business within the borders of one country. By their own admission, they sell sex by moving women and girls from one neighborhood, city, or region of the country to another. It is hard to imagine that rapists and child molesters would get their own guidebooks or that mainstream publishers would produce a book called *International Sex Trafficking: The Laws of the Game*. Yet they promote books by traffickers like Ken Ivy's because, for the most part, pimping has few negative connotations in our society.

Ironically, while pimps are often glamorized, the prostituted women who provide their profits are more likely to be demonized.* "I don't know of a single word, since the time of the Bible, that connotes such shame and contempt as 'prostitute,'" says Dallas cop Byron Fassett.

In the Bible, a "harlot" is a damned woman, to be stoned or "burned with fire" for the "abominations and filthiness of her fornication." Through the ages, that attitude has not improved much. These days, in the biggest-selling video game of all time, *Grand Theft Auto IV*, you can pick up a prostitute, have sex, then kill her and get your money back. YouTube offers over fifty videos from various *Grand Theft* players who discuss their favorite ways of killing the women, from stabbing to a simple bullet in the head.

"This is the number-one-selling game at Wal-Mart and Target?" asks Vegas vice cop Aaron Stanton. "What does that tell young girls and young women about their lives, and what does that tell young boys?"

The problem isn't a simplistic connection that suggests playing the game will make men want to go out to maim and murder prostitutes. What's disturbing is subtler and more deeply ingrained. The game designers, sensitive to the demands of the market, know that such content will be popular with today's youth. A major commercial success, *Grand Theft Auto IV* broke industry records by grossing over five hundred million dollars in revenue in its first week alone and has gone on to sell over ten million copies worldwide.

The demeaning of prostitutes and idealization of pimps has long been a staple of Hollywood movies and TV shows as well, reaching new heights in 2006 when the Academy Award for Best Original Song went to "It's Hard Out Here for a Pimp" from the movie *Hustle and*

---

* They are also much more likely to be arrested than the pimps. How pimps and prostitutes are treated in popular culture reflects how they are treated by the law. The Chicago Alliance Against Sexual Exploitation found that the women made up 65 percent of the prostitution-related arrests between 2003 and 2005. Fewer than 1 percent of the arrests were of pimps.

Flow. The premise of the song and the movie is that a pimp's life is made that much harder because of whining women:

> *You know it's hard out here for a pimp*
> *When he tryin' to get his money for the rent*
> *For the Cadillacs and gas money spent*
> *Because a whole lot of bitches talking shit*

After the rap group Three Six Mafia performed its song on Oscar night to an audience of millions around the world, host Jon Stewart quipped, "You know what? I think it just got a little easier out here for a pimp."

Vice cop Gil Shannon, from Las Vegas, was outraged when he saw the show. "Our children were watching this in the same living room as we were," he says. "Daughters, nieces, mothers, aunts—everyone has someone female in the family that they care for, and they're saying it's tough out there to be a pimp? How about it's tough out there to be a victim of prostitution? It's tough being beaten and raped and exposed to sexually transmitted diseases and being told that if you don't earn me money, I'm gonna kill you?"

The legend of the pimp lives on. With obvious pride, Pimpin' Ken writes that "the pimp has reached near mythical status." Perhaps that status is best personified by TV actor, rap musician, and former pimp Ice-T, popularly known for his portrayal as tough, streetwise cop Odafin "Fin" Tutuola on TV's famed *Law and Order: Special Victims Unit*. Ironically, the program is renowned for its sensitive depiction of sexual crimes, often against children. One episode, entitled "Underbelly," used the murder of three teenage girls forced into prostitution to expose the plight of runaways and children in group homes. Ice-T himself twice earned the NAACP Image Award for his work on the series.

But when he is not wearing his pretend badge on TV, Ice-T boasts of his days as a pimp, and he continues to glorify the business. In 2003, he narrated and rapped in a movie called *Pimpin' 101*, which its makers billed as "one of the most famous XXX hip hop porn films ever made." In the opening song, performed over pictures of naked

women doing various sexual acts, he singles out two of the locations
Maria and other girls knew all too well:

See me in Vegas... Swing through Hunts Point
Throwing dollars at those hos and strippers

Ice-T grew up in New Jersey's tough gang scene, graduating, as he
put it, from "small-time hustler" to big-time jewel thief. Then, inspired
by a famous pimp called Iceberg Slim, he saw the benefits of getting
women to do the work for him. "That's where I got my name," he says
in an interview at the end of the movie. "I had the pleasure of being in
the pimp game for three years."

Ice-T shares some of the lessons he learned selling women as he
narrates *Pimpin' 101*. "Any ho sitting out there too long is not being
a good bitch," he explains at the start. "You ain't supposed to see my
bitch because my bitch supposed to be in a bedroom somewhere getting some motherfuckin' money."

And she has to make that money regardless of the risk. The movie's
first "lesson" shows a cheaply dressed woman about to enter a car with
two mean-looking bikers—"the kind of cats that like to do the wrong
shit to a ho," Ice-T chortles. "But hey, pimpin' ain't easy but hoing ain't
hard." The woman is then brutalized sexually and tossed out of the
car.

As a bonus on the DVD, Ice-T gives a rambling interview about his
life, prostitution, and the women who are trafficked. "I've had no moral
thoughts... about it being wrong," he concludes. "They like it."

■ ■ ■

NOWHERE IS the image of young black men as pimps who exploit
prostituted women so heavily promoted as in modern-day rap music.
Pimp language, pimp dress, and pimp words that denigrate women are
a recurring beat in many top songs and music videos.

Snoop Dogg and 50 Cent could not have been more explicit when
they performed a song called "P.I.M.P" at the 2003 MTV Video
Music Awards:

Bitch choose with me, I'll have you stripping in the street
Put my other hos down, you get your ass beat

To drive their point home, the rappers led scantily clad women around the stage on leashes and were joined on stage by Snoop Dogg's so-called spiritual adviser, none other than the real-life poster boy for the pimps, Bishop Don "Magic" Juan. The final insult came right after the performance, when Chris Rock, the well-known comedian who was hosting the awards show, sarcastically noted, "Today is the anniversary of Martin Luther King's 'I Have a Dream' speech. Isn't it nice to see his dream has finally come true?"

It may have been tongue-in-cheek, but Rock's observation was sadly accurate in the sense that pimps were indeed trying to spin their mistreatment of women as part of nothing less than black liberation. In rap music and on the streets, pimping is portrayed as empowerment, a route for black men to succeed. That's why Don Juan could get away with claiming that pimping was a way for "a guy with a third-grade education to be driving a Rolls."

Activists like Vednita Carter call this "toxic propaganda" that distorts the collective identity of black people. Carter had her hands full as the founder and director of St. Paul's shelter and recovery program Breaking Free, but when she was not helping young women escape the bonds of prostitution, she found the time to take the battle to the cultural front. For more than a decade, her writings have appeared in legal and academic journals, anthologies, and the feminist press nationwide. Behind the pimp mythology she saw the sorry legacy of slavery and racism that through the ages inevitably led to prostitution becoming so prevalent in the black community and, in some quarters, accepted.

As slaves, Carter noted in one of her published studies, African women and girls were paraded around naked, their bodies easily accessible to their captors at all times. "Few black women reached the age of sixteen without having been molested by a white male," she wrote. "Many of the biracial female children that resulted from these rapes were sold to brothels as young as ten years of age. Called 'fancy girls,' they were given food, blankets, and a place to sleep in exchange for performing sex acts each day with numerous strangers."

Emancipation only altered the form of exploitation. Carter remembered her grandmother talking about what life was like back in 1863, when Carter's great-grandmother was only twelve and the slaves were freed. Many fled north, where a woman, if she could not find work as a servant, was often forced to trade sex for food, shelter, or clothing for her family. "Nobody blamed her, nobody judged her," Carter says. "It was just a silent thing that happened because we couldn't do or say anything about it."

By the 1920s and 1930s, every Southern city had its red-light district on the "other side of the tracks," in the black ghetto. In the ensuing decades, Carter notes, racist stereotypes in the mainstream media and in widely accepted porn portrayed black women as wild animals, ready for sex anytime with anybody. She was struck once walking into a store to see the level of violence and brutality on the covers of porn magazines featuring black women. "Looking at the women's faces, I could see they felt shame, embarrassment, hopelessness," she wrote. "Seeing these black women shackled, spread-eagle, or hog-tied made it seem as though this part of history—the history of my family's enslavement—was repeating itself all over again."

Strip joints and massage parlors are typically zoned in black neighborhoods, which, Carter argues, gives the message to white men that it is OK to solicit black women and girls for sex. "Like slave women on the auction block, African American women are displayed on the streets or in strip clubs, surveyed like cattle, and selected to perform at the orders of a stranger," she wrote.

It was a powerful, unsettling message, not one that everyone in the black community wanted to hear. As she spoke out at community meetings and in churches, she endured snickers and snide comments. "This is a taboo topic, even today," she says.

But she would not stop. "This is not a joke; this is what's happening to our women and girls," she told her audiences. "Black men need to unlearn the lessons of slavery; we are not their bitches, we are not their hos, any more than we are the bitches and hos of white men, on the plantation or in the 'hood. We need to educate ourselves about our history and how it affects who we are now."

Ironically, it was the death of a white police officer that helped galvanize the Twin Cities of Minneapolis and St. Paul and drew attention to the plight of their forgotten children of the night. Sergeant Jerry Vick was a fourteen-year veteran of the police force, the only officer to be twice awarded the medal of valor, the department's highest honor. In one incident during his first year on the job, he dragged a three-year-old boy from a burning house in 1990 and then crawled back in to rescue a fifteen-month-old girl.

But Vick always felt his biggest award was working the streets of his city as a vice cop. "He was passionate about ending the violence of prostitution and human trafficking," says Vednita Carter. "He was an extraordinary officer who did not look at prostituted women as willing participants of oppression. Many who knew him saw him as their guardian angel."

In the early morning hours of May 6, 2004, Vick was working undercover in a bar on the east side of St. Paul, less than a ten-minute drive from the Breaking Free headquarters on University Avenue. He was checking out reports that minors were being prostituted here. As he and his partner exited the bar, they confronted two men on the street who turned out to be convicted felons. One of them pulled a gun and fired at Vick several times, killing the forty-one-year-old officer.

The murder shocked the city. But what was unusual was that a cop's death led to an outpouring of grief from an unlikely source—the women he had arrested.

"You were a different kind of cop; thanks for not revictimizing me," said Candy, in a special Breaking Free memorial dedicated to the fallen officer.

"Sergeant Vick arrested me many times," added another, Lisa. "Although I was angry at being arrested, he always acknowledged me as a human being. He told me I didn't deserve to stand out on the street; he said I was better than that."

Vick's death helped raise the public profile of prostitution. His family joined volunteers and police officers for a fund-raiser for a transitional residential program that Breaking Free was setting up. "Jerry understood that if women didn't get off the street, they never had a chance at a better life," said his mother, Maggie Vick.

Not long after, Breaking Free's House of Hope opened its doors, standing discreetly on a tree-lined street in a quiet neighborhood in east St. Paul. Inside, there are six bedrooms, with a spacious common living room, a dining room table, and a well-equipped kitchen. On the wall next to the fridge, a whiteboard lists the weekly activities, everything from lessons in how to make tacos to workshops for writing job resumes. The women share in the household tasks and must attend regular counseling and addiction sessions.

Around the supper table one evening, two women talk about employment prospects. One, a white woman in her thirties, says she knows the manager at a local clothing store and is heading out the next day for a job interview. Another resident, a black teenager cradling a baby, asks if she can come along. A third woman heads out the door for a "Dress for Success" buying trip sponsored by a local church, giving her a chance to get some decent clothes as she hunts for a steady job.

Near the front door of the House of Hope is a small bronze plaque with Jerry Vick's picture to remind people the home is "dedicated to his memory." In the corner of the plaque is Breaking Free's symbol, a woman's fist, breaking the chains—invisible or not—that bind her.

Around the same time the House of Hope opened its doors in 2006, the mayor of St. Paul declared November 2 Breaking Free Day in the city, in honor of the organization's tenth anniversary. "Prostitution tears at the fabric of our community, ruining lives, devastating families," the proclamation read.

Vednita Carter had good reason to be proud of her work. At least in one city, the myth of a harmless, happy-go-lucky pimp culture was being challenged.

. . .

PIMPS ARE expert manipulators. And they know it.

Las Vegas cops Aaron Stanton and Woody Fieselman once had the opportunity in a courtroom to talk informally with a particularly boastful pimp they had just helped convict.

"How many girls are out there on the tracks working without a pimp?" they wanted to know.

"I don't like that word," he said.

"What word?" they asked.

"Pimp."

"What would you prefer? Sexual entrepreneur? Money manager?" Fieselman said.

"Nah, street psychiatrist," said the pimp. "I seek out girls who need my help."

Like wolves to the scent of blood, pimps can sense the vulnerability of young girls, zeroing in on the weaknesses and needs of their targets. Dallas police sergeant Byron Fassett wanted to show the girls—and other cops—just how manipulative a shrewd pimp could be. He decided he would do it with the pimps' own words.

Fassett saw an opportunity when his team busted a hustler named TC in 2003. TC faced two counts of sexually assaulting a minor, and as a witness the cops had his teen victim, Danielle, who had been in the life since she was fifteen. It was still early in Fassett's campaign to help prostituted children, and the state attorney's office was just beginning to develop an expertise in prosecuting these cases. So when he learned the prosecutors had offered TC a deal—eight years in exchange for pleading guilty and cooperating with authorities—he slipped one more condition into the package: the pimp had to speak candidly in a videotaped interview about his methods and manipulation.

For three hours, Fassett filmed TC and Danielle separately. The result was a gripping and revealing portrait of the pimping world. "I want to give an inside view of the prostitution game," TC says by way of introduction. Wearing a neat short-sleeved shirt and an expensive wristwatch, he boasts that over his career he's made close to a quarter million dollars exploiting forty women. Easily 60 percent of the girls on the street are under seventeen, he concedes.

With remarkable frankness, he then proceeds to give a detailed outline of how a shrewd pimp spots his potential next recruit, lures her in, and keeps her under his thumb. "Someone with low self-esteem is going to be your first choice," he explains. More often than not, he says, the girls will have been molested already—by a boyfriend, an uncle, a father, their mother's boyfriend. "That's the main reason why they left home," he continues. "You have females who can't deal with the pain and pressure at home and would rather take their chance with me.

"A pimp's whole persona is selling people the dream. I tell you whatever it takes to get what I need out of you."

When Danielle appears on the screen, she is reserved and withdrawn, her braided hair falling loosely over her left shoulder. She clasps her hands frequently as she talks. Sexually abused by a cousin, she took to the streets, and when she met TC, she believed he was going to make everything OK, that he was going to be her protector. "Knowing my past, he used that against me," she says. TC convinced her to prostitute herself because he was temporarily short of money, she says, "just this once so he could get back on his feet.... But then it was every day, all day."

The beatings started when she didn't meet his demands. A broomstick. A gun fired at her. A near drowning in a bathtub. "He was beating me just to make me weak, so wherever I go I will always be afraid of him," Danielle says. Twice she went back home only to flee again. "The more you run away, the more you get down talked," even by the people who are supposed to love you, she says. "They don't see the person you is. Just a ho."

When Fassett showed the video to young girls in a shelter for runaways, they cried. They saw too much of themselves in Danielle, and they had never before heard a pimp talk so brazenly about how he manipulates them.

TC neatly summed it up in one phrase, ugly but painfully true: "Fuck the head, the body is going to follow."

Brutal, but no doubt more honest than Bishop Don "Magic" Juan's public relations spin at the Players Ball about all the "blood, sweat, and tears" he and his fellow pimps have to endure to earn their diamonds and fancy cars.

■ ■ ■

FOR ALL their flash and street smarts, pimps can be wimps. Fassett was always struck by how the tough-talking hustlers often caved once they were sitting across the table facing a cop with a mountain of evidence.

"It is always amazing when you listen to these girls talk about these guys. They almost seem bigger than life. They take on an almost God-like persona for these girls," Fassett says. "It is not hard to be a man when you are slapping around a fourteen-year-old girl. But when we get them in the interrogation room, they back down. Pimp after pimp after pimp. They are basically cowards."

But Fassett wants the girls to see their tormentors as the pathetic bullies they are. "I wish those girls could see that this guy is not all-powerful," he says. "I wish that the girls could see them for the wimpy ass pieces of crap that they really are."

Which does not make them any less formidable as adversaries for the police. Byron Fassett shows TC's candid confession at law enforcement training conferences to shake up the officers and force them to respect the street smarts of the pimp.

"I truly despise him, but I am fascinated by him," Fassett tells his audience. "He has no letters out after his name [for a college degree], but he has a firm grasp of child psychology. Pimps are expert in human nature. They are expert in manipulation and seduction."

Children do not end up in prostitution just by chance. They are made and molded into objects of exploitation. Fassett shows the audience a diagram that displays stages of a girl's slide from independence to submission as links in a chain, an eerie echo of Vednita Carter's analysis of prostitution as slavery. When the child is first recruited, she has her own identity. As she buys into the pimp's dream, she loses a part of herself.

"Like a husband who abuses his wife, the pimp wants to alienate his target from all avenues of support," Fassett explains. "The best victims are the ones who don't know they are victims."

This deep psychology of dependence makes it all the harder for the police to help girls break away from their pimps. "More often than not," says Fassett, "when I arrest their pimp there are tears—not of joy, but of sadness."

"Where do I go now?" the girls will ask.

FBI agent Dan Garrabrant had the same experience. "What do most of these girls have to look forward to—a bad foster home? An overcrowded group home? Or back to some family situation where they're being abused? So when I walk through that door, it's not like: 'Thank god you found me!'"

The pimp cuts a girl off from her friends and family, all too easy in many cases where often there is little love at home. He makes her believe that he has her back, that he and he alone loves her, and when that is accomplished, he brings out the weapons of violence, the fear, drugs, and degradation.

"If we can't break the chain, she becomes the offender," he warns. Indeed, Danielle became TC's "bottom girl," helping him control and discipline other women, until she was arrested at age nineteen. Just like Knowledge had his women actively recruiting younger girls into his stable.

"The amount of control is indescribable," concludes Fassett. The girl is left with a simple message from her pimp: *I own you now.*

That ownership is marked, literally, by a tattoo. Matthew Thompkins, for example, had his girls branded with such labels as KNOWLEDGE IS THE KEY TO MY LIFE, KNOWLEDGE BORN BITCH, and KNOWLEDGE.

"How deep does that branding go?" Fassett continues, who prefers to use the word "branding" over "tattoo" when he testifies in court to make it clear this is a form of sex slavery. "How do you remove that tattoo in the brain? Every morning when she looks in the mirror, what does she see—that she is property.

"How," Fassett asks, "do you dig down in there and take that out?"

· 6 ·

"He Was Untouchable"

CAESAR STANDS erect, his shoulders square and his chest thrust out, daring any man to be as tough as he is. As if there weren't enough testosterone in Atlantic City.

The white marble statue of the Roman emperor, bedecked in gold and surrounded by four stallions, dominates the entrance to the casino that bears his name. Tourists mill about looking for some gambling as men of all ages walk down the Strip looking for some sex. The pimping scene around the casinos picks up after midnight and stretches into the early morning hours. "The pimps want the girls out late because they want the guys drunk," the FBI's Dan Garrabrant explains. That makes the johns perfect targets for the sex the pimps are selling. "If they won at the casinos, it gives them something to celebrate. If they lost, it lets them feel good about something."

On a cool April night, Maria was also hoping to strike it lucky as she stood outside Caesar's. She had ignored Knowledge's warning to stay away from his tracks, and she kept renegading, trying to drum up business on her own. Maria thought she spotted a potential john when she caught sight of a Hispanic man in the distance. "So I went up to him like he was a trick, and I said, 'Hey, Papí, you want to do something?'"

"Bitch," came the cold reply. Instantly, Maria recognized the man. This wasn't a tourist looking for a pickup. It was Tracy, her first pimp and Knowledge's business partner, and it was testimony to how conflicted she was about her life that instead of fear she felt nostalgia.

"A part of me still loved him so much that I wanted to run to him," she says.

But Tracy didn't have romance in mind. Maria screamed and kicked as he lifted her up and threw her into his car. First he drove her to the woods on the outskirts of Atlantic City, and she was terrified he was going to kill her right then and there, in the dark, where no one could hear. But they continued on to Galloway, right to the front door of Knowledge's three-story home. He had several luxury cars parked out front, and his rottweiler paced in a cage out back.

Maria walked through the dark oak front door. Several of the women in the stable were inside. Then Knowledge sauntered down the long stairway just past the foyer. He was dressed casually in a T-shirt and sweats, and a small smile broke across on his face when he saw her.

"I just knew it. I knew it inside: *Fuck, I am going to die*," Maria recalls. But she wouldn't die here, in the house, in this white neighborhood, with other people watching. "He was going to kill me in New York."

■ ■ ■

IT HAD been more than a year since Maria's return to Atlantic City after her arrest in Las Vegas. And though she didn't know it, Dan Garrabrant's FBI investigation of Knowledge was about to kick into high gear.

All Maria knew was that she was in trouble. Big trouble.

She yelled for help at the top of her lungs, but nobody came. The neighbors were too far away to hear anything.

"Stop screaming in my fucking house," Knowledge said calmly. "Hear me out."

"OK," Maria said. He sent all the women away and had Maria join him and Tracy in the living room.

"Isn't this ironic," he said to Tracy. "Look who started everything, the one bitch that you thought would never turn on you."

"I don't know what you're talking about," Maria interrupted. "I told you, I didn't say nothing."

"Bitch, shut up! Just shut the fuck up," Knowledge shouted.

"You shut the fuck up!" Maria shouted back, surprising herself by her own courage. *I got balls*, she thought. But she had only a few seconds to gloat.

Whack! Tracy swung out and struck her hard in the face, leaving his handprint, red and burning.

Knowledge glared at her. "Who are you going to fuck with? Are you going to fuck with me or are you going to fuck with him?" He was asking her to choose up, decide whom she wanted to work for, ostensibly inviting her back into the fold.

For Maria, it was an easy choice. She pointed to Tracy.

"They were going to kill me anyway. Whoever I picked, it was going to happen," she says. "But if I picked Tracy, it would be a little easier to get away from him because Knowledge was too smart."

"Well, all right," Knowledge grumbled and walked back upstairs.

Maria felt only slightly safer with Tracy. She had heard that he had been arrested the previous year for pimping a minor, after one of the women working for him had squealed to the police. "He was crazier than before he went to jail," Maria says. "Now he had this grudge. Against bitches, because a bitch did him wrong."

Tracy then introduced Maria to his newest acquisition, a light-skinned African American named Joanie, a waif from Philadelphia who was only fourteen years old. She looked it too, with straight hair and a body so thin even her breasts and hips had not yet filled out.

"She was just so scared," says Maria, recognizing much of herself three years earlier in the eyes of the frightened yet hopeful runaway. Maria thought of the scars on her body, remnants of the knife wounds from violent johns, and the bruises from pimps. She wanted to shake Joanie and wake her out of her daydream. "So many things happened to me, I wanted her to not have to go through that," she says. "I just wanted to grab her and run."

Tracy startled Maria out of her own reverie. "OK, we're going back home," he announced. He meant New York, where he and Knowledge had their pimping headquarters. He turned coyly to Maria. "You happy to go back home?"

"Yeah, babe," Maria said, forcing a smile.

Five of them piled into the Hummer. Goddess, the reliable veteran in Knowledge's stable, was in the driver's seat, with Knowledge beside her, while Maria was squeezed between Joanie and Tracy in the back. They sped off onto the Garden State Parkway toward New York, and Maria knew she had less than two hours to figure a way out. "They weren't going to hold court on me or anything," she says, referring to the practice of two pimps working together to beat a woman. "They were going to beat the shit out of me and then kill me."

Maria came up with the only ruse she could think of. "I really have to pee," she announced. She figured if they stopped on the side of the road, she could run out in the middle of the highway and try to stop traffic without getting run over. Or if they pulled into a rest stop, she could maybe make her break there.

The white Hummer took exit 76 into the Forked River service area, jammed with trucks, RVs, and cars. The women's washroom was just past the busy Starbucks. Knowledge ordered Joanie to accompany Maria as Tracy stood guard outside in the parking lot.

Maria had just a few minutes. She stopped the first woman who walked into the washroom. "Excuse me, ma'am, I am being kidnapped. Can I use your phone?" she boldly asked.

The startled woman complied. Joanie stared at Maria, wide-eyed.

The older girl was impatient. "Look, you want this to be the rest of your life?" she asked. "This is going to be your life. You know that, right?"

Joanie was flustered. "No, I love my daddy," she said of her pimp.

"Whatever," Maria muttered in reply, thinking that there was no time to waste worrying about this kid. All she could do was save herself—maybe.

Never one to trust the police, Maria called a sometime boyfriend she had met a few months ago, but he refused to come pick her up.

Maria was on her own. Brazen, she walked up to Tracy and put on the performance of her life—a performance *for* her life—knowing this was her best and last chance.

"I called the cops, and they are going to come and get you," she declared. "So if I were you, I would leave now."

"Bitch, you didn't call the cops." Tracy tried to call her bluff, but Maria sensed a hint of uncertainty in his voice.

"I know you're going to kill me," Maria said angrily.

"No way, babe," Tracy pleaded, shaking his head. "You're my number one."

Maria ignored him and walked out to the Hummer in the crowded parking lot, hoping to make as big a scene as possible. "You fucking nasty little piece of shit," she yelled at Knowledge, who sat looking somewhat stunned in the front seat. "That's why you've got that little girl with you," Maria continued, pointing to Joanie, who by now had dashed back to her keepers.

"I just start talking so much shit," Maria recalls. "Trying to attract as much attention as possible. I wanted everybody to see it."

The ploy worked. With all the bystanders and surveillance cameras, the men decided a discreet departure was the better part of pimp valor. As they pulled away, Tracy rolled down his window. "You're going to pay for this, you know," he warned.

"Forget her, she's a snitch," Knowledge said to his buddy. He then turned his face to Maria. Her pimp, master, and daddy for the past four years just stared at her in ominous silence. He looked calm and relaxed.

"It was like he was untouchable," says Maria.

■ ■ ■

DAN GARRABRANT had not heard from Maria in more than a month. Then his cell phone rang, and he got an earful.

"Fuck you!" Maria blurted out over the phone. "I hate you people! You nearly got me killed, you motherfucker!"

To make her way home from the rest stop, Maria had called the state police and made up a story about being abandoned by her boyfriend after a fight. She was not going to tell the cops that she was an underage prostitute on the run from her pimps, who wanted to kill her. Once safely back home, though, she unloaded her fury at the FBI agent. It was all his fault, this position she found herself in. She vented, she cried, and she accused.

Though Garrabrant didn't realize it at the time, he had corroborating evidence of Maria's story. Two weeks after Maria's escape at the highway rest stop, Garrabrant got a call from the Atlantic City Police Department. They had picked up a prostituted teenager on the streets of Atlantic City who stood out because she was so obviously underage. She readily talked to the FBI man about being trafficked by a pimp named Tracy from Philadelphia to work in New York and Atlantic City. Unbeknownst to Garrabrant, this was Joanie, the fourteen-year-old in the Hummer with Maria. But at the time she made no mention of the highway incident. It would be months before Garrabrant made the connection between Joanie and Maria's kidnapping.

"For her, what Knowledge was trying to do with Maria was just another small horror show, a fleeting thing," Garrabrant later surmised. "I don't think she got what was going on." Garrabrant managed to find Joanie temporary shelter at a group home and added her name to the list of minors they could use as evidence in prosecuting Knowledge and Tracy.

Handling Maria would not be as easy. Garrabrant promised to keep a closer eye on her—and on Knowledge's whereabouts. But she was far from convinced. According to FBI logs later filed with the courts, she "indicated that she did not want to cooperate any further because she believed [Knowledge and Tracy] were going to kill her."

Certainly, Knowledge was relentless. One way or the other, through sweet talk, pressure, or outright violence, he had to eliminate Maria as a threat to his operation. He called her constantly on her cell phone, asking her to meet with his lawyer in Atlantic City and retract the statement she had given the Vegas police. "This is what a lot of pimps do," Garrabrant says. "Get a female witness to go to a lawyer that he would pick because that's his out: 'Hey, look, she lied to the police and now if we go to court, we have got doubt.'"

Maria stalled. "I didn't refuse, I just kind of forgot and never went," she says. The frightened girl, as usual, was torn—she didn't fully trust the police, but she knew they, unlike her pimp, would not try to kill her. "I knew that I would rather have the FBI on my side than Knowledge."

Once Knowledge even told Maria he was going to make a special trip from New York to Atlantic City to see her face-to-face. "Listen, bitch, I am coming down to see you," he said on the phone.

Maria panicked and called Garrabrant, reaching him on his cell phone while he was in a rural area with poor reception. Worried he would lose the signal, he pulled his car over and spent the next hour trying to calm the girl and marshal the FBI's forces at the same time. They put surveillance teams both on her house and on Knowledge's Galloway home.

Sure enough, Knowledge showed up outside his home. He wasn't bluffing: he had come to confront Maria. What worried the FBI was that Knowledge, who had a fleet of personal cars to choose from, had come down to Atlantic City in a vehicle that was not registered in his name.

"It was scary," says Garrabrant. "We thought he might have done that because if he did pick her up and do something to her, he wouldn't want to be in a car that could be traced back to him."

But the Bureau and Maria had one thing going for them—Knowledge had never known precisely where she lived. In the past, he would just call her and tell her to meet him someplace. So on this occasion, Knowledge kept calling Maria on her cell. Garrabrant countered by staying on the phone with her as well for as long as possible.

"He's calling, he's calling," she said nervously as the telltale clicks of another incoming call kept interrupting their conversation.

"Don't answer," Garrabrant kept saying. "Don't leave. Don't go to his house." The FBI agent knew this moment was an important test. She had to learn to put her faith in him and the Bureau once and for all.

Knowledge eventually gave up and drove back to New York without seeing the girl he had once controlled as Suprema. For Garrabrant, it was a turning point in winning over Maria. "She just became more comfortable and had more confidence in me," he says. "I was someone who always answered the phone and listened to her. And I think for Maria and a lot of the young women out there, not many people besides their pimp have ever taken the time."

Maria was troubled, though. How could she be talking to the FBI on one line and her pimp on the other? She was almost eighteen now and trying to figure out her life. But she felt that she could not break completely free of Knowledge's orbit. His words kept coming back to haunt her. "You can't live in both worlds," he'd once said. "You know that. You're a ho or you're a square. You can't have it both ways."

"You know, Daddy, I'm a ho," she had assured him then, even as she thought, *I am not a ho.*

Now Maria wasn't so sure. Was she destined to be a ho all her life? "I didn't know what the fuck I was doing," she says. "I was just lost."

■ ■ ■

MARIA'S INTERNAL turmoil came just as the FBI was about to launch a full-scale operation against Knowledge's empire. Garrabrant's probe against Knowledge was one of several ongoing investigations that reflected the bold new approach that the Innocence Lost program brought to the battle against prostituted children: treating pimps like organized crime bosses and going after them with Mafia-style anti-racketeering laws. In Michigan, the FBI closed in on a pimp named Blue Diamond who was trafficking girls as far away as Hawaii. In Pennsylvania, the FBI began investigating another far-flung truck-stop prostitution ring led by a hustler who called himself Silky Red.

Garrabrant was ready to add Knowledge to that target list. By late spring 2005, he had gathered enough material to get his FBI superiors and the Department of Justice prosecutors in Washington to authorize an official federal probe of Knowledge for operating a criminal conspiracy. "We had to show that we would need wiretaps and surveillance and a major operation," says Garrabrant. "Otherwise, Knowledge would have the money and resources to get away."

He successfully made the case that not only had Matthew Thompkins's suspected crimes crossed state lines but also that his network operated with a level of sophistication that made it largely impregnable to the limited resources of a local police vice investigation.

With the official go-ahead, Garrabrant's next step was to put an operational team in place, starting with the prosecutors. Too often in the past, Garrabrant felt, some prosecutors were reluctant to take on complicated cases against pimps. "If I went to any federal prosecutor in the country and said, 'Listen, I have a thirteen-year-old girl who was kidnapped, forcibly taken from her home, and forced to have sex with a forty-year-old guy and then sold to other men,' they would be saying, 'Bring it on.'" But Garrabrant found that if he took that same scenario and instead described the girl as a prostitute working for a pimp, prosecutors got cold feet. Their attitude was that if some young girl wants to go do that, there is nothing to be done.

The first designated prosecutor in the Knowledge case went on maternity leave, then a second one had to leave to handle a Mob trial. The file eventually landed in the lap of Jason Richardson, an assistant U.S. attorney in New Jersey who had a reputation for being methodical and determined.

"As a prosecutor, I never have enough evidence," says Richardson. "I don't care whether you catch the guy standing over the body, covered in his blood, on tape with the gun in his hand, screaming to the heavens that he did it. I still want more."

Like most prosecutors, however, he had little prior exposure to the pimping world. "The only thing I thought about was the character Huggy Bear from *Starsky and Hutch*," he says, referring to the cartoonish huckster featured in the classic 1970s cop show. When he first was assigned the Knowledge case, Richardson wondered, tongue in cheek, if he was going to see the bell-bottom pants and fedoras.

But Garrabrant was pleased by how quickly Richardson saw the criminal nature of commercial sexual exploitation. He showed Richardson the size of Knowledge's enterprise, the lives being destroyed. "Jason saw right away that these girls are beaten into submission," says Garrabrant. "This is not a real choice. It's done through force."

To assist Richardson, the Department of Justice sent in trial attorney Sherri Stephan, an experienced prosecutor from the Child

Exploitation and Obscenity Section. "You very rarely get the pimps," she says, noting that Knowledge had been operating for sixteen years before he even got arrested. "He organized it as a business, so we looked at this as a criminal enterprise and started at the top."

Rounding out the team was Tara Bloesch, from the U.S. Postal Service's Office of Inspector General. Bloesch had been an FBI agent for seven years before becoming a postal investigator in 2004, so she was a natural choice to probe Thompkins's postal employment. "I was very surprised at the combination of an active mailman being able to engage in this level of criminality," says Bloesch, who eventually rejoined the FBI's ranks after her short stint with the USPS.

Bloesch found out that Thompkins often lent money to other postal employees and allowed them to pay off their debts by covering for him and delivering the mail on some of his routes. He flashed his money around when he showed up at the Manhattanville post office and at times had the women working for him waiting in his car outside during his visits. Bloesch was able to show how Thompkins profited from his knowledge of the details of postal regulations. He knew that anyone purchasing a money order over three thousand dollars had to show government-issued picture identification and fill out a form, so he instructed the women to send him their earnings with postal orders under the reporting limit.

Garrabrant was determined to lay bare the full workings of the pimp's empire. "I wanted to know what Thompkins was going to do before he even knew he was going to do it," he says. "We were scrambling to get every bit of intelligence, from what Matthew likes to eat for breakfast to where he sleeps at night. You want to know everything, every house, every car, every place he's been, every cop that's ever stopped him."

To get that comprehensive picture, the FBI agent used additional subpoenas for financial records, more surveillance teams—and wiretaps. Few investigative tools in law enforcement are as hard to get as a Title III warrant for electronic surveillance because Congress and the Supreme Court ruled that police must show they have exhausted every other method of inquiry. But Garrabrant would eventually get permission for wiretaps on two of Thompkins's cell phones, even if that meant he and Richardson had to renew the surveillance requests every thirty days, with affidavits setting forth what they had learned and what they still needed to find out.

"The case took up 110 percent of my time," says Garrabrant. He was only partly joking; he took off only one day between the spring of 2005 and the end of the year, in mid-July, when his son was born. "People said I was crazy, but there was just too much riding on it," he says. "You can't just walk away."

• • •

DESPITE HIS heavy workload, the FBI agent tried to set aside time for Maria. As a member of the Bureau's Violent Crimes section, Garrabrant still had to handle his share of serial killers, cold cases, and even terrorism files. At any given time, he would find himself with as many as twenty open cases. But always he fought to make sure that at least 70 to 75 percent of those were child prostitution investigations. And on top of the pile would always be Maria.

In May 2005, Maria turned eighteen; that simplified things considerably for Garrabrant. She was no longer legally a minor, and he could contact her without her parents' permission, keep tabs on her, ask local police and casino authorities to watch out for her—in short, all the surveillance activities that he couldn't do under FBI policy when she was a minor.

Her age also made it easier for Garrabrant to do something he found distasteful but necessary—lie. It was the only way to protect her and his investigation, he'd concluded. The FBI was certain Knowledge was going to take another run at Maria because she posed too much of a threat. And that put Garrabrant in an untenable situation. If he told Maria the truth, that thanks to her original tip and the deepening probe the FBI was closing in on Knowledge, she could be in danger. Because if either Knowledge or his people ever confronted her on the street and she revealed, even unwittingly, that the investigation was active, they'd know she was a witness. And if she was a witness, she was a problem—one that would have to be eliminated.

"On the other hand, if they thought the case was dead, and she convinced them it was dead because that's what she believed, that was the best way of keeping her healthy and safe," Garrabrant explains. "We ended up having to tell Maria that the case fell apart. We had to make her believe it was completely dead in the water."

Garrabrant's dilemma was heightened by the fact that Maria had a mind of her own, as she had so ably proven to Knowledge and Tracy. At times, his contact with her was fleeting. "I would be able to easily get a hold of her for a while, and then for a week she would be in the wind," he says.

It was not as if the FBI man had anything concrete to offer her. "She had nowhere to go. And we had nowhere to put her," he says. Garrabrant was grappling with the same dilemma that police and community workers across the country faced when working with girls trying to exit the life: a woeful lack of services. Often the choice was between jail and an insecure group home from which the girls could easily flee. He tried sending Maria out of state to stay with some of her friends, but she soon returned to the Strip on Atlantic Avenue.

In July, state police and the Division of Gaming Enforcement—the investigators tasked with keeping the casinos safe and honest—conducted a sweep that picked up more than a dozen prostituted women, by chance including Maria. As a matter of course, Garrabrant was called in to interview younger women in the group. He spotted Maria at the police station, and they talked briefly, but for her own safety he didn't let on that he knew her. He managed discreetly to arrange to get her released on a summons, instead of being forced to appear in front of a judge and post bail.

That same night at the station, Garrabrant interviewed a young woman named Cream. She also was cooperative and got an early release. What Garrabrant did not know was that Cream worked for a Boston pimp named Noel "Finesse" Lopez, who in turn was close to Knowledge. Word got back to Knowledge that a friendly cop named Dan had helped Maria out. Now, unbeknownst to both Maria and her FBI guardian, she was in more danger than ever before.

Only a few weeks later, the FBI got authorization from a federal judge to start the wiretaps on August 5. It was just in time.

■ ■ ■

DONALD TRUMP never met Maria, but his gaudy casino in Atlantic City was like a second home for the teenager.

Over the years, she had conducted a lot of business underneath the crystal chandeliers of Trump Plaza Hotel and Casino, parading up and down the polished marble floors. Towering thirty-nine stories above the city, the resort prides itself as being at "the center of the Boardwalk, the heart of the action." It certainly was the center of a lot of action for Knowledge's women, and it was not surprising Goddess knew she would find Maria there.

Knowledge had dispatched Goddess to confront the former member of his stable. On August 11, six days after the FBI wiretaps began, agents picked up a disturbing conversation between the two. The pimp wanted the wayward Maria good and scared.

It had been only three months since the attempted kidnapping and her narrow escape at the highway rest stop, and since then Maria had defied Knowledge's orders to keep away from his track. Worse, Knowledge now suspected that she was on good terms with at least one cop. Knowledge did not know Garrabrant's full name; more important, he had no idea yet that Maria's friend Dan was not just a local cop but an FBI agent, a red flag that would have signaled how seriously the authorities were taking his case.

So Knowledge gave Goddess strict marching orders to pull Maria into line.

"You want to not be too animated," he told her over the phone. "You want to be calm and to the point."

"Yes," she said obediently.

He told Goddess to call Maria Dynasty instead of Suprema, a sign that he'd demoted the younger girl in his hierarchy. And he gave detailed instructions on what message to deliver, as if it were a script for Goddess to memorize. "Who is the officer Dan-whatever-his-name you called when you got locked up? What's his last name? Dan who?" he told her to ask.

"Rumor has it that you called him so you could get out from getting arrested and that you were speaking to him about my peoples," Knowledge continued. "He gets you out of jail because he wants you to do this and he is supposed to be subpoenaing you to court and you have to go. All this crazy shit you talking about. You running your mouth telling all these people all this bullshit and now it's stirred up a whole big controversy around here."

Knowledge ended by telling Goddess to give Maria a firm warning. "You need to think twice about what you're saying. Because everything comes with consequences."

Two days later, on August 13, Goddess did her best to carry out Knowledge's orders. She confronted Maria just inside the Trump Plaza, at the busy valet parking circle.

"Listen, I know that you spoke to Dan or whatever," she said.

"Goddess, there is no case," Maria insisted, stating what she believed was true but was in fact the lie Garrabrant had been forced to tell her. "They don't have enough evidence for the case. There's no case anymore, that's what I am trying to say."

"I know you spoke to him," Goddess persisted, trying to stick closely to Knowledge's script. "Just think twice about what you're doing."

But Goddess never got a chance to pass on more of Knowledge's threats. A Trump Plaza security officer rushed up out of nowhere and grabbed Maria.

"I don't know what's happening," Goddess sputtered in disbelief to the casino authorities, her conversation with the girl so rudely interrupted. "I was just talking to her. I don't know what's going on."

"She's eighty-sixed from Trump Plaza," the security man said as he dragged away Maria using the entertainment business term for barring someone from the premises. Maria, having been stopped multiple times for attempted prostitution at Trump Plaza, was on the casino's blacklist. But this time, being "eighty-sixed" turned out to be her lucky break because the arrest got her away from Goddess and her prying questions.

In a panic, Goddess made a frantic call to Knowledge. Once more, their conversation was caught on an FBI wiretap as part of the investigation that, contrary to what Maria believed, was very much alive.

"Hi, Daddy, I seen Dynasty," Goddess said, the words spilling out in a rushed and nervous patter. "I was doing what you told me to do. And while we're talking the head of security comes and tackles her to the ground and puts handcuffs on her." Goddess was clearly rattled. "The whole thing is just not sitting right with me right now," she continued. "Like right now, she is being held in handcuffs in the back."

Impatient, Knowledge cut her off and pushed for the only information that interested him. "What was she sayin' to you?"

"She said to me that the case was no longer in effect," Goddess replied.

Knowledge abruptly hung up. He was furious, convinced more than ever that his problems with Maria were far from over. The next day, his partner Tracy bumped into Maria in another casino and was brutally blunt with the teenager. "I don't know why Knowledge was being so soft on you," he said, according to police files. "If I had my way, you would already be in a body bag."

Maria tried to shrug off the threat with her usual grit. But she was shaken. Her FBI benefactor took what comfort he could from the fact that the confrontation at the Trump Plaza seemed to vindicate his strategy of temporarily deceiving Maria. "She told them exactly what we told her, because she thought it was true—that we had no case against Knowledge," Garrabrant says. "But we also knew that if she didn't believe that it was true, she would have got hurt."

* * *

THE TRUMP incident was just one small part of the picture of Knowledge's operation that the FBI caught through their extensive wiretaps. The monitoring would go on for another fifteen weeks.

Almost every one of Knowledge's calls with the women in his stable and his fellow pimps was captured on tape. Seven days a week, for a total of 110 days, they tracked no fewer than fifty-seven thousand phone calls, more than six thousand of which were deemed "pertinent," or related to criminal activity. At its peak, the FBI probe had fourteen investigators in the Northfield office working the wires full-time.

From the wiretaps, Garrabrant learned the names, the where-abouts, the actions, and the earnings of Knowledge's many women, of Goddess, Lotion, Madonna, Slim Shady. He got a glimpse of how Meredith kept them and the books all in line. The wires also gave investigators a snapshot of Knowledge's cruelty. On October 12, 2005, White Diamond, Meredith's younger sister, called her pimp from one of his cars after turning a trick. She was weeping uncontrollably.

"I'm lost, I don't where I am," she blurted out between sobs.

"You better shut the fuck up while you're driving my car," Knowledge barked back. "Are you deaf?" he asked when all he heard was quiet crying. "Let me know when you hear me. You acting like a stupid ass bitch. You better learn how to fucking speak to me when you're on the phone, bitch. Who the fuck do you think you're talking to—"

"I didn't think—"

"Shut the fuck up!" he yelled, as the wiretap captured the girl's endless whimpering.

It was a petty dispute, but it illustrated how vindictive Knowledge could be and his insistence on total control over his women.

From the wiretaps also came serious leads—names, business asso-ciates, and contacts that spread across the country, allowing the FBI's Atlantic City office to feed information to police in Boston, New York, Las Vegas, and Miami. Listening and sifting through the hours and hours of chatter among Knowledge, his enforcers, and his women were already time-consuming. The investigators also had to make sense of a complicated system of code words Knowledge had every-one in his pimping business use, inspired in part by his Five Percenter ideology. When one of the women reported in at the end of a night, all the wiretaps would pick up was a cryptic message like "Divine Allah, I pulled all mine from the See-Allah-Savior. I only did one on the True Ruler."

It took some time before the FBI cracked the code. Knowledge him-self was known as Divine Allah. The "track" on the street became the "True Ruler." Other words would replace letters—"see" for C, "Allah" for *A*, "savior" for *S*. So the woman was really saying, "Knowledge, I earned all my money last night at the C-A-S-ino and only did one job on the track."

To report their incomes, the women also spoke in Five Percenter code: "Divine Allah, I made Knowledge followed by Three," they would say. "Knowledge" stood for *1*, and "followed by Three" meant *000*, so it meant they had pulled in one thousand dollars that night.

Aside from security, the secret language and codes made the women feel special. Two of Knowledge's women could be in the supermarket talking about their business, and no one would have any idea what they were talking about. "It was like they were a special group of superprostitutes, working for the superpimp," Garrabrant says.

Garrabrant and some his colleagues became so adept at interpreting the Five Percenter terminology that they would sometimes chatter away in code at work, much to their supervisor's distress and general laughter in the office. It was a welcome respite from a grinding investigation that was consuming Garrabrant's life.

■ ■ ■

THE FBI probe caught an important break in Las Vegas that summer, when another girl caught in Knowledge's web broke free.

It began on July 21, 2005, when the Las Vegas cops got a call from a concerned mother who lived on the West Side. The cops were more used to coming out to the troubled neighborhood for homicides or drive-by gang shootings. This time was different.

"She told us her daughter had returned home, and she thought she might have been involved in prostitution," says Aaron Stanton, the cop who had first interviewed Maria when she was arrested in Vegas.

When Stanton and his partner, Woody Fieselman, showed up at the home, they found a pretty if somewhat sullen fourteen-year-old sitting uncomfortably with her mother and grandmother. Sandy was the girl who had run off with Slim Shady. Once in New York, though, she had found the life of selling her body for Knowledge less romantic than she had imagined. One night while she was riding with Knowledge in his Escalade she found several cell phones when he stepped out to go shopping. She managed to reach her mother. "It scared her being that young and alone in New York," says Fieselman. "She wanted out."

It was not clear if she told the pimp what she had done and Knowledge feared her mother would contact police or if he simply decided his latest underage recruit was becoming more trouble than she was worth. Either way, the next day Goddess had driven Sandy from Atlantic City to New York and put her on a plane back to Vegas.

Two weeks later, she found herself staring at two Vegas vice cops in her living room. Fieselman surmised she was "a bit irritated" when her family expected her to do the right thing by talking to the police. "She was very quiet, really reserved," adds Stanton. Sandy wasn't sure she wanted to say anything to the detectives, but she at least agreed to sit down with them. When she began describing a pimp from the New Jersey–New York area who used elaborate codes when speaking with his girls and forced them to keep detailed journals and accounts, Stanton and Fieselman looked at each other, excited.

"The lightbulb goes off," says Stanton. "I knew right then and there who she was talking about."

Eager to check with the FBI's Garrabrant and get additional background on the Knowledge case before talking in more detail with Sandy, they told the girl and her family they would return to do a more formal interview. Once back in the office, they called Garrabrant with the news.

"We have another juvenile," Stanton told him. Garrabrant agreed to send them any photos he had of the women associated with Knowledge, and he helped them review the case file. A few days later, the Vegas cops went back to get Sandy's testimony on tape.

They wanted her alone, knowing she would feel uncomfortable talking about her experiences in front of her family. They walked to her bedroom, at the end of the hallway. She sat on her bed, and Fieselman crouched on the floor, the tape recorder in his hand. "She laid out a very detailed statement of her time in New York with him, what kind of car he drove, how much she made for him," Fieselman recalls.

The Vegas cops showed her various photos of Knowledge's women. "If you recognize any of these women, write down what you know," they asked Sandy. They pulled out a picture of Knowledge that Garrabrant had sent them.

Sandy's eyes widened. "That's him!" she exclaimed.

The circle was closing in on Matthew Thompkins.

• • •

THE CIRCLE also appeared to be closing in on Maria. Garrabrant remained on alert for any sign she was at risk. "We were monitoring her, trying to call her every day and talk to her. And we had police in the casinos and on the Strip so if we heard there was something going on, we could immediately jump on it," he says. "But it was a balancing act."

A balancing act that grew more and more precarious.

On September 1, the FBI wiretaps picked up a conversation between Knowledge and Noel "Finesse" Lopez, his Boston-based partner. It had been one of Lopez's women who first tipped off Knowledge that Maria had been friendly in jail with a cop named Dan. Lopez was one of several pimps who were part of Knowledge's informal network. They would exchange information on the best cities or neighborhoods to market their women. And Knowledge was a great persuader; if one of Lopez's women was "getting out of pocket," as the pimps termed it, Thompkins would sweet-talk her into staying.

But there would be no sweet talk for Maria. In fall 2005, she was still renegading, and Lopez was angry that she was disrupting business on his track.

"Them bitches wanted to fight the queen bitch," Lopez reported.

"Who?" Knowledge asked, not sure at first whom he was talking about.

"Dynasty," came the answer.

"Yeah, you know, because they know all their secrets is out," Knowledge said, trying to explain the women's animosity toward a girl they thought had betrayed them to police.

Lopez reported that his patience with Maria was running out. "I'm going to go out and say something," he said. "Fuck that."

"Definitely," Knowledge ordered. "What you got to do is go out there and threaten Dynasty."

Lopez did exactly that. According to police logs later filed in court, "Lopez then approached [Maria] and told her . . . that he wanted to kill her and cut her into pieces."

For all his tough talk and threats, Knowledge must have realized he faced a dilemma. He could not be sure if Maria was telling the truth when she claimed the police probe into his enterprise had stalled, but he also had to consider that eliminating a girl whom he knew had been in contact with the police could bring down a lot more heat than he needed.

Neither the pimp nor Maria knew that by this point Garrabrant was close to wrapping up the case. Thanks to Maria's initial tips, the wiretaps, and the thousands of pages of bank and property records they had obtained, the FBI had put together a detailed flowchart of Knowledge's enterprise. They knew the real identities of most of his girls, the locations of all his homes, and the plates on all his vehicles.

They were getting ready for the final takedown. The only question was whether Knowledge would fall before he decided to get rid of the girl who had caused him so much grief.

· 7 ·

Takedown

B Y DECEMBER 2005, the FBI's Innocence Lost initiative was just over two years old and beginning to hit its stride.

The number of field offices investigating child prostitution had nearly doubled, from fourteen to twenty-five. Arrests in 2005 rose to close to four hundred, more than triple the number in the previous year. The FBI was on the verge of carrying out its largest coordinated sweep to date, taking down child prostitution rings in Ohio, Pennsylvania, Michigan, Hawaii, and the Atlantic City–New York corridor.

In Michigan, the Bureau teamed up with local and state police to go after Robert Lewis Young, a pimp who used the street name Blue Diamond and brought women, including several minors from Hawaii, to Detroit and Chicago. He hid his substantial profits with the help of co-conspirators including a wealthy dentist in Chicago who laundered over four hundred thousand dollars for the pimp. To delve into his operations, police did everything from sifting through his trash to tapping his cell phones to setting up a surveillance camera in a tree outside his house. (When the leaves came out in spring, they had to go out at 3:00 A.M. one morning to surreptitiously trim some of the branches.)

In Pennsylvania, the FBI began investigating a ring led by Franklin "Silky Red" Robinson, who operated an interstate sex trafficking service out of the Gables of Harrisburg truck stop. Harrisburg was the hub of the network because five major highways converge there, providing a steady stream of customers. It was such a popular site for prostitution that online chat boards for truckers were filled with news about the "lot lizards," as the women were called. Silky Red moved dozens of women across a sprawling network that spanned at least ten states, from Maryland to Arkansas. One girl was as young as twelve. He also "purchased a seventeen-year-old for approximately $600" from a fellow pimp, according to court filings. The girls were largely recruited from Toledo.

Like most pimps, Silky Red was candid about the violence he used to keep the women in line. When one of them made only fifty dollars one night, he beat her so hard he fractured his hand. He bragged that another time he hit a woman so hard that "both my hands were swelled up because I beat the bitch so much." It was all part of ensuring a steady flow of money. At one point, Silky Red boasted he had just put down ten thousand dollars cash on a Cadillac and still had seventeen thousand dollars in his pocket. His operation was moving money through wire transfers totaling $183,000.

The cash also continued to flow into the bank accounts of Matthew Thompkins, thanks to his extensive operations in New York, Atlantic City, and Las Vegas. But like Blue Diamond and Silky Red, Knowledge was in the FBI's crosshairs, and perhaps more so than his fellow pimps in Michigan and Pennsylvania, he sensed that the feds were after him.

At the start of their probe, Dan Garrabrant and his team had been discreet, but by late 2005 their footprints were more obvious. They had interviewed many women in several cities—"a lot of girls, not just on his track," as the FBI agent put it—and word from the street would have filtered back to Knowledge.

But Knowledge had no idea about the wide scope of the investigation, much less its progress. He must have assumed that the FBI was getting nowhere. Maria, after all, had talked to the Vegas cops two years earlier; if the authorities had enough proof against him, they would have surely arrested him by now.

"He still thought he was safe, that the case was dead," says Garrabrant. "I don't think he believed that we would ever get him. He just thought he was invincible."

■ ■ ■

THE FIRST sign of trouble for Knowledge came on December 2, 2005. It was on the domestic front, but it was an indication that there were cracks in his pimping empire.

Meredith—the woman who had stuck with him since she was a teenager, given birth to two of his children, seen him through the expansion of his empire, cooked his books, and helped keep his women in line—left a disturbing message on his voice mail. As the most senior of his women, she might have had the right to claim the pimp as hers. But she also had the experience to know better. She should have known that one of the biggest mistakes she could make was to think her pimp really loved her.

Knowledge had claimed for years that he was too businesslike to sleep with the women under his control. "It's a perk for them, not me," he once said dismissively. "I'm a big dude, but it's a privilege for a bitch to do anything with me." If Meredith had her doubts about that claim over the years, she kept them to herself. But when she heard that he had fathered other children, that may have been her breaking point.

"Hey, listen," her phone message began. "Best believe if you have another kid that's not biologically mine, I'm going to kill it."

She lashed out at his philandering. "Keep your little Goddesses and your Madonnas," she said, referring to other women in the stable. "Because you're a fucking liar. You telling me, 'No, I'm not having sex with nobody. No, that they haven't reached that level with me. I'm not even thinking about it.' All this nonsense that you're dropping on me, you need to be truthful to me about what's going on between me and you."

Her voice began to crack as she took stock of her entire sad life. "You don't have to feel bad because you turned me out at fifteen," she said, alluding to Knowledge's recruitment of her as a child. "I don't give a shit. I don't care that much no more. I don't care what you do because of you lying to me and because you keep leading me on to believe all this other bullshit."

The wiretap picked up the beep at the end of the message, then the melodious tone of the recorded operator. "If you are satisfied with your message, press 1."

Meredith hung up.

Two days later, FBI wiretaps picked up a phone conversation Knowledge had with a fellow pimp. Knowledge's friend had beaten one of the women under his control so badly that she had filed a complaint with the cops.

"What's happenin'?" Knowledge began.

"Just going through some bullshit," his colleague replied. "The bitch ran to the police and got protection and all this bullshit.... I fired the bitch."

"Yeah, fuck her," Knowledge said in support.

"Bitch was just playing games," the other pimp noted. "I can't afford to go to jail. I just got too much on the line to lose for this one punk-ass bitch."

Knowledge agreed. "As long as you keep it moving," he told his pal. The two pimps shared a confident chuckle.

Still unaware of the storm fast gathering around him, Knowledge thought nothing could stop his ascent in the pimping world. His confidence was buoyed by his appearance that month in the "third annual sex issue" of the rap magazine *Ozone*. He was the featured star. Entitled "Sex Sells: A Day in the Life of a Real Pimp," it was a fawning portrait written by the magazine's editor. "His name carries heavy weight on the streets," she wrote, describing what she called his "whores" as "young and fairly attractive." They had nothing but praise for their pimp. "Whatever money I make goes to him and he makes smart decisions," said one. Another said, "I learned from the best."

Knowledge thought he was being crafty. He had gambled on the big-time publicity generated by a major rap-scene publication, but to protect himself he insisted on choreographing the story. He made sure the magazine changed his name and altered his description.

"The ABC boys will never be able to figure out who I am," he laughed over the phone, using code letters for the FBI. Knowledge did not know about the wiretaps on his cell phones, but he took precautions just the same. The joke was on him, though: the "ABC boys" were listening as he plotted his big magazine write-up.

Knowledge no doubt gloated when the magazine came out screaming "Pimps and Hoes!" on its cover. But it would end up as his swan song. "The only boundary he refuses to cross is the age of consent," the *Ozone* article reported, taking Knowledge at his word when he claimed that he would never force a minor into prostitution. "Anyone who pimps a woman under eighteen deserves to go to jail," Knowledge told the magazine.

Matthew Thompkins, businessman, pimp extraordinaire, and Divine Allah, was more prophetic than he ever could have wished. Because on December 9, just days after the magazine hit the stands, FBI agent Dan Garrabrant swore out a criminal complaint against him for "conspiracy to transport minors to engage in prostitution."

■ ■ ■

Two years of hard work, of befriending Maria, of protecting and respecting her, of listening to her when she gave Garrabrant his initial leads, had finally paid off. The FBI was now ready to strike with an indictment targeting not just Knowledge and his longtime partner Demetrius "Tracy" Lemus but also his enforcer, Noel Lopez; his business administrator, Meredith; and four of the senior women, Goddess, Slim Shady, Madonna, and Fortune. "It was the object of the conspiracy to recruit and transport minor girls and others between various cities, including Atlantic City, New Jersey, Bronx, New York and Las Vegas to engage in prostitution," Garrabrant charged in his indictment.

The complaint spelled out many of the offenses Knowledge and Tracy had committed against Maria (identified only as "Minor Girl 1"), including their recruitment of her, trafficking her in Atlantic City and Las Vegas, attempting to kidnap her, and making threats against her life. In addition, Garrabrant detailed the abuse suffered by Sandy, or "Minor Girl 2," in Las Vegas and New York. Finally, the indictment cited the case of "Minor Girl 3," Joanie, the fourteen-year-old whom Maria met the day Knowledge and Tracy tried to drag her to

New York. Joanie had ended up prostituting for Tracy in Wildwood, Atlantic City, and New York. "The investigation revealed the defendants… managed a large-scale prostitution ring that operated in several states," the FBI agent concluded in the indictment, noting that Knowledge and his co-conspirators derived "substantial income from the prostitution of minor girls."

The U.S. District Court of New Jersey issued the arrest warrants the very day the complaint was sworn out, on December 9. The FBI scheduled the takedown three days later as part of a coordinated national sweep of several other pimps. Garrabrant knew it had to be carefully stage-managed because Knowledge had more than a dozen people working for him in several cities scattered across at least three states, and if word of an impending raid got out, he and Tracy could flee and destroy their records.

So the FBI set an elaborate ruse in motion. Working undercover, Garrabrant and another agent approached Madonna. Thanks to wiretaps, they had her cell number, but they told her they had gotten her contact information from a previous client who had described her as "hot." She eagerly agreed to meet them at the Hilton bar in Atlantic City, where the men told her they were planning a major Christmas party and they wanted her to bring as many of her friends as possible. "She went back to the other women and said there was a lot of money to be made," Garrabrant recalls.

The goal was to lure as many women in Knowledge's stable as possible to the same place at the same time. But the FBI also hoped that with the huge amount of cash at stake, Knowledge himself would show up to greet his wealthy customers and keep the girls in line. "We thought that he would have to come because if you've got eight or nine women going out to make fifteen to twenty thousand dollars, you want to make sure the party goes OK and that when it's done, they come back to you and give you all the money," says Garrabrant.

At first, everything appeared to go as planned. The women started showing up for the big party in a casino hotel suite the FBI had rented. The bureau was keeping track of Knowledge's cell phones, and it had surveillance teams posted on his homes and cars, including agents hidden in the bushes outside the house in Galloway, just in case he stopped there en route from New York to the party in Atlantic City. Garrabrant coordinated the operation from a command center in New Jersey.

At the last minute, a snag threatened to bring down the entire operation. Late that night, Knowledge was on the phone, promising the women in Atlantic City he was on his way. But the tracking on his cell phone indicated to the FBI that he was lying; he was still in New York. It now looked like they would have to take down Knowledge there, and fast, too. Because if he got wind that there was something amiss in New Jersey, it was over.

As it turned out, Knowledge was heading toward a recording studio in Manhattan—a legitimate one, unlike his dubious venture of Hoodlum Records. The NYPD and the FBI scrambled to find him. Thanks to wiretaps on his cell phone, they could listen in as he talked about where he was headed and could get a general fix on his location by tracking the cell phone towers he was hitting. But they did not know precisely which one of his many cars he was driving, which could make a vehicle arrest difficult. At the command center, Garrabrant tried to keep track of him, notifying the surveillance teams of his movements based on the cell phone GPS signals. Finally, one of the teams spotted him in a Mercedes, pulling into a public parking lot in Midtown Manhattan. As he stepped out, agents grabbed him. It was just after midnight.

"I was breathing a whole lot easier," says Garrabrant. "My fear was that he was going to becoming a fugitive."

At the same time, back in Atlantic City, undercover cops arrested Goddess, Madonna, and several of Knowledge's other women. Tracy, the pimp who had first gotten Maria into the game, was under constant surveillance at the Liberty Inn, a cheap hotel on White Horse Pike on the outskirts of the gaming resort town. There was a brief burst of panic when, about fifteen minutes after Knowledge's arrest, Tracy came out and got into his car. *We got burned*, Garrabrant thought. He feared Tracy was making a run for it. It turned out he was only driving to a nearby gas station to fill up. When the police cars moved in, Tracy did try to flee, speeding away down the highway.

But the chase ended within minutes as the police cars surrounded him and the pimp surrendered.

In all, the police that night executed warrants at six locations used by Knowledge and Tracy's prostitution ring in New York, New Jersey, and Nevada. In Vegas, Woody Fieselman led the team that raided the Upscale Exotics service Knowledge had set up to accept credit cards just off the Strip, at the seedy intersection of Industrial and Stardust. They found that the office was more industrial than stardust, a ten-foot-by-ten-foot room with a telephone on a desk and a two-drawer filing cabinet. There were piles of business cards announcing various "exotic girls," but all the numbers were routed to the same phone in the office. "He had more escort services operating than you could shake a stick at," says Fieselman. He carted up the evidence and prepared to ship it to Garrabrant.

In New York, teams moved into Knowledge's New York City apartment on Holland, where Meredith had long guarded the company files, his home on Tall Tulip Lane in Yonkers, and his sister's house in the suburb of Scarsdale. In Galloway, agents searched his $325,000 home on Second Avenue and seized a silver 2000 Mercedes-Benz and a black 2003 Range Rover. The fleet of cars in other locations included a 2002 BMW, a 2003 Hummer, a more recent 2003 Mercedes-Benz SL500, a Lexus RX300, a 2002 Cadillac Escalade, and a Ford Expedition. And, for good measure, the police also grabbed cell phones associated with ten numbers, computers, and computer-related equipment.

．．．

FOUR DAYS after Garrabrant's team arrested Knowledge and Tracy, the FBI publicly announced "one of the largest coordinated enforcement actions ever taken against child prostitution rings in the United States." Garrabrant's arrests of Knowledge and Tracy in New York and Atlantic City were part of a wider sweep the Innocence Lost program was carrying out in a half-dozen states. Nineteen people were arrested in all; another dozen were charged but remained at large.

In Pennsylvania, Franklin "Silky Red" Robinson and the multistate trafficking hub he ran out of the Gables of Harrisburg truck stop came to crashing halt when he and fifteen other defendants were indicted on charges ranging from sex trafficking of children to conspiracy to engage in money laundering. Robinson later pleaded guilty and got twenty-five years behind bars.

In Michigan, Robert Lewis "Blue Diamond" Young saw the collapse of the prostitution network that he had established between Detroit and Honolulu. He was charged with twenty-seven counts of violating federal statutes including sex trafficking by force and transportation of a minor for criminal sexual activity. The wiretaps revealed a particularly gruesome cruelty on Blue Diamond's part toward the women he controlled. He had impregnated one of them, Doll Baby, with twins and then beat her so badly she had to go to the hospital with broken ribs.

"My feet are so sore, I can't even stand on them," a woman named Star complained over the phone.

"Bitch, you better shut your fucking mouth," Blue Diamond shot back. "I don't want to hear about your sore feet, bitch. You hear me. You better get out on the track to make me more money."

A later wiretap caught the sound of Star being beaten for allegedly pocketing some of her earnings instead of handing it over to her pimp. "You piece of shit!" Blue Diamond yelled during the beating. "Get your ass back on your feet, get back to where I told you, bitch."

Young would have no women to beat up or boss around anymore— he got twenty-five years in prison.

In Ohio, a rare kidnapping-for-prostitution case ended with the arrest of four people and freedom for two terrified teens. Two teenage cousins, aged fourteen and fifteen, were walking to a fast-food restaurant in Toledo on a rainy day in May 2005 when they accepted a ride from a man in a white Lincoln Continental. One of the girls thought he looked familiar, perhaps a friend of her father's. Instead he turned out to be a convicted Detroit pimp named Deric Willoughby. Willoughby and three associates gave the teens clothes and fake identities, then took them to hotels around Toledo and forced them to perform sex acts with clients. Ten days after their kidnapping, their abductors took the girls to a truck stop in Michigan. By coincidence, the police—tipped off about prostitution at the truck stop—happened to make a raid that day and discovered the girls in a rig with a trucker. Willoughby got eight years in prison. The girls were returned to their families.

In all, more than thirty children were identified in those FBI busts of late December 2005, including the girls in Knowledge's network. That brought the total number of child victims rescued to more than two hundred since the Innocence Lost initiative had begun two years earlier. It was an impressive and gratifying number. But FBI assistant director Chris Swecker noted somberly on the day the arrests were announced, "The FBI and its partners cannot restore the innocence lost from those children who are lured into childhood prostitution."

"This is a crime of hidden victims," added John Rabun of the National Center for Missing and Exploited Children. "Many think child trafficking is only a problem in foreign countries, but nothing can be further from the truth."

■ ■ ■

THE FULL truth of the seriousness of the charges against him were just beginning to sink in for Matthew Thompkins as he sat in a holding cell in New Jersey, where he had been brought after his arrest in Manhattan.

A few hours after the raids, Garrabrant walked in to confront the pimp he had been chasing for two years. It was the first time the two men had met face-to-face. The 380-pound man towered over the diminutive federal agent. Ever the smooth operator, Knowledge was at first unfailingly polite. But his mood soured as he discovered the extent of his troubles.

This was no simple pimp bust. Knowledge had been read his rights, and Garrabrant assured him he did not have to talk to the FBI if he didn't want to. But Garrabrant had a few things to say. One by one, the special agent named every person who had worked with Knowledge and identified how many of them had been arrested that night. In measured tones, the agent pointed out that even as he sat there, police officers were busy seizing the pimp's possessions—his cars, his houses, cash, *everything* he'd owned only three hours earlier was now in the hands of the authorities.

"He was completely shocked," Garrabrant recalls. "I think he probably knew that someday an arrest would come. All pimps have to worry about that. But thinking you might get popped and then actually getting popped, that's a whole different story."

All the more so because Knowledge realized this was no ordinary local police bust. He was not looking at what most pimps expect when they get busted—easy bail and, at worst, a few months in jail. The full weight of the federal government, the Department of Justice and the FBI, was crashing down on him. He was being hit with child trafficking and money-laundering charges, and it dawned on Matthew Thompkins that he faced years, maybe even decades behind bars.

"I don't think Knowledge ever expected that one day the FBI would come knocking on his door," says Garrabrant. "His reaction was *Holy shit, it's the feds that have got me.*"

· 8 ·

"She's Not Your Ho Anymore"

JUST AS the FBI was jailing Knowledge in New York, in Dallas Byron Fassett and his High Risk Victims and Trafficking unit were seeing the first signs of progress in their attempts to put the pimps in their city behind bars. After an initial year building up their forces, starting their first cases, and clearing up the backlog of juvenile prostitution files neglected in the past—"just wading through the mud, learning from mistakes," as Fassett puts it—the team's hard work began paying off in big numbers. By the end of their second year of operation in 2005, the team had identified 136 high-risk victims. From that pool, investigators had opened eighty-three investigations and filed fifty-three felony cases on forty-two suspects.

Fassett was running eighteen police officers spread over three teams: four detectives tackling Internet crimes, ten more handling the more traditional crimes of abuse against children, and then his four-person team for high-risk victims. As the sergeant in charge, Fassett of course could assign himself to any one of those squads, but his passion was for the heartache and heroines he found working with young girls forced into prostitution.

Not that it didn't take its toll. He had just finished a grueling week-long trial and managed to get home by 5:00 P.M. on a Friday to catch up on chores. Before he got started, he had to leave on an emergency call about an abduction of a ten-year-old. He made it back home late that evening, only to return to the police headquarters at 3:00 A.M. when two underage girls were picked up on the streets. The sergeant was back in his bed by 5:00 A.M. when the phone rang with news about another girl his squad had picked up.

"Sometimes I sit on the edge of my bed," Fassett admits, "and wonder, *Am I getting too damn old for this?*"

"You don't have to do this," his wife had said to him on more than one occasion.

"Yeah, I do," was Fassett's response. "I can't explain it. But I do have to do it. Because these kids have no one. They really are the voiceless. They have nobody to speak for them."

For a partner to help run the squad, Fassett recruited Cathy De La Paz, an equally no-nonsense cop from Mississippi who had made her way up through the male-dominated ranks by taking on the hardest jobs in the force—undercover narcotics and internal affairs. The mother of two young children, she shared Fassett's passion for rescuing the girls on the street no one else seemed to care about. "We were getting better at investigating these cases," she says. "Now you can't dismiss these kids. Somebody is watching them."

Still, try as they might, Fassett and De La Paz could not watch over every endangered child in the Dallas area. The brutal kidnapping and sexual assault of one young teenager would test their team's resolve almost to the breaking point.

■ ■ ■

FELICIA HAD learned to survive by her wits at a young age. She was born in Mexico, and her father died when she was just three. At age seven, she crossed the border with her new stepfather to join her mother who was already working in a restaurant in Dallas. It was a blur for a frightened child. "I came in a car, that's all I remember," she said.

Felicia was one of nine children in a simple home in a poor neighborhood of North Dallas. She enjoyed her classes at Vivian Field, a decent if overcrowded middle school where most of the five thousand students were Hispanic, black, or Asian. "She always had these really big dreams," says Stephanie Lovelace, a juvenile probation officer who would later handle Felicia's case. "She fantasized about being a cheerleader. But there was no capacity for her to do that."

For one thing, Felicia had health problems that went undiagnosed for years because no one at home or in school ever bothered to find out what made her so quiet and distracted. Only when Felicia got caught up in the gears of the juvenile justice system did basic medical attention reveal that she suffered from depression, attention deficit disorder, and bipolar disorder. "I hear people whispering," she said.

Little wonder Felicia never made it past ninth grade. Whatever may have caused her illnesses, her home life didn't help. From the age of seven until she was at least eleven, Felicia was sexually abused by her stepfather. "He molested me. He went to jail," was all she was willing to say later. The details remain shrouded in sealed court documents. He served only nine months in jail on a charge that was plea-bargained down to a misdemeanor, an all-too-frequent occurrence in a domestic sexual assault case where the child was reluctant to testify and the mother was not eager for the details of a sordid home life to come out.

Despite promising authorities she would protect her child and that the man who'd abused her daughter was out of her life, Felicia's mother never made him leave the house. "She chose that man over Felicia," says Lovelace, the probation officer. She says that Felicia's mother, who blamed her daughter for bringing trouble and the authorities into her home, also hit Felicia frequently.

By the time she was thirteen, Felicia had run away from home about a dozen times. Once she and two "homeboys" from her neighborhood, as she described them, were caught trying to burglarize a high school. That earned her a juvenile record and a probation requirement to return home every night by 5:30 P.M. Every time she ran away from home, she violated her probation. Yet her home life was precisely what drove Felicia into the streets. "I kept missing curfew and I knew I was going to eventually get locked up," Felicia later testified. She was caught in the spiral of abuse and detention that trapped so many runaways, the same depressing circle that Fassett's team had been trying so desperately to stop.

During one of her runaway episodes in the late summer of 2005, Felicia had heard on the street that an easy way to pick up some quick cash was to head down to the Dallas Municipal Center and pretend to be a refugee from Hurricane Katrina, which had just devastated neighboring Louisiana. She tried to get a fake ID under the name Alicia Hernandez. The scam didn't work because the authorities took her fingerprints, ran them through the system, and discovered her real identity.

In a way, though, it didn't matter. She liked the idea of being Alicia from Louisiana, of being anyone but who she was. Casting her real self aside meant a lot for an abused teenage runaway trying to make it on the streets. "You can just pretend to be somebody," she said.

Ironically, the very day Felicia was at the municipal center trying to scam a fake ID, Fassett and his HRVT members were there to help out with the flood of refugees. They were in uniform, on crowd-control duty, not doing their usual job of looking for runaways. If they had bumped into Felicia back then, she would have looked like just another teenager. It would be many months before she and Fassett again crossed paths, this time meeting face-to-face in a detention center.

Those months would almost prove fatal for her.

■ ■ ■

BY FALL 2005, it had become a revolving door at home. Felicia, by now fourteen and a half years old, spent as little time as possible there, struggling instead to survive on the streets. She knew her mother would call the cops on her every time she came back.

"I know I can't go back home," Felicia said later. "My mother probably called me in as a runaway already so I just stayed out." At first she survived by panhandling, but she was always on the lookout for a place to stay and someone to take care of her. In other words, she was the "ideal victim for a pimp," as one youth counselor would later testify in court.

In rapid succession, she passed through the hands of three street-wise hustlers. There was Demarcus "Marvelous" Jones, a man with two misdemeanor convictions for theft and criminal mischief but no convictions as a pimp, even if his name was all too familiar to the vice cops. "You heard his name a lot," said De La Paz. "He was busy." Felicia would later tell police Marvelous had sold her on the prospect of dancing, but when it turned into prostitution, she left.

Then she was lured by Bobby Hall, whom police described as an "old-style" operator in his fifties. Felicia eventually climbed out of a window at Hall's home, leaving behind what few clothes and belongings she had, and escaped.

By December, Felicia was on the streets again, hungry and alone. She had ten dollars in her pocket when she ran into Trina, a girl she had met in juvenile lockup. Together they made their way to the Greyhound bus station, "doing nothing, just sitting there because it was open twenty-four hours and we could stay."

Trina wandered off and came back after a few minutes with news that she'd found a place to stay for the night. And she introduced Felicia to a lanky, scruffy-looking African American man who called himself Peebo.

"What's your name?" he asked, and Felicia told him. He seemed friendly enough, so she didn't hesitate to get into the backseat of his car, which was already packed with seven people.

Peebo, in his forties, was smitten by this fourteen-year-old whom he'd later describe as "this cool little old girl." He first left her at an apartment in North Dallas, where he asked her to babysit for an infant girl whose mother was a stripper and a heroin addict desperately trying to get into Peebo's circle. But for Felicia it was a warm place to stay, and there was food. And maybe a decent job that didn't involve sex.

She didn't know Peebo had other plans for her.

His real name was Stephen Lynn Buggs. His nickname came from a girl who called him Sweet Pea back in sixth grade; on the street he wisely toughened that to Peebo. A dropout by ninth grade, Buggs was a pill-popping alcoholic and, as he liked to boast, "a pretty good hustler." Cars, dope, women—it pretty much didn't matter what he was selling as long as it put cash in his pocket. "I know how to make that money work for me," he said. And it showed. He made enough from his criminal activities to redo part of his house in marble tile.

In the pantheon of pimps, however, Peebo was a bottom-feeder when compared with a high-stakes player like Knowledge. He was typical of the thousands of small-time hustlers who populate the streets of American cities and prey on vulnerable women and girls. Where Knowledge was a business manager with a countrywide vision, exploiting dozens of women to pull in hundreds of thousands of dollars in casinos from Vegas to Atlantic City, Peebo ran a couple of women at a time in strip clubs and massage parlors in the Dallas neighborhoods he knew. And where Knowledge tried to lay low and had no criminal record until the FBI busted him, even Peebo admitted he'd had "way too much involvement with the criminal justice system," doing stints in jail for the previous sixteen years for everything from drunk driving to gun charges.

In the street parlance of the business, Peebo was a "guerrilla pimp," favoring fists and bottles broken over heads to keep his women in line. His wife of nine years left him because of repeated beatings. "I didn't want to get killed," she later testified. Buggs found a new partner he could victimize just two weeks after finishing another stretch in prison for assault in 2001. Her name was Cheryl, a twenty-one-year-old woman from Cheyenne, Wyoming, who had come to Dallas in search of a better life. She ended up working as a medical assistant by day and stripping by night at the Men's Club. Peebo beat her just as he had his wife, "so many times that I don't remember," Cheryl said, "but I just kept staying with him out of love."

Cheryl was less than pleased when Buggs announced to her that he wanted his new fourteen-year-old acquaintance to move in with them. A couple of days after dropping off Felicia to babysit at the North Dallas apartment, Peebo returned to tell her he was now taking her to his home. Cheryl was not impressed when she first set eyes on the disheveled teenager: a backpack, one change of clothes, and a pair of shoes with no laces. "She was a mess," Cheryl remembered.

It was competition, not compassion, that fueled Cheryl's concern over Felicia. "I didn't want her in the house because she was on my territory," she would later explain. But once Felicia settled into a small upstairs guest room, Cheryl warmed somewhat to the visitor. "I grew to like her," she admitted, giving the teenager cute clothes she had been saving up for her sister.

Buggs, meanwhile, warmed to the girl in his own way, later admitting in court he had a "sneaking like on her."

When Cheryl caught him one morning in the living room with Felicia's leg lying over him, he rushed to the kitchen to explain. "Baby, it's not what you think." But it was exactly what she thought. Buggs used Felicia for his own sexual pleasure and to sell sex.

He soon announced he had found the fourteen-year-old a "job." She started stripping at a prostitution den known as the Penthouse Club. Any money she made, she gave to Peebo. Felicia toughed it out for a short while before she bolted. She tried to survive on the streets for a few days by herself but was forced to give up. "I didn't have no money and I was hungry," she said. "There was no food."

Back she went to Buggs, who took advantage of her desperation, this time putting her to work in a down-in-the-dumps massage parlor with the high-class name the Swedish Institute. The customers who walked through the doors shortly ended up across the street with Felicia in the Crowne Plaza Hotel. She would service five to six of them a night at fixed rates: $175 for an hour, $135 for a half hour. Of course Buggs got his way with her for free. Felicia said he had sex with her at least twice in December at the hotel.

Buggs also put the teenager out on the streets, driving her around in his Avalanche and making sure she had a steady supply of condoms. For good measure, he also supplied her with cocaine, marijuana, and some "handlebars," street slang for Xanax, a prescription antianxiety medication. Felicia described her routine in a resigned monotone of acceptance. "I would walk and some guy would say something and then we would go back and have sex and then he would give me money and then I would give it to Peebo."

Peebo later insisted he had no idea Felicia was a minor, but that seemed doubtful considering that he was the one who conveniently gave her a fake ID that showed she was twenty-three. Her childish behavior, if not her age, was plain for all to see. Once, when he saw the young girl laughing at a cartoon show on TV, he remarked to Cheryl, "The little bitch is just a kid."

Buggs wanted that "little bitch" all to himself, and that was what sparked the incident that nearly cost Felicia her life. It began late one night in January 2006, when Buggs took Felicia and Cheryl to a seedy neighborhood bar in the city's north end. Next to the cut-rate liquor stores, auto-parts outlets, and burrito joints, the Red Lion beckoned its customers with a simple white sign painted over cracked red bricks. The bar, located next to a popular strip club called Lipstick, didn't need much advertisement; it had long been frequented by pimps.

After buying Felicia a vodka, Buggs started to hit the booze heavily himself. At one point, he dispatched Felicia to hunt for a client outside. "Y'all can walk around and see if y'all can find somebody," he said. A short while later, he caught Felicia talking to a rival hustler—her former pimp, Bobby Hall. "He thought I smiled at him so he got mad," Felicia said.

Mad was an understatement. The drunken Buggs was seething with rage. He ordered everyone into his Avalanche. "She's trying to get over us, babe," he said to Cheryl. As the car sped away, he exploded with anger against the younger girl. "He was just cussing me out and calling me names and stuff. Peebo was just screaming," Felicia remembered.

Felicia thought the worst of Peebo's fury would be over by the time they got home.

■ ■ ■

HOME WAS a redbrick, two-story house on a dead-end street in a high-crime area. Ten feet from the house, there was a rusted NEIGHBORHOOD WATCH sign, battered and bent over.

When they pulled into the driveway, the pimp shoved Felicia out of the car so forcefully she fell on the cement. Once inside, Cheryl, much to her professed regret later on, went upstairs. "I should have had them both separate but instead I just walked off into the bedroom. That's when I heard all the noises coming from the living room. Yelling and screaming."

Alarmed, she came back downstairs only to witness a slugfest in the living room. "He was hitting her just everywhere," she later testified. "She just stood there and took it."

But it got even more violent. First Peebo threw a Buddha statue at Felicia. Next he smashed two Corona beer bottles over her head. Then he made her strip, grabbed some metal ceremonial swords that were displayed on the mantel, and started to beat her so hard on her arms and legs with them that one of the swords broke.

"I'm going to kill you!" he yelled. "I could just stick this into you and kill you!"

"He hit me again and again. He made me lie down and then he grabbed a cigarette and he burned me," Felicia would later say. "I was afraid of dying."

His eyes aflame, Buggs turned to Cheryl and barked out, "Get the gun!" He hit Felicia repeatedly with his pistol and pointed it at her head.

"I'm going to kill you!" he threatened again.

"No, don't! Don't kill her because you'll catch another case," yelled Cheryl, apparently more concerned her pimp would add to his lengthy criminal record than with Felicia's fate. Later she would try to justify her inaction. "I sat there and I watched this happen in the living room because I was afraid he would turn on me next."

Buggs had one final torture left. He grabbed one of his swords and shoved it forcefully into Felicia's vagina. Cheryl's account of the rape is chilling in its clinical detachment. "He pushed it up her pussy," she said. "He would do it and then he would tell her to push it up her. And he just told her to keep pushing."

When the beating was over, Felicia was near unrecognizable, with both eyes badly swollen and one completely shut. There were burns on her chest, and her limbs were cut all over.

"I'm going to put you in the garage," Buggs announced. Then he thought better of that, fearing Felicia could probably get away. Instead he turned to Cheryl. "Baby, I'm going to show you how you hog-tie somebody," he said. He got some electrical cord and bound Felicia's wrists and ankles behind her back, cut off her hair with a pair of scissors, and covered her mouth with tape. The best place to dump her, he decided, was a small closet in the bedroom.

"Put the bitch in the closet!" he yelled.

And Cheryl did, closing the door behind her.

Felicia lay there in the dark, crumpled on the floor in a semiconscious state. Her head was pounding, her bound wrists and ankles throbbing. At least she managed to scrape off the tape Buggs had slapped over her mouth by rubbing it against the closet's dirty carpet. She could still barely breathe. "There was like a pile of clothes—my face was in the carpet and stuff," she later said. "I was just scared."

Buggs, drunk and spent of rage, immediately fell asleep. "I don't remember nothing but passing out," he said.

Cheryl, though, couldn't close her eyes. "I didn't go to bed. I was laying there. She was calling my name out."

Felicia begged for some water. Cheryl opened the closet to check on her. "I could tell she was uncomfortable. All her weight was just on one side." But all Cheryl did was lift Felicia up a bit to help her shift her weight. Then she closed the door again.

Forty-five minutes later, Cheryl could hear the girl whimpering again, calling their names. "I can't feel my arm," she cried out at one point. It was enough to prod Cheryl into action, if only briefly. "I could tell she was cold so I threw like a blanket over her," she said. "And I closed the door again and I went back to bed." Cheryl's guilty conscience apparently had its limits.

In the early hours of the morning, the household stirred awake. Buggs let Felicia crawl on her knees to go to a nearby bathroom. "I just peed on the floor," Felicia would recall. As she lay there in her own urine, she caught a glimpse of herself in the mirror. "Horrible. My face was puffed up. My eye was closed down."

Felicia crawled out and collapsed on the living room couch. Everyone slept until the early afternoon.

Hung over, Buggs was contrite once he awoke. "I can't believe I did this to my baby," he told her. He would later claim that everything had returned to normal in his household. "Cheryl cooking pancakes. All of us eat on the couch like nothing happened." Cheryl remembered it differently, but then she was the one who had to clean up the blood, the broken glass, and the clothes strewn everywhere. "It was just a mess in the living room," she said.

Felicia was even more of a mess, and Buggs seemed more worried about the state of his investment in the girl than the state of her health. Cheryl gave the girl a few tablets of ibuprofen, some Neosporin for her cuts and scrapes, and witch hazel for the swollen eyes. For days, Felicia just lay on her bed in the cramped upstairs bedroom, too sore to even navigate the stairs to the kitchen.

"Her legs were beaten to a pulp," Cheryl said.

■ ■ ■

IT WAS a while before Felicia was able to walk again. But, aching and groggy from the painkillers, she still had the strength of mind to plot her escape.

Buggs had ordered Cheryl to stay home and watch over the battered teen as she healed. After a few more days of recuperation at his home, Buggs drove Felicia back to his "trap," an apartment in East Dallas where she had prostituted for him before. She told Buggs she was well enough to go out to walk the streets for him. "I said I was going to go out and work," she later recounted.

Instead she walked out and never came back. Battered and bruised, she managed to make her way back home. She knew it had never been much of a haven for her. But she also knew it was better than being her pimp's punching bag. Her mother, as always, seemed at best indifferent to her daughter's fate.

"I'm hurting, but I'm OK," Felicia told her.

"Go rest a little bit and we'll see what we will do in the morning," her mother said.

It was 10:00 P.M. The next morning, after they had breakfast, her mother called the police in Carrollton, north of Dallas, where they lived—not to report the beating but to report her child for repeatedly running away. When the cops arrived, they simply arrested Felicia for violating her probation orders. They took the battered girl to the police station. Her mother went to work.

(When, several weeks later, Fassett and De La Paz found out officers from a neighboring police force had arrested Felicia instead of helping her, they were beside themselves with fury. "It is just systemic, unadulterated apathy," Fassett says. "It's a mind-set that says this child is a criminal." Even a drunk lying injured on the street gets medical attention from police and a call for an ambulance, De La Paz points out. "This is a child with fresh cigarette burns on her chest. You can lie about a lot of things, but not cigarette burns.")

Once again the fourteen-year-old was alone, forced to fend for herself. It was 7:30 A.M. on January 25, 2006. She was cold, sitting in the Carrollton police station. It had been more than two weeks since her beating, but the brutality was still evident. Her right eye was black; her left eye was still bleeding. She had scrapes and cuts on her knees and bruises on her hip, both thighs, and shoulder. On her chest were the three distinct burn holes where Buggs had tortured her with his cigarette.

"They were some of the worst injuries I have seen," Detective Angela Lundy, who took charge of the girl, would later testify. She took photographs of Felicia's wounds that morning. Yet despite the girl's obvious battering, the Carrollton police did not bother to send her to the local hospital for a checkup. It was a callous oversight, one that would come back to haunt the authorities when Stephen Buggs would claim that her injuries could not have been that severe if police decided she did not need medical attention. Nor did the police bother to do a rape kit.

Detective Lundy did give the shivering girl a jacket along with a muffin and a soda. Then, with the police camera rolling (as was standard procedure), she began to question the runaway. They spoke for over an hour. Felicia gave only the broad outlines of her story. She said she had been taken from a bar to a house where she had been stripped naked and tortured. She did not name Buggs, much less admit that he had made her sell her body in strip bars and massage parlors and on the street.

Lundy asked the girl if she was involved in prostitution. Felicia, no doubt frightened, ashamed, and already deep in trouble with the law, denied it. "It wasn't emphatic, she just said no," the detective said.

Felicia was shipped off to the nearby Lone Star Juvenile Center. Even in jail, she received no medical attention, not even X-rays to determine the extent of her injuries. "That's only if you like have major stuff," she would later say, all too used to being ignored and neglected by the system—and her family. In the nine months she was locked up, her mother never once came to visit.

In the eyes of the law and even her family, Felicia was a criminal— a repeat runaway who broke her probation rules. She would have stayed in jail, silent and forgotten, had it not been for two Dallas cops who saw her through different eyes.

■ ■ ■

BYRON FASSETT and Cathy De La Paz were slowly getting the message out to the rest of the police force that runaways were a priority, not a nuisance. To reach out to more and more officers, they kept making adjustments along the way, some cosmetic, others more institutional.

Fassett tweaked the cards his team handed out to patrol officers. The name of his unit—on the cards only, not officially—was changed from the High Risk Victims Unit to the Juvenile Prostitution Unit. Fassett personally found the popular police designation of the victims as "juvie prostitutes" to be denigrating, but he did not want to raise any eyebrows among the more cynical or more traditional law-and-order street cops. "Otherwise, they would joke that I have become a social worker," Fassett says. Which, in many ways, he had.

It was an example of Fassett's flexibility in navigating the treacherous waters of the justice system's politics—firm on principle, more fluid on tactics. Anything to get help to "my kids" as he liked to call them.

Fassett also tapped into the MIRs, the miscellaneous incident reports that patrol officers wrote up when they had arrived at the scene of a call but there was no obvious offense. Most of the MIRs went into a dead file that nobody ever saw. But Fassett convinced the department to flag any MIR that had a reference to runaways or high-risk victims. Hundreds of reports began flooding across the desks of the High Risk Victims investigators, not all of them actionable, but

there were enough leads to open up fifteen to twenty new investigations every month.

The MIRs helped change the way Fassett's team operated. Typically, most child-protection squads in any police force find their cases
through the usual reporting channels: a complaint, an arrest, or a
detention sparks an inquiry that might lead to the rescue of a child.
But fewer and fewer of the HRVT cases were coming from that route.
Most filtered up through the hundreds of daily encounters police
around Dallas were having with young people.

"It means the word is getting out," Fassett explains. "Our team of
four people has only eight eyes. But locally and nationally, there are
hundreds if not millions of eyes coming in contact with kids every
day."

In one typical MIR, a young girl was reported as a runaway:

> She... was living with two suspects; they had just been evicted from
> the Budget Suites for an instance involving prostitution. The adult
> female suspect has been arrested for prostitution before. It appears
> that this complainant may be an exploited child being forced to
> prostitute.

Fassett was struck by the terminology in the report: "an exploited
child being forced to prostitute." The cops on the street were changing their wording because they were changing their attitudes. "This
kid in the past would have been treated as just another runaway and
locked up," Fassett notes. "But when you educate the rank and file and
put in mandated reporting across the system, a case like this can't fall
through the cracks."

But Fassett and his investigators also learned that if they wanted to
nail the pimps, they were going to have to be more than cops. "I'm a
cop, and I want to put the pimp in jail," Fassett says. "But to do that, I
have to be Mom, Dad, and, yes, a social worker. You have to take care
of that kid's immediate needs—physical and psychological—before
you can do anything else."

It meant turning traditional policing on its head. Cops are used to going after bad guys, and if they can help a victim along the way, so much the better. But Fassett's people were aiming for the exact opposite: to turn victims' lives around, which would let them nail the bad guys. "My priority is to locate, identify, and remove the child from danger," he says. "If a successful prosecution happens after that, that's great."

They discovered the small things were what mattered. In their office at police headquarters, the team collected a pile of sweatpants and shirts and gave them to the often scantily clad girls when they came in after an arrest. Originally, that served a dual practical purpose—it was inappropriate for the male officers to be talking to such sparsely dressed teenagers, and the air-conditioned rooms could be frigid, especially in the middle of the night or the early morning hours when a lot of the girls were picked up. "Those poor little things were shivering in there," Fassett recalls.

But the casual outfits had another, unintended benefit. "What we found is that it put them back in kid mode," says Fassett. Given a chance, the girls become girls again.

"They become comfortable. You can almost see them change from a kid in an adult world who is on the street having to work to now just a kid, all curled up in her sweats," says Fassett. "This is how teenage girls are supposed to sit. It really changes their mind-set."

As more and more girls started coming into their offices, the cops also had to change their own mind-sets. One morning, Cathy De La Paz stepped out of an interview room where she was querying a new arrival.

"You have a couple of quarters?" she asked Fassett.

"What for?" her boss asked.

"For a machine in the washroom," she answered curtly.

"Hey, if she needs a Coke I'll get her one later," Fassett said.

"No," De La Paz shot back, letting the next word—"stupid"—go all but unsaid. "For a machine in the women's bathroom they don't have in men's bathrooms."

"Oh," said a suddenly uncomfortable Fassett, who finally realized they were talking about tampons. Fassett couldn't get the money out fast enough.

The squad soon decided to keep a supply of feminine hygiene products on hand. It became so routine that Fassett did not even notice when one day he was walking with his police chief down the corridors with a tampon in one hand.

"Well, this is a sight," the chief remarked.

"One of my kids needed it," he explained. The casual description of the girls brought in off the streets as "my kids" was indicative of how much Fassett took this personally. Behind the tampons and the sweatshirts lay a deeper, almost seismic shift in police attitudes.

"What are the main reasons a child gets involved in this?" Fassett would ask himself and his team. "Love, affection, and attention. It has nothing to do with drugs or survival. It's about filling a void. This child has an enormous void in her life."

It was not by accident that the young girls forced into prostitution called their pimps Daddy.

"That's where we have to play such an important role," says Fassett, himself the father of two children. "When we yank this child off the street, we have to step in and fill that void. You got to go in that room and you have got to quit being a cop. Sometimes you just have to listen to the kid."

• • •

IF EVER there was a girl who needed someone to listen to her, it was Felicia.

Her case would have disappeared into the mountain of files, one of hundreds of girls ignored by the system, were it not for some good groundwork laid by the High Risk Victims and Trafficking unit. As part of its outreach program, Fassett's team had alerted probation officers at the juvenile center where Felicia was being held to be on the lookout for potential victims of prostitution. The new rules worked, because they eventually did send Felicia's name to the Dallas cops. Meanwhile, a geographic stroke of luck occurred at roughly the same time. The Carrollton police decided to send Felicia's file to the HRVT unit as well, since some of the events she recounted had taken place in Dallas.

Felicia had been locked up in the Lone Star youth detention facility for a month before both reports on her crossed Fassett's desk. By coincidence, he and De La Paz planned to go to the youth jail to interview other detainees, so they added Felicia's name to the list. It was early on Thursday, February 23. On the ride out to Lone Star, they randomly divided the names of the girls. Fassett drew Felicia.

These were what the cops called cold interviews. No hard facts, no formal allegations, just a list of girls who fit the profile of potential victims of prostitution: repeat runaways who have been out on the street for a long time. Felicia was Fassett's first encounter of the day. Like most girls who knew the streets, the fourteen-year-old had no reason to trust cops. More often than not, talking to the police meant getting arrested. After all, that was how she had ended up in this juvenile center in the first place.

Fassett knew that the traditional police model for interviewing crime victims would not work. "Our system is built for people who tumble into problems and want out. Ninety percent of these girls don't think they are victims," he says. "She doesn't want our help, and she is mad as hell, and she is going to fight us tooth and nail."

So Fassett looked for the trigger incident or series of events that had set the girl down the path she was on. Most police victim interviews are based on what Fassett calls "a prior outcry," when a citizen calls for help and police investigate the crime. With these girls, each case requires a lot more digging. "You have to go back to the time when they were happy and see what turned," he explains. "Inevitably, there was abuse or neglect, and it wasn't dealt with or, more likely, dealt with improperly."

That scenario fit Felicia perfectly. Fassett found the girl sitting across from him in the detention center briefing room that morning to be remarkably relaxed. Jail was nothing new for her. "She was happy-go-lucky, nonchalant," he remembers. "This was just another day in her life."

But Felicia was disarmed by the smiling, fatherly figure who seemed uncharacteristically free of judgment about her situation—especially for a cop. Soon, she was sketching out the basic details of her days on the streets. She threw out names like Marvelous. That caught Fassett's attention and gave a ring of truth to Felicia's story. Fassett recalled his partner De La Paz had once worked a case against Marvelous. When Felicia showed him the cigarette burns, Fassett knew this was serious. He pushed his chair back, got up, excused himself for a moment, and went to the other interview room to interrupt De La Paz. "You might want to sit in on this one," he told her.

What does he think is so important? De La Paz recalls thinking.

She got her answer the minute the two officers got back in the room with Felicia and Fassett asked her to show his colleague her wounds. De La Paz was momentarily speechless. "Cigarette burns are just the most violent thing," she says. "You just don't do that without raping somebody. It goes together. And that is when I realized this is going to be something."

For the first time, Felicia opened up and told her full story. For ninety minutes she shared her secrets with the two officers. She admitted she had been forced into prostitution. She explained how her pimp, Peebo, had dragged her from the bar to his house, where she had been stripped naked and tortured.

The intricate details of her detention and torture not only gave Felicia's story the air of legitimacy, they also convinced the cops that the girl's evidence gave them a good chance to track down a notorious pimp. But they had to move fast.

Fassett hated interviewing prospective witnesses in jail. It reinforced the stereotype of them as criminals instead of victims. If he and De La Paz were going to win Felicia's trust and nail Buggs, she had to be relaxed and comfortable. What's more, she would have to be out on the streets with the police, pointing out the scenes of the crimes. "We needed to get her out of there," Fassett says.

They sent a message to the district court judge presiding over youth court to request a temporary release order for Felicia. But that was simply not done, they were told. Against regulations. She was a juvenile, and there could be too much liability if something happened to her.

"No" is not a word the HRVT team likes to hear, much less obey. "We are just so ornery and stubborn," says De La Paz. "A lot of people will just say, 'You can't.' And I will not have people tell me that. If it is something that furthers a child abuse investigation, then it has to be: 'Yes, you can.'" They were dealing with unconventional victims, and that called for unconventional methods, even if it meant bucking a justice system that was blind to the problem.

"It comes back to this systemic mind-set," says Fassett. "They are not seeing what we see."

The battle with various bureaucrats dragged on for a week. Finally, Fassett and De La Paz asked for an audience with the judge, and on Friday, March 3, they walked into court. Usually a judge will beckon for officers to approach the bench at the first break in any proceedings, but the HRVT cops were made to wait until the end of the day. It was not until around 3:00 P.M. when the judge finally agreed to talk to them. They were on delicate ground, for they were just cops, and they were challenging a magistrate who had already made his ruling.

"I don't think you have been provided with all the facts," Fassett said with as much tact as he could muster. "These guys are hurting children. I just want to point out that if we are not allowed to move Felicia, this investigation will end now. It is my belief that additional children are being hurt or could be hurt." Fassett knew he was putting the judge on the spot, but it worked. Sort of.

"All right, you have six hours. Firm," the judge said. "I will hold you in contempt of court if she is not back in six hours. And the clock starts now."

It was ludicrous. It would have been hard enough to do a proper investigation in six weeks, much less six hours. The Dallas cops had until 9:00 P.M. that night to check out several potential suspects and crime scenes spread across the sprawling Dallas metropolitan area and surrounding towns. But Fassett and De La Paz were not going to waste time complaining. After dashing to the detention center, they lost an hour just processing the paperwork to get Felicia released. Finally, with the girl in the backseat of the car as De La Paz frantically took notes, Fassett sped his way through the worst of the city's Friday afternoon rush-hour traffic.

They first made it to Plano, north of Dallas, where Felicia pointed out Bobby Hall's house. Then they hurried to the Pleasant Grove neighborhood on the eastern tip of Dallas so she could show them Peebo's home, where she had been beaten. They managed to squeeze in a look at a couple of motels where her pimps had made her work. When they stopped for a bite to eat at a fast-food joint, Felicia— famished and tired of detention center grub—wolfed down as much as she could grab, only to promptly vomit it all up on Fassett's feet on the way back to the car. The girl was mortified, more by the thought of all that good food going to waste than the state of Fassett's shoes.

As night fell over the city, Fassett and De La Paz raced back to police headquarters. They wanted to record Felicia as she phoned her former pimp, hoping such one-party-consent calls, as they are known, could provide valuable leads and possibly even some incriminating statements. Buggs didn't answer when she called him, but she had little trouble getting Bobby Hall on the phone. He talked extensively with Felicia about his dealings with her. As Felicia chatted away, Fassett nervously kept tapping his watch to signal to De La Paz that time was running short and they had to get the girl back into custody.

They managed to return to the detention center by 9:01 P.M., just a minute over their six-hour limit—deliberately. Fassett was not above sticking it to a stubborn judicial system whenever he got the chance.

Now the hard work began. They had to prove Felicia's allegations. The team had to evaluate which of the three pimps to target first. Buggs moved easily to the top of the list. He appeared to be the most violent, and the allegations against him were the most detailed.

But time was running out. "We needed to get critical evidence before it was lost," Fassett explains. They were starting late, several months after Felicia's beating. The Dallas team managed to retrieve the photographs of her wounds from the Carrollton police files. Over several nights, De La Paz and three other officers worked surveillance on Buggs's home on GlenCliff Drive, watching the pimp's comings and goings. De La Paz was able to track down fourteen traffic tickets the Dallas police department had issued to Buggs to verify his registered residence was indeed the house on GlenCliff. They confirmed his identity, his habits, and the hours he kept. By March 9, 2006, just over two weeks after the cops had first met Felicia, they had enough evidence to secure a search warrant and an arrest order.

They didn't want to take down Buggs when he was in his house, where he was known to have a gun and could barricade himself. Fassett followed him to a gas station and then called in what he jokingly calls an "air strike." The police moved in to arrest the surprised pimp.

Meanwhile, De La Paz started to do the crime scene canvass at his home, where she found much of the evidence that corroborated Felicia's story. On a decorative stand in the living room were three swords of hardened metal. One of them was broken, and its handle lay atop the entertainment center. (Later the police would compare the shape of the sword with the bruises on Felicia's body in the photograph, and they matched up perfectly.) In a drawer was the electrical cord Buggs had used to tie up Felicia, while behind the headboard in the downstairs bedroom they uncovered the pistol he had pointed at her head. Three bullets lay next to the gun. De La Paz sent the broken blade, the sword case, and the cord to the laboratory for DNA analysis. The tests would later confirm traces of Felicia's blood.

Fassett was struck by how special that made Felicia's case. More often than not, girls would come forward with similar stories of physical violence that could not be verified. "As horrific as the abuse sounds, most people find it unbelievable, literally to the point where they just don't believe it," he says. But Felicia was luckier than most—because of quick work by a specialized team dedicated to helping prostituted children, there was hard evidence to back up her claims in the form of photographs of her injuries and DNA-tested bloodstains.

Fassett says, "What her case did is that it showed people that everything we've been saying about what these kids go through is true."

As a result of Felicia's disclosures, the Dallas High Risk Victims team laid seven felony charges against Buggs, ranging from compelling a minor into prostitution to trafficking in humans and aggravated kid-napping. A week later the police arrested Bobby Hall and raided his home. They found the clothes Felicia had left behind. He was charged with trafficking and compelling prostitution under the Texas Penal code.

When De La Paz and Fassett first walked into Buggs's holding cell, he was stunned. He could not believe the cops had gone to this much trouble over a teenage girl, a runaway, a throwaway who nobody seemed to care about.

"All this over some little ho?" he asked.

De La Paz glared at him, her lips tight. Her words came out in icy anger. "She's not your ho anymore."

"Like Attacking the Mafia"

Back in New York, Matthew "Knowledge" Thompkins was, like Stephen Buggs, furious that he was behind bars because of "some little ho." He had always known there were risks in the game, but he figured he was smart enough to beat the odds. When police raided one of his many homes, they found a mock New York license plate with the number PIMPN8EZ.

Pimpin' Ain't Easy.

Except that, in reality, pimping is easy. Prosecuting pimps is hard. The FBI's Dan Garrabrant and prosecutor Jason Richardson had to demonstrate to the courts that pimps are not just petty criminals. The two lawmen were after a bigger prize—they wanted to nail Knowledge and his partner Tracy for being part of a large-scale "criminal enterprise" that trafficked in human beings.

In a justice system that all too frequently sees prostitution as a "victimless" crime and therefore of low priority, Garrabrant knew he was lucky to be partnered with Richardson, the assistant U.S. attorney in Camden, New Jersey, the kind of prosecutor who saw his work not so much as a job as a calling. On the wall above the prosecutor's desk was a framed cutting from a *Harper's Weekly* of 1865, detailing the story of John R. Rock, "the first colored lawyer accepted before the Supreme Court." Next to it was a collage of images of the famed jurist Thurgood Marshall. Richardson had recently added another picture, propped up in a corner on one of his overstuffed filing cabinets: a photocopy of Knowledge's mock license plate, PIMPN8EZ.

Richardson had no experience in prosecuting pimps, but he was nothing if not a quick study. Going over the mountains of files and the hours of wiretaps, he was impressed by the skills of the man he was trying to convict. "I didn't realize how organized this was," he says. "Knowledge was very empathetic and could pick up on what people needed to hear. He could size someone up and figure what would work and then follow it through. Then he played on each of the women's emotions to get them to compete against each other for supremacy within the stable itself."

Richardson knew that in the past the courts had often failed to take the crime of pimping seriously. "We don't do prostitution cases, we don't do hundred-dollar hookers" were the dismissive words Richardson remembers hearing in the halls of justice. The prosecutor wanted to show that modern-day prostitution networks had grown into sophisticated businesses that used violence to trap vulnerable minors and that there were federal laws on the books to send these kinds of offenders away for years.

Richardson pored through the thousands of pages of wiretap transcripts, studied the surveillance reports, and carefully examined the extensive tax and property records the FBI had collected. Follow the money. That has always been the best rule in criminal investigations.

Knowledge made no secret that his business was all about money, not sex. It was only fitting that the money trail would help bring him down. He was charged, after all, not just with child prostitution but also with conspiracy to engage in money laundering.

"We started pulling the financial records, and that is when it becomes interesting," says Richardson. "Knowledge was someone who was living off the radar, but when you started putting together his assets, the amount of property that he owned, the houses and expensive cars—anytime you have a sophisticated criminal enterprise, it gets exciting."

The case was a huge learning curve for the prosecutor and the FBI agent. "This was a very big, organized group, and we had to attack it like we were attacking the Mafia," says Garrabrant.

No detail was too small or insignificant. When the prosecutor was listening to a wiretap conversation, he caught mention of Knowledge bragging about a new luxury car. "Have we subpoenaed the Mercedes-Benz dealer to find the records, to find out what he is saying on those applications, to find out if there are any bank accounts that we are missing, how is he claiming a legitimate source of income?" Richardson asked of the FBI.

On a visit to the county probation office in Atlantic City, Garrabrant came up with another valuable nugget. "You'll never believe what we got," he told the prosecutor, showing him a letter from Hoodlum Records that claimed one of the women from Knowledge's stable who had been arrested was employed as a "clerical worker" at his front company. That way she could claim she had a legitimate job while in reality she pulled in more cash for Knowledge by working the streets.

Richardson wanted a successful prosecution of Knowledge to serve as a warning to other pimps. "We both knew the damage this guy did," he says. "How do we make him an example?"

■ ■ ■

IN THE end, despite all the financial paperwork and electronic wiretaps, Richardson knew his case would stand or fall on the testimony of the young women and even younger girls who worked for Knowledge and Tracy. And that was going to be a problem.

Were the women victims, co-conspirators—or both? From a strictly legal point of view, even an underage girl like Maria, though exploited, was also committing a crime. "She was out there selling her body for money, breaking the law," says Richardson. But he and Garrabrant nevertheless made a sharp distinction between the older women who were adults under the law and the girls who had been exploited by Knowledge when they were under the legal age of consent. There was no question in their minds that Maria and the other minors were victims, not criminals. And their testimonies would be the pillars of the trafficking case against Knowledge and his fellow pimps.

Maria gave a detailed statement to police about her work for Knowledge in Atlantic City, the Bronx, New Jersey, Florida, and Nevada dating back to 2003. If the case ever went to trial, she would make a powerful witness.

The second underage witness was Joanie, one of last recruits of Knowledge's partner Tracy. She had been in the Hummer with Maria on the New Jersey expressway in spring 2005 and had witnessed the attempted kidnapping by Tracy and Knowledge. By coincidence, police had picked her up as a prostituted minor on the streets of Atlantic City months before the takedown of Knowledge's operation. But Garrabrant had no reason to connect her to the case at that time.

The pieces began to fall into place after the sweep of Knowledge's network. Once she was under arrest, Goddess, the woman who was driving the Hummer the day of the attempted kidnapping, identified Joanie as the girl who had been sitting in the back with Maria. "Holy shit," Garrabrant exclaimed. They had stumbled upon an important witness but had not realized it until that moment. Now Joanie's testimony could corroborate Maria's story and help seal Knowledge's fate.

The third and final pillar in the case against Knowledge for trafficking minors was the testimony of Sandy, the fourteen-year-old from Nevada. She could testify about the elaborate operation to whisk her out of Las Vegas to Knowledge's New York headquarters—providing, of course, that the police could find her. It wasn't easy.

"It's rare that you rescue these girls and they go back and everything is peachy clean," says Vegas vice cop Aaron Stanton. "They're on the streets because they have problems in the first place, so they often keep running."

That's what happened with Sandy. Long after she had fled Knowledge's network, she was lured back to the tracks. Once she showed up at the Las Vegas hotel Excalibur dressed in a sleek white top and pants, gold sandals, and her hair braided down to her waist. But at heart she was a scared child. She walked up to a security guard, revealed she was a minor, and gave him Aaron Stanton's name. The Vegas cop came down to pick her up and bring her back home.

When Sandy bolted again in the late fall, the Vegas cops put flyers in the casinos and gave out her pictures to the vice enforcement cops. "Everybody was looking for her," Stanton says. This time, she eventually turned up at the juvenile detention center where Stanton spotted her while he was talking to another minor. He was relieved she was safe. The cops already had Sandy's testimony against Knowledge on tape; that was enough for the grand jury indictment. But for Stanton, she was more than just another witness, and he hoped that one day she would break free and put her life back together.

The prosecution team would keep the testimony from the three teenage girls as a weapon in reserve. Having them recount their stories in open court was something to be avoided at all costs. "We didn't want to victimize the girls twice," says Garrabrant. "Think about the degrading things these girls had to do on the street. And then you are going to put them on the stand and make them relive all of that?"

But Knowledge and Tracy would know that if they didn't agree to a plea bargain and if the prosecution felt it had no choice, the court would hear from three very angry and very eloquent young girls.

■ ■ ■

THE SITUATION was more complicated with the adult women in Knowledge's stable. After all, Meredith, Goddess, Madonna, Fortune, and Slim Shady had helped to enlist and train the minors; indeed, Meredith had assisted Knowledge in running his entire operation.

Richardson made a tough call. He charged them as co-conspirators, which would ensure that if found guilty they would do some serious time in jail. "They may have started out as minors, but they were out there recruiting more girls into a life of prostitution," he explains.

At the same time, these women suffered some of the same abuse as Maria and the other underage victims: beatings, sexual humiliation, and financial exploitation. In some instances, their physical abuse was even more severe. So Richardson hoped they would agree to give evidence against their former boss in return for lighter sentences and a chance at a new life.

Selling them on the idea of testifying against Knowledge was not going to be easy. Richardson and Garrabrant had to gain the trust of women who had been under the thumb of their pimp and deeply suspicious of the law, in some cases for more than a decade. But Garrabrant had a street cop's experience in dealing with women "in the life," while Richardson drew on his years of dealing with traumatized victims and witnesses. "What causes someone to go out on the street?" he asks. "You've got to listen to their story."

He was still a prosecutor, not a social worker, and he had a simple but forceful message to deliver. "This is a chance for you to change your life," he told the women. "This is really the time for you to square your shoulders, take a deep breath, and help yourself. And it is on you to make that decision."

But Richardson and Garrabrant offered the women something they had not experienced during all their years on the street—dignity. "They don't get treated like people out there," says the FBI agent. "We were going to treat them with the respect they deserved, no matter what they decided—whether they were going to get on board or not."

It worked. In the end, every single one of the adult women in Knowledge's stable made the decision to plead guilty and help the prosecution. It was a crucial victory. Getting their sworn testimony meant their statements could be used even if they changed their minds by the time Knowledge's trial began. Richardson also knew Knowledge was not above trying to intimidate any woman who dared to consider crossing him, as he had done with Maria. It later emerged in court testimony that the pimp had indeed tried to sway at least three of the women under arrest. He hired an attorney for Fortune, sent money to Slim Shady along with a letter that stated she could ask for anything she wanted if she did not cooperate with authorities, and got a message to Meredith that "it's too early to plead."

This time, Knowledge's sweet talk did not work. None of the women backed out. His grip on them was finally cracking.

But Richardson was not yet out of the woods. He recalled the sage words a senior prosecutor offered him at the start of his career: "If a crime happens in a church I will bring you priests and nuns. But if a crime happens in the ghetto I will bring you winos and bums." Richardson knew that if or when his case against Knowledge went to trial, most jurors might find the former prostitutes exuded what he diplomatically called "a little bit of street, a little bit of edge." But he also believed the jury would see past their rough exteriors. He told them to be themselves. "You have to be who you are," he said.

Then again, with any luck there would not have to be a trial at all. If he could get enough damning evidence in front of the courts beforehand, maybe he could pressure Tracy and Knowledge into accepting a plea. One by one, the women appeared before Judge Freda Wolfson, an affable federal judge with a reputation for frankness and efficiency. There were no other witnesses or cross-examinations because they were all pleading guilty. None of the women made statements; instead they gave short answers to questions from the judge or the prosecutor. But the stories that unfolded were dramatic and full of details, and, for the first time in public, Knowledge's conspiracy was laid bare by his senior women.

Madonna was the first to appear, on January 2, 2006. She admitted that she and her co-conspirators had recruited and transported minor girls between several states for prostitution. She told the judge how she had helped Knowledge arrange for Maria to travel from New Jersey to Las Vegas on the fateful trip in December 2003, which led to Maria's arrest. She explained how, in early July 2005, she first helped Sandy buy clothes and then traveled with her to Atlantic City for her initiation into the sex market in the casinos.

Madonna's older sister, Fortune, was next up. Fortune confirmed that she had been brought into Knowledge's stable at age seventeen and then, when she was an adult, had in turn recruited Madonna when her sibling was still a teenager. The pimp "wanted all the women working for him as prostitutes to bring home potential girls and women to work for him and [made] a competition of it," she explained. Fortune also acknowledged she taught Maria how to work the Atlantic City casinos.

Knowledge was a relentless taskmaster who had his girls work at least twelve hours every weeknight and fourteen hours each night on the weekends, Fortune recounted. Knowledge forced all the women "to keep journals of your activities, including the number of 'dates' you had and how much money you made," she said. And he beat them for the smallest infractions, she told the judge, "like not following his rules, for talking back, or for looking at the wrong man."

Goddess, the tall brunette who had so impressed Maria the first time she saw her step out of Knowledge's Mercedes-Benz in New York City, revealed the seamier side of being in Thompkins's employ. She testified that, when she was first recruited, the pimp taught her "the rules of the game," right down to "what outfits to wear and what prices to charge for sex," and then dispatched her to a "whore-house" in Manhattan to "learn the business." Once, she said, he had instructed her and Tracy to rent a house in Manhattan so he could open a brothel. She told the court that at any one time he was running "between eight to fifteen women" and that in the entire time she worked for him he had profited from "over two hundred" women in his stable.

Knowledge's penchant for violence came to light when Goddess testified how he kept the girls and women in line, beating them with "belts, extension cords, or dog chains." As the driver in the white Hummer, Goddess confirmed the details of Maria's kidnapping and her dramatic escape at the highway rest stop; she also confessed that she had confronted Maria at the Trump Plaza on Knowledge's orders to scare her into submission.

Knowledge's greed was the focus at the end of May, when Slim Shady got her day in court. She told the judge that Knowledge had put her on the street when she was only sixteen and that by seventeen she was posing for his sex ads in local papers. Knowledge made the trek out to Hunts Point in his black Mercedes in order to force her to work longer hours as a black "duck" to earn her keep. Even though Slim Shady pulled in close to a quarter of a million dollars in one year for her pimp, Knowledge still insisted she call him for permission to go to the store, and he kept her on a tight budget of twenty dollars per day for expenses.

Perhaps the most emotional testimony came from Meredith. In many ways, her journey had been the longest and the hardest, from a child recruit to chief administrator to key witness against the man she had been with for more than sixteen years, the man who had fathered her two children. She had begun working for him as a teenager, and she was the closest thing he had to a wife. "It was really tough for her," says Garrabrant. "She was really his first conquest. The hard thing for her was finding out a lot of things about Thompkins that she didn't know." Or chose not to know.

More enraged than the other women because Knowledge's betrayal cut deeper for her, Meredith held nothing back in her confession to the judge. She confirmed that he taught her how to prostitute herself in the Bronx when she was fifteen and that, no more than a year later, she was working out of a brothel he ran. As Knowledge's business manager, she gave the court special insight into the inner workings of his enterprise. She explained how she traveled to Las Vegas with him to "obtain a business license, open a merchant account, rent office space, and place ads in the Yellow Pages" to set up Upscale Exotics as a credit-card center for sex. She said Knowledge gave her the "receipts, bills, and trap money . . . earned by the prostitutes" and that she kept the "ledgers and journals of all of Thompkins's financial activities." She acknowledged that she also created "fake leases and fake log books" to claim rent payments from the women in the stable "in case the 'feds' busted him." Further, she admitted her own sorry role in helping Knowledge recruit minors, having brought her own sister into the fold as White Diamond. In case there was any doubt that Knowledge knew the exact age of the minors he exploited, she stated that she kept copies of several of the girls' real identification, including Slim Shady's high school transcript and school ID.

Meredith also helped Knowledge cover up his crimes in other ways. She knew he beat the women with "various instruments . . . including cords, chains, and other metal objects," but she said whenever she found any of these "headcut toys" she would throw them away in disgust and anger. She also confirmed that, upon Maria's return to New York after her Vegas arrest, the pimp instructed Maria and Meredith "to shred and burn various items, including bills, invoices, and photographs."

While she echoed what many of the other women had said, her testimony—coming from the woman who had been so close to Knowledge, who had sometimes shared his bed and always shared his business secrets—carried with it an added poignancy and power. "She has turned a major corner in her life. She's renounced the activities that she's been involved with for sixteen years," her defense lawyer told the judge. "She's done that because she wants to make a clean break with the person who brought her into the conspiracy. She's showing enormous courage."

Each woman's testimony was a personal saga of oppression and betrayal at the hands of a pimp, but taken together their experiences made up a damning indictment of Knowledge and his business. On August 3, faced with the overwhelming wiretap and surveillance evidence and the incriminating testimony of Maria and the other women, Demetrius "Tracy" Lemus, Knowledge's partner, sometime enforcer, and the pimp who had recruited Maria in the first place, gave in. He pleaded guilty to a "conspiracy to transport minors in interstate commerce to engage in prostitution." Worse, from Knowledge's point of view, he confirmed and amplified the women's allegations, divulging the inside details that only a co-conspirator could know.

That left the last man in the conspiracy, the one who started it all: Matthew "Knowledge" Thompkins.

● ● ●

FOR SEVERAL months, he wavered. He stalled, steamed, and weighed his chances of going to trial.

Thompkins had gambled in Atlantic City, and he had played the casinos in Las Vegas. Would he be foolish enough to roll the dice in court?

In lengthy pretrial negotiations, Richardson spelled out what Knowledge faced. "This is what we have," he told the pimp and his lawyer. "Not only do we have pictures and videos and documents, but everybody who was sitting with you the day you were arrested—all your women—they are now sitting on the prosecution side." If Knowledge opted for trial, the prosecutor warned, "I will track down as many of the minor girls and adults out there that I can find, and the jury will see you for what you are. The judge at the end will be convinced that you need to go to prison for the rest of your natural life, for all the people you victimized." On top of all that, the prosecutor continued, there were the money-laundering charges. "We have binders upon binders of money orders, all the financial data that the FBI agents put together," he said.

These were not empty threats. If the pimp opted for a trial and was convicted, he faced life in prison. There would be no parole. Knowledge was a gambler, but he was not stupid. "He realized it was over," says Garrabrant.

On the morning of October 27, 2006, Matthew Thompkins stood before Judge Freda Wolfson, his wrists handcuffed and his feet in shackles. "We would be presenting witnesses including at least three minor girls that worked for the stable in 2003, 2004, and the beginning part of 2005," Richardson told the court, referring to Maria, Sandy, and Joanie. "We are prepared to present flight records and travel records to show how the women moved, particularly through JetBlue, between New York and Las Vegas.

"We had several of the recordings from the over five thousand wire interceptions... financial documents, as well as a large section of postal order receipts," he continued. "The estimated total at this point in time the stable made between 1998 and 2005 was in the neighborhood of eight hundred thousand dollars."

Now it was Judge Wolfson's turn. For the next twenty minutes, she peppered Thompkins with a series of detailed questions about his operation. The once loquacious and boastful pimp was reduced to monosyllabic admissions.

"Between 1999 and December 2005, were you a pimp, that is, did you run a prostitution enterprise business?" the judge began.

"Yes," Thompkins replied.

"As part of your prostitution business, did you have girls and women working the 'track' in various places including Atlantic City, New Jersey, Philadelphia, Pennsylvania, and Bronx and Manhattan, New York?"

"Yes."

"At various times, did you recruit minor girls and women to work as prostitutes for you?"

"Yes."

"Did you 'turn them out,' that is, teach them how to be a prostitute and tell them what to charge for various sex acts in the various locations that you had them working?"

"Yes."

"Did you instruct your prostitutes to recruit other women and minor girls to join your stable of prostitutes?"

"Yes."

"Between 1999 and December 2005, did you have more than five minor girls working as prostitutes for you?" Judge Wolfson continued, getting to the heart of the conspiracy.

"Yes."

"Did those minor girls travel to or from Atlantic City, New Jersey, and New York and Nevada?"

"Yes."

The judge then asked Knowledge to confirm his trafficking of Maria, known as Suprema in the court records. Her story took only a few minutes of the court's time, but it was enough to seal her former pimp's fate.

"Did you instruct Suprema to travel from New York to Las Vegas on or about December 2003 to work as a prostitute for you?" the judge asked.

"Yes."

"After you learned that Suprema gave information to the Las Vegas Metro Police Department about your illegal activities when she was arrested... did you instruct your prostitutes and other pimps to confront her and have her retract her statement and stop giving information to police?"

"Yes."

"Did you subsequently instruct other prostitutes in your stable to destroy or remove documents and other items from two apartments you maintained in Las Vegas, Nevada, and property in New York?"

"Yes."

Finally, Judge Wolfson looked up from her papers and stared directly at Knowledge. "Mr. Thompkins, how do you now plead to Count 1, the conspiracy to transport minors to engage in prostitution?"

"Guilty."

"And as to Count 2, the conspiracy to engage in money laundering, how do you plead?" she asked, referring to his skillful use of postal money orders and other schemes to hide his prostitution wealth.

"Guilty."

Thompkins's public shaming was not finished yet. He had to listen as the judge outlined his elaborate money-laundering schemes, and he had to confirm that his houses, luxury cars, and close to a three-quarters of a million dollars in cash in the bank had all come from the "proceeds of the prostitution activities." As a final indignity, the judge asked him if he agreed to forfeit "all of those assets."

"Yes," said the man who once had reveled in showing off his silver Benz and his white Hummer.

It was over. Thompkins was led out of the courtroom, shuffling because of the shackles. He would have to wait in a jail cell five more months before appearing again in front of the judge to find out how much more time he would have to spend behind bars.

■ ■ ■

HE HAD been defeated and disgraced, but Knowledge was no fool, as even his victims and his foes acknowledged.

Despite what he put her through, Maria still admires him as a smart man, one who could, she says, have even been president "if he just used all his smartness for good and not for evil." The words sound trite, but they ring true, coming as they do from a girl who saw his evil up close. "But I guess he was just addicted to the game," she continues. "Because you do get addicted to the game."

The FBI man who put him away could not help but concede his adversary was smart and shrewd. "He was looking for an endgame," Garrabrant says, adding that he figures Knowledge had been planning to "go straight" by investing some of the value of his home properties and the hard-earned cash his women had made in his Hoodlum Records company. "If that had happened, he would have been out of the game, and we would never have caught him."

It didn't turn out that way. But Knowledge, ever the slick operator and up against the wall, still had one more trick up his sleeve. The estimated value of his forfeiture was $1.9 million. He had already had to give up his eight luxury cars and four homes, all of which were seized the day he was arrested. But there was a clerical error in the original indictment, which omitted his accounts at both the Municipal Credit Union on Lafayette Street and the Chase Manhattan Plaza. So authorities had to spend two extra days to get a superseding order from a grand jury in New Jersey that sat only one day a week. That time was all Knowledge needed, for when police arrived at the banks they found that everything—savings, checking, and money market accounts worth $778,000—had been cleared out by someone. It appeared that, even though the pimp was already under arrest, he still had friends and accomplices on the outside. To this date, the money has not been retrieved.

The adult women who had earned that money for Knowledge faced their own challenges. In testifying against Knowledge, they were taking a chance. They were pleading guilty to crimes that carried a stiff penalty; the charge of trafficking minors for the purpose of prostitution carried a minimum mandatory punishment of five years behind bars and a maximum of forty, while the money-laundering charge had no minimum but a potential twenty-year sentence. In theory, the plea agreement they signed offered them no immunity or even a promise to reduce their sentences.

In the end, all five women got sentenced to time served, which meant from four to eighteen months in prison. The catch was that they would be put on eight years of supervised release. "It was an effective and equitable compromise because it punished the women for colluding in the exploitation of the minors but gave them a chance to make a break with their past," Richardson explains. "The goal was, 'What can we do to get them some structure in their life, to help them move on?'"

There was strong incentive to make that break. Supervised release meant that if they fell back into prostitution and thereby violated their parole conditions, they were looking at going back to prison for a lengthy period.

So far, the plea agreement seems to have worked. Meredith has been pursuing her college studies. Goddess sent Garrabrant a note from jail. "Even though I am behind bars, I never felt so free," she said. "Thanks for treating us like people." Slim Shady sent a card to Garrabrant, Richardson, and postal investigator Tara Bloesch. "Thank you for saving my life," it said simply.

"It is remarkable what these women went through. They got their lives back," says Garrabrant. "I've been in law enforcement for eighteen years. But I never got a thank-you note from someone I put in jail."

■ ■ ■

MARIA WAS in a tougher spot—no closure, no forgiveness, no chance to start a new life.

Knowledge and Tracy were behind bars awaiting sentencing; the older women were either finishing up their jail time or beginning afresh on the outside. But what was a young girl like Maria supposed to do? Richardson and Garrabrant were grateful for her assistance, but they could do little to help Maria find a place to live or a job. True, she had been spared the indignity of arrest and jail time. But at least the women who testified against Knowledge had a chance to speak out against their former pimp, to publicly turn the page. Maria, the girl whose arrest had spurred the collapse of Knowledge's empire, had remained silent. There had been no public redemption. No release of her anger and grief. She was left with only fear and guilt.

In the time between Knowledge's arrest and his conviction, Maria turned twenty. For all of her teenage years, from age fourteen to nineteen, she had known nothing but a street life in which she sold her body to get by. She still felt shunned by her family while her other "family" of pimps and prostitutes had been jailed in no small part because of her actions. As much as she had come to see Knowledge for what he was, she was still wracked by guilt. "That life was a part of me for years," she says. "You bring down the kingpin of pimps, and even though I know it was good, you feel horrible inside."

She felt even worse for the women she believed she had betrayed. "I snitched on them. I feel like the worst person in the world—a rat," she says about her feelings at the time. "If I could just rewind the tape, I would, I would just not say anything. I would never have told."

Even with Knowledge in jail, Maria was frightened—and for good reason. The pimps in Atlantic City knew who she was and taunted her with words that stung and scared her: *You fucking snitch, you fucking bitch.*

One of them warned her there was a contract out on her. "There is a nice amount of money out there if somebody kills you," he told her.

In her small one-room apartment, Maria went to sleep every night after wedging a couch against the door. "I got sticks on all my windows, so that you can't open them," she explains. "Every time I go to sleep hoping that I wake up alive the next morning."

She was too frightened to keep renegading. Stripping seemed like a safer option. It didn't mean she was leaving the life for the square world, but maybe, Maria hoped, it offered a way for her to make it her own.

She started at Bare Exposures, across the street from Caesar's casino, where she had drummed up business for Knowledge. She eventually moved to other clubs that offered "extracurricular activities" to customers who wanted more than a dance. She toughed it out for two years, until her independent streak got her into the same kind of trouble with the strip-joint managers as it had with her pimps. When the managers imposed a rule that the girls had to kick back one hundred dollars for every trick they pulled backstage, sometimes leaving the women with only a few dollars at best, Maria balked and stormed out.

But that left her at age twenty-two without a job and with little cash. She had survived on the street with little more than her wits and courage to protect her, and in all that time she had managed to stay away from any hard drugs. Now, for the first time, she turned to cocaine. "I was in a bad way," Maria says. "I didn't want to talk to other people. I just did the drugs to numb the pain."

Alone, frightened, and hooked on drugs, Maria was at her lowest point.

"My whole life was fucked up because of this," she says. "I just wanted to die."

· 10 ·

In the Dead of the Night

IN THE depths of her depression, Maria may have thought about dying. Some women caught up in the trade had no choice in the matter.

Like Princess, the woman who first met Maria in Atlantic City back in 2000 and introduced her to the pimping world. Though she had no proof, Maria was convinced she had been murdered. She once witnessed a pimp burning Princess with a hot iron. Then one night she saw the two leave for Hunts Point, the notorious pimping area in the Bronx. A few hours later, only the pimp returned. "He had blood all over him and this crazy look in his eyes," Maria says. She was too frightened to ask what had happened to her friend.

Aside from Maria's account, FBI agent Dan Garrabrant had no evidence Princess had even been killed, much less any proof that a pimp was involved. Women on the tracks disappear all the time—and not necessarily because they have been killed. They get sick, they get "traded off" to another pimp, or they flee to newer territory.

But the FBI agent had no trouble believing Princess could have been killed by somebody—or something. Drugs, disease, and death were the costs of what was ironically called "the life."

■ ■ ■

ON A cold fall night around midnight, Dan Garrabrant stands next to the muddy stream that runs along the ditch near Black Horse Pike, one of the main roads that lead into Atlantic City. Rusted pipes, the carcass of a car, and a few old boxes litter the grass. A few feet away, a tattered sign advertises fifteen-dollar-a-night rates at a hotel where the faded pink and green paint looks as old as its dilapidated doors and battered walls.

"This is where the bodies were found," the FBI agent says, pointing to a stretch of brown dirt and yellow grass. "Four women that no one seemed to care much about."

The bodies turned up around Thanksgiving, November 2006, a month after Matthew Thompkins had pleaded guilty. That's what Garrabrant's job was like: put away one bad guy and before you have time to catch your breath, there are more victims. Four corpses scattered over a hundred-yard area in the deep, dirty grass. The oldest corpse had lain there for a month; the freshest body had been dead less than a week. In death, they provided a portrait gallery of the disparate women forced into commercial sexual exploitation: all were white, ranging in age from twenty to forty-three years old. They hailed from Delaware, Florida, Pennsylvania, and New Jersey, from the slums of Atlantic City to the rich neighborhoods of Philadelphia. One had gone to college; the others had dropped out of high school. Two had children. One was married. Prostitution knew no boundaries. The street did not discriminate.

At forty-two, Barbara V. Breidor was the oldest victim and the wealthiest. She had grown up in an affluent Philadelphia suburb and used to summer with her family in a beach town not far from the Atlantic City casinos. As an adult she worked in a jewelry shop owned by her mother, then got a job as a waitress at the Tropicana casino. That is where her slow descent began: an addiction to prescription painkillers, then heroin and cocaine. She supported her expensive habits by selling her body.

Kimberly Raffo, also a waitress, was forced into prostitution after getting hooked on crack. At thirty-five, she seemed to have the most stable background and the most precipitous fall—she left behind a twelve-year-old son, a fourteen-year-old daughter, and a husband in Florida. Comfortably middle-class, she had begun an affair, taken up cocaine, and then suddenly fled to what she doubtless hoped would be a freer life in Atlantic City.

Tracy Ann Roberts was the prettiest of the four women, standing five feet, eight inches in a slim 120-pound frame with an elegant butterfly tattooed on her back. The twenty-three-year-old danced at a local strip club. She had drifted here from nearby Delaware after breaking up with an abusive boyfriend, only to find herself with a pimp who punched her so hard in the throat she vomited blood and was hospitalized.

The youngest of the four victims was Maria's age. Molly Jean Dilts was a twenty-year-old from a small town just outside Pittsburgh. For Maria it had been a single event—her rape at age twelve—that pushed her away from her family and over the edge into a life of prostitution. For Molly, it was apparently a series of tragedies: the death of her mother from cancer, the suicide of her brother, the birth of a son from an unknown father. There was a descent into drink and drugs, her favorite being crack cocaine. Depressed, desperate, and alone, she made her way to the streets of Atlantic City, where she called herself Amber or Princess. To look more attractive to customers, the somewhat chubby girl tried to control her weight by making herself throw up.

"She was just someone who was lost," a cousin who was her closest friend told reporters after Molly's body turned up. "I know she was crying for help in the last months in life, and we just brushed it off as some kind of phase she was going through."

Local police handled the case; this wasn't an FBI investigation, but Garrabrant kept tabs on it. There were few leads. The same man likely had slain the women, given the proximity of the bodies to one another, but there could have been multiple killers. The bodies of three of the women were so badly decomposed that determining how they died was impossible. Tracy Ann Roberts, whose bloated body lay in the ditch for only a week, had been strangled to death.

To this date, all four murders remained unsolved.

"How can people dare to call prostitution a 'victimless crime'?" Dan Garrabrant mutters as he kicks away the dirt and walks away from the ditch.

...

SINCE AT least the time of Jack the Ripper, prostituted women have always been seen as fair game.

They have been the preferred targets of some of the most famous serial killers in America. In November 2000, Gary Ridgway, the "Green River Killer," pleaded guilty to forty-eight counts of aggravated murder in Washington State, although he claimed that he had killed over ninety women in all. Most were prostituted women; thirty-one of his victims were teenagers. Ridgway picked them up along Pacific Highway South and strangled them. The choice of victims was easy, he told the judge, "because I thought I could kill as many as I wanted to without getting caught."*

Many serial murderers don't get caught. In the small North Carolina city of Rocky Mount, nine women—all of them poor, many of them forced to sell their bodies—have gone missing since 2005. In the southwestern corner of Louisiana, near the town of Jennings, the badly decomposed bodies of eight women who had a history of drugs and prostitution have been discovered in the past five years. In Baltimore, four prostitutes were strangled in as many months in spring 2008 in a string of murders that remain unsolved.

In Milwaukee, as far back as October 1986, police found two prostitutes strangled to death just one day apart. Six years later, another prostitute turned up dead. In all, twenty prostitutes were found strangled over the next twenty years. But it wasn't until May 2009 that police took things seriously to investigate the possibility there was a serial killer. They finally linked the DNA of a suspect to at least

---

* Just north of the border in British Columbia, Canada, Robert Pickton was found guilty in 2009 of murdering six women and originally faced charges for the slaying of twenty more, most of them prostituted women from Vancouver. He disposed of the bodies at his pig farm and, according to court testimony, bragged in jail that he had killed a total of forty-nine. The case sparked outrage because initially police paid little attention to the disappearance of the women, many of them Native Canadians. Pickton's first alleged victim disappeared in 1995; he was not arrested until seven years later.

nine of the deaths and tested about two dozen other unsolved prostitute homicides. But many outraged parents of the victims complained that for years no one cared about their daughters. One retired policewoman admitted bitterly to the local paper that many cops saw the women as "disposable."

"Who gives a crap about them?" she asked.

The callousness of men who murder prostituted women never ceases to startle even seasoned cops like Las Vegas's Gil Shannon. He has a collection of crime scene photos he often shows to young girls in custody, to hotel security staff at training sessions, and to politicians, in the hope that he can shock them into facing the reality of domestic sex trafficking. One photo depicts a petite sixteen-year-old on the floor of a hotel room, her hair askew; the bruise marks on her neck indicate she was strangled. Her killer turned out to be the son of a police chief from California brought to justice because he foolishly used his credit card to book the room.

Another disturbing photo shows a young woman with burn marks all over her head. Her john had taken her out to the desert, became frustrated when he could not get an erection, and booted her out of the car. When she refused to return his money, the enraged client ran her over with his car. The girl was pinned under the automobile, and the burn marks came from the heat of the muffler pressed against her face as she died.

In summer 2008, Las Vegas police found the mutilated body of a seventeen-year-old girl in a shallow grave in the desert, stuffed into a hockey bag. Her tattoos had been cut off and her teeth broken in an ultimately futile attempt to prevent identification. Nichole Yegge, a runaway suffering from bipolar disorder, had met up with a thirty-one-year-old drifter who had been booted out of the army and his twenty-one-year-old girlfriend. Police alleged the couple pimped Nichole out as a prostitute, using the Internet to advertise her services. The couple was charged with first-degree murder and kidnapping.

Across the country, the statistics are frightening. An analysis published in 2004 in the *American Journal of Epidemiology* found that the mortality rate of women in the trade was an astounding two hundred times greater than the population at large.* Given their daily exposure to violence and abuse, it is a wonder more are not killed. Dr. Melissa Farley, a clinical psychologist and one of the most respected researchers on human trafficking, runs the Prostitution Research and Education organization. When she conducted interviews with 130 prostituted women in San Francisco, she found that more than 80 percent had been threatened with a weapon or physically assaulted. More than two-thirds had been raped—indeed, 59 percent had been raped four or more times. Life on the streets for the youngest girls was just as bleak. A survey by the National Runaway Switchboard in Chicago found teen runaways were three times as likely as at-home children to have been robbed, assaulted, or physically abused.

Faced with those odds, death for many can only be a matter of time. By some estimates, life expectancy after becoming involved in prostitution can be as little as seven years. Even if they survive the threats from their pimps, clients, or strangers on the street, women in "the life" face a slow demise through drugs or sexually transmitted diseases. A study of prostituted women in the Twin Cities found that 46 percent of them had attempted suicide.

Maria was not alone in her thoughts of ending her life.

■ ■ ■

DAN GARRABRANT tries to remind every young girl he meets who is trapped in prostitution about the dangers. Not that many of them listen. They're young and distrustful of outsiders, and, like most teens, they think they are immortal.

Perhaps the Hispanic girl he found sulking in the Atlantic City youth shelter reminded Garrabrant a little of Maria. At sixteen Rebecca was just a year younger than Maria had been when she first

---

* The study looked at close to two thousand prostitutes in Colorado Springs over thirty years. Twenty percent of the women who died were victims of homicides. The homicide rate for prostitutes was 204 per 100,000 compared to 4 per 100,000 for female liquor store employees and 29 per 100,000 for male taxi drivers. (See the "Fact Sheet" published by University of Rhode Island's Donna Hughes at http:www.uri.edu/artsci/wms/hughes/pubtrfrep.htm.)

crossed paths with the FBI agent. Hardened by three years on the track, Rebecca shared Maria's toughness and brazen confidence in her ability to survive the swamps of the street.

When the local police picked her up, they notified Garrabrant as they did every time they took a minor into custody. She was, Garrabrant recalls, "talkative, funny as hell, a practical joker with a bubbly personality." But even less cooperative than Maria. "She was aware of the game and the dangers of the street, but she felt she had no other place to go," he says.

She told him that, like most girls he had interviewed, a trigger event had pushed her into the streets—she was raped by a relative when she was twelve.

As he got up to leave, Garrabrant turned to the teenager to plead with her one last time. "Do me a favor, just give me some time. Give me forty-eight hours to try to figure something out," he said. He knew he had little chance of finding her a safe place to stay. There was Rachel Lloyd's GEMS shelter in New York, but it was almost always full. Sometimes the best Garrabrant could do was to come back in a couple of days with a warm cup of coffee and the names and phone numbers of some shelters.

"Don't run away because bad stuff is going to happen to you," he begged Rebecca. "I've seen cases where I meet a nice person like you and the next thing I know I'm getting a call that you're dead."

It was the same warning that he had given countless numbers of girls before. He gave Rebecca his card, but in his gut he felt there was little chance she would heed his words. "She wasn't ready to make the break," he says.

When Garrabrant returned the next day, Rebecca was gone. At first he feared she had fled, but later he found out the shelter had tracked down her family and put the teenager on a bus. Except that "family" meant a mom addicted to crack. Within days, she had run away again.

Seventeen days after Garrabrant had pleaded with Rebecca for more time, the police found her body in an industrial area outside Baltimore. Murdered by an unknown assailant. Stabbed to death.

Rebecca had kept Garrabrant's card; the local police found it in one of the pockets on the dead girl's body and notified the FBI agent. "I was very upset," he admits, choking up in an uncharacteristic display of emotion. "We missed this one. This was someone we let down. And that sucks."

. . .

GARRABRANT TOOK his victories where he could find them. The fall of 2006 had been clouded by several murders, but he took solace in the fact that Knowledge's empire had been brought down. The underage girls Knowledge had exploited were no longer a part of his stable. Joanie, the fourteen-year-old, was in a shelter on the West Coast. Sandy was back in Las Vegas. Maria was still in the sex trade, but at least she was safe from the two pimps who she was convinced at one point had tried to kill her.

Then, in early 2007, Maria and Garrabrant got some welcome news. On March 27, Judge Freda Wolfson handed down the sentences in the case. Tracy was sentenced to eight years in prison, and there would be no leniency: in the federal system, there was no parole. Wolfson was much harsher on Knowledge. She sent the "Pimp of the Year" away for twenty-three years behind bars.

Matthew Thompkins would be near sixty years old before he would ever cruise along the Strip in Las Vegas or strut down the Boardwalk of Atlantic City again.

· 11 ·

"Judge People by Courage"

STEPHEN "PEEBO" Buggs did not flaunt his money in Atlantic City and Las Vegas the way Knowledge had. But the Dallas pimp turned out to be the more daring high-stakes gambler; he decided not to plea bargain but to take his chances with a judge and jury.

By the spring of 2007, just as Knowledge was being sentenced in New Jersey, Buggs was set to stand trial in Dallas for trafficking and assaulting Felicia. Because of the usual court delays, it had taken almost eighteen months since his arrest for the case to wind its way through the system. After firing his first lawyer, Buggs ran out of money to pay for a new one. That earned him the right to court-appointed counsel, and in Texas, the state frequently calls upon outside private defense attorneys to take on such cases. It was a big break for Buggs because rather than an overburdened public defender he got T. Price Stone, a smart and talented criminal lawyer with more than thirty years' experience.

Stone didn't much like his client when he first met him in the jail cell. "He was a very arrogant, know-it-all type of person, not any fun to deal with," he says. "He was a hustler."

But this wasn't a popularity contest. It was a criminal trial. Buggs told his lawyer he was sure he could beat the rap, and his confidence was not entirely misplaced. After all, this was not an FBI investigation, as Knowledge had faced. There were no wiretaps or surveillance records, no financial statements or business papers. Although Byron Fassett and his team had gathered some impressive physical evidence to support Felicia's story, it was largely Buggs's word against hers—and she was a runaway, a drugged-out teen with a criminal record.

The stakes were huge for the principal protagonists. Buggs faced spending much of the rest of his life behind bars if he lost. For Felicia, it was her best chance to reclaim her life. But the trial also had a wider significance because it laid bare two starkly different visions of the girls forced into prostitution: blame them, or blame the pimps and the society that had disowned them. By the time the proceedings were over, it was not just Buggs who stood accused. The trial also exposed flaws in the police department and the juvenile justice system as well as the public's own prejudices toward the children themselves.

■ ■ ■

TIM GALLAGHER knew these cases could be difficult to win. A tall Texan with a patrician bearing, Gallagher was one of the first prosecutors Fassett had approached back in the mid-1990s when he began to go after pimps. A decade later, Gallagher was assistant district attorney, and his office had gained an impressive amount of experience in these types of trials. "When you decide to prosecute a child prostitution case, you make a conscious decision that you're not going to take the easy road," Gallagher says.

When he first sat down to talk to his future chief witness, Gallagher was struck by how young and vulnerable Felicia looked. "She was still a child," he says. But a terrified one, frightened of having to confront her pimp in court.

"I don't want to see him," Felicia told Gallagher.

Gallagher was used to that terror. "What they fear the most when they're on that witness stand is looking at the person who has profited from them, beaten them, and sexually exploited them," he says. Gallagher patiently won her confidence, assuring her he would always be there in the court to protect her. "Once she realized that we were going to do what we said we were going to do, then she trusted us."

Felicia also felt tremendous guilt and shame in revealing the deepest, darkest moments of her sexual history to a courtroom filled with strangers. But Gallagher stressed that she was a child who had never been given a chance to say yes or no. When the jurors learned that, he assured Felicia, they would see her as a victim, just like he did. It would not turn out that simply.

Defense lawyer Stone saw Felicia in a dramatically different light. The fact that she was a minor didn't hold much weight for him. "The government portrays them as poor little waifs," he says. "They're all saints from their point of view. But frequently they are not. Many of them are hustlers also. My guy was terrible, but they are not far behind."

That appraisal was reinforced once Stone learned the full details of Felicia's background through pretrial disclosure and his own inquiries. "She was a con, frankly, like Mr. Buggs," he says. "Lying, cheating— you name it, she had done it. She had been in all kinds of trouble. This was a bad news girl."

Stone knew the best defense was a good offense and to win he was going to have to go after the teenage girl's character. "She is going to be the critical witness. If you can show that she is an inherently lying type person, we had a chance," Stone says. "If she comes across as truthful, there is a problem."

■ ■ ■

PROSECUTOR GALLAGHER, along with police officers Byron Fassett and Cathy De La Paz, spent months with Felicia preparing the case. They went over every detail of her story, every event she remembered, every encounter with Buggs and his fellow pimps. "I thought I knew everything personal there was to know about this girl, like she was my daughter," says Fassett.

Then, with just a few weeks to go before the trial, there was a startling revelation. Felicia had already told the police that Buggs had beaten her with a sword, and the photographs of her bruises backed up her story. But she had not yet disclosed to the police one particularly gruesome part of the assault because her shame still ran deep: the fact that he had raped her with the weapon. It was Peebo's live-in girlfriend, Cheryl, now ready to testify against her former pimp and partner, who first revealed that horrific detail during her own pretrial preparation. At one point she was discussing the beating with the swords with De La Paz when she offhandedly remarked, "And that's when he stuck it up in her."

De La Paz tried to make sure the shock didn't register in her eyes. She did not want Cheryl to know this was the first time the cops had heard of this, so that Cheryl's account of the incident would come out unfiltered and uncontaminated. After Cheryl finished her description, De La Paz and Byron Fassett rushed over to see Felicia, who was still being held in the juvenile detention center for violating her probation. Again, they did not want to prejudice any testimony by showing their hand, so they began obliquely, explaining that they had been talking to Cheryl. "I found out something that you didn't tell me," De La Paz said softly. And both cops waited.

Felicia started crying and spilled out the full details of what Buggs had done to her with the sword that night. "'I had a horribly sickening feeling in my stomach," says Fassett. "It obviously had such a traumatic impact on her that she suppressed it." The incident showed him how patient police had to be with victims of commercial sexual exploitation. Here was a girl who had been in the safety of police custody for months, not frightened and alone on the streets, and still she had been reluctant to fully reveal what her pimp had done.

In the days leading up to the trial, Felicia was about to turn sixteen. De La Paz went out to buy a cake and walked with it into the room where Felicia was meeting with police and prosecutors. Felicia was stunned. De La Paz lit the candles and told the girl to close her eyes and make a wish. She did that and then just stood there with her eyes closed.

"Well, blow out the candles," the detective prodded gently as they all waited.

"I can't," Felicia said. "My eyes are closed; I can't see them."

It dawned on the cops—who thought they had seen it all—that Felicia had never had a birthday party before and simply did not know what to do.

"No one ever got me a cake before," the teenager explained. She started crying, but this time they were tears of joy.

Sixteen birthdays and not a single celebration. Finally, Felicia had found people who cared for her. During the investigation, De La Paz had made repeated attempts to try to reach Felicia's mother. At one point, a Spanish-speaking officer even got the woman on the phone to explain how they were trying to help her daughter. She hung up.

Now Felicia had a family of police officers from the Dallas High Risk Victims and Trafficking unit in her corner. They took up her cause with the judge even before the trial started. As the jurors were being selected, Felicia was brought to a courthouse conference room to be ready the moment the trial began. Fassett and De La Paz were appalled at what they saw. Felicia wore a white jumpsuit with the words DALLAS COUNTY JUVENILE CORRECTIONS emblazoned on the back. Worse, she was shackled in handcuffs with chains around her ankles.

"She was the victim here, and she was made out to look like a criminal," says Fassett. "How was that going to look in the eyes of the jury?"

It was a sign of the contempt with which the justice system treated prostituted children that these arrangements did not seem to bother anyone else. Rules were rules. Once again the cops had to raise hell to get the rules to work for a prostituted child, not against her. They insisted the restraints come off. The court authorities refused, suggesting a compromise that would have Felicia walk in with leg irons before the jurors were seated so they wouldn't see them. The cops stood their ground. The court then offered to remove the leg chains but keep the handcuffs on her wrists. No way, insisted Fassett. He knew that all the defense lawyer would have to do with Felicia on the stand was hand her a document to read, and as she held out her shackled wrists the jurors would be reminded she was a "criminal." Instead Fassett offered to have an officer from his unit be in court eight hours a day to watch over her. The judge relented, and Felicia was free of chains.

That still left the prison uniform. De La Paz rushed out and bought Felicia some black pants from Wal-Mart and from home retrieved one of her daughter's white shirts and a pair of shoes. The girl was now as ready as she could be.

• • •

ON TUESDAY, May 8, Stephen Buggs walked into the courtroom on the sixth floor of the Dallas County District courthouse wearing a dark suit, a light shirt, and a simple patterned tie. No prison outfit for him.

He looked more like a businessman than a pimp. Then again, maybe in his eyes there was not much difference between the two. No matter how much he seethed inside about Felicia turning on him, he appeared calm and confident, a done-wrong man determined to put things right. Byron Fassett and Cathy De La Paz, on the other hand, were nervous. They feared that it would be Felicia and not just her former pimp who would be on trial over the next few days.

The trial would be brief but intense, with nine witnesses testifying over just four days. Judge Rick Magnis opened the proceedings with the standard question. "How does your client plead?"

"Not guilty," defense lawyer T. Price Stone said firmly.

Right from the start, Felicia's truthfulness became the central issue. The first witness was Detective Angela Lundy, the Carrollton police officer who had questioned her soon after her escape from Buggs. Prosecutor Tim Gallagher needed her testimony to accomplish one thing—namely, to introduce the jurors to the extent of the savagery Felicia had endured. After he entered into evidence fourteen photographs the detective had taken of the girl that January morning, Lundy matter-of-factly described each one—the bleeding in the left eye, the bruising and scraping on the left thigh, the burn marks on the chest.

For Stone, his cross-examination of Lundy was an excellent chance to launch his first attack on Felicia's credibility. The defense attorney got the police officer to acknowledge she had videotaped the interview with Felicia. It was an early triumph that led to the judge ordering Gallagher to enter the tape into evidence. Through pretrial disclosure, Stone knew that when she first spoke to the Carrollton police after her beating, Felicia had denied being forced to sell her body. Felicia did not fully disclose her story until several weeks later, when she opened up to the Dallas High Risk Victims cops. If the jurors could be shown that the chief witness against Buggs had lied once, maybe they would believe she was lying again.

"Would it be correct you asked her about various things she might have done while she was in this runaway status?" Stone asked.

"Yes, sir," the Carrollton detective replied, telling the court she explicitly asked Felicia if she "had prostituted herself."

Stone pounced on that opening. "Her response, if I am not wrong: no, she had not done that?"

"That's correct, she said no," Lundy confirmed.

"She said no, [she] had not prostituted herself," Stone repeated triumphantly.

That was all Stephen Buggs's lawyer needed. He let the officer off the stand, and the court was adjourned for the day. It had not gone well for the prosecution. Gallagher had succeeded in laying out the brutality of the attack, but the defense had already undermined the victim's trustworthiness. The next morning, it was De La Paz's turn to be grilled. At this stage, her testimony would be sub rosa—without the jury—as the lawyers sparred over the admissibility of evidence seized at Buggs's home. It was Felicia's allegations to the police that had sparked the raid. If the girl could be shown to be a dubious witness, the search warrant and evidence gathered as a result of her disclosures could be thrown out—along with much of the case.

"Did you find her to be a truth-telling or truthful person?" he asked.

"There was nothing for me to check about her background that would tell me that," De La Paz replied, skillfully deflecting the question by noting that the background check did reveal Felicia's history as a runaway and "a victim of sexual assault."

Stone asked if she had questioned the girl about her frequent run-ins with the law, including burglary.

"I talked to her about her victimization, which is why I was there," De La Paz shot back.

Now the judge, in an unusual move, stepped in. "Were you aware she made inconsistent statements?" he asked the detective.

"I'm aware of the interview with the Carrollton officer," De La Paz answered cautiously.

"You had some reason to think that she's not a completely truthful person?" Judge Magnis came back at her.

"No, not at all," she replied firmly. "I didn't think that at all."

"You were aware she told one story and then told a different story," the judge kept pushing.

"I deal with these victims often," De La Paz explained. "I find that very common with victims of prostitution, and I don't feel that is cause to believe that they're liars."

"You believe that's an honesty issue?" the judge persisted.

"Very often, children don't want to tell on their parents or authority figures, people that have done things to them, out of fear, loyalty," De La Paz said, hoping to get the court to grasp how a pimp could dominate a girl. "You often see that."

"You're going beyond the scope," the judge said, cutting her off and returning to his only concern. "You were aware she had said one thing and changed her story?"

"I was aware she told me *more* than she told the Carrollton officer," the Dallas detective answered deftly.

It was a dialogue of the deaf. The judge, no doubt like the public at large, saw a runaway who lied to police while De La Paz was speaking to the shame and fear of an abused girl.

Gallagher tried to rescue his star police witness by assuring the judge the tape of Felicia's interview at the Carrollton police station would be entered into evidence. "The witness in the video was consistent about the beating and the aggravated kidnapping. She never denied that," he said. "The only thing she denied was the prostitution."

But the judge retorted that defense lawyer Stone "was asking if there was any reason to believe she was not a truth-teller. I think it's fair that this be brought out."

Whatever his doubts about Felicia, Judge Magnis apparently felt the police had not been out of line in at least investigating her allegations. In the end, he ruled that the search warrant and evidence seized were valid. It was a crucial victory for the prosecution but one that came at a high cost—the sustained attacks on Felicia's character. And it would only get worse.

■ ■ ■

PROSECUTOR TIM Gallagher's next witness was Sam Quattrochi, the superintendent of the Letot Center, the primary care facility in Dallas for runaways and exploited children. The Letot staff worked closely with Byron Fassett and his team. As he was battling to set up his High Risk Victims unit, Fassett's frequent visits to Letot and long talks with Quattrochi had helped him gain an understanding of child prostitution. Now Gallagher hoped he could do the same for the judge and the jurors.

Quattrochi's credentials were impressive. A certified probation officer with a bachelor's degree in psychology and a master's diploma in social work, he had been running the center for twenty years. He estimated he personally had helped hundreds of girls as a counselor, while his staff had helped thousands. But, he explained to the court, these girls were extremely reluctant to cooperate with police or pretty much anyone else.

"Typically as a result of their own family experience, they're extraordinarily distrustful of adults in general," Quattrochi said. "There's a great deal of fear about consequences should they provide information about criminal activity and associates. Fear of their life, basically."

"Pimps condition them to look at themselves as criminals, isn't that right?" the prosecutor asked.

"Yeah," Quattrochi agreed. "That's to put the fear of God into them. Fear of their own arrest, conviction, incarceration. The pimps are highly skilled at manipulating these victims."

"How do the pimps control the girls?" Gallagher prodded.

"They make sure that they secure a targeted girl that's really wounded," Quattrochi explained, pointing out that 80 percent of the prostituted teens he saw were runaways. "They're going to target a kid that doesn't usually have any kind of support system."

The Letot director gave specific details about Felicia's fragile physical and mental health. He told the court his center had handled her no fewer than three times as a runaway, with one stay lasting twenty-six days. She had been diagnosed with bipolar and attention deficit and hyperactivity disorders and had been treated surgically for an overactive thyroid, all within the preceding ten months.

"This girl is a poster girl for prostitution," he concluded. "She has all the characteristics of a child that is going to be a target for pimps. She's an ideal victim."

Quattrochi had given the court a nuanced and insightful picture of Felicia and her life. Stone had to try to undo the damage.

"Would it be fair to say that girls that are involved in this are not real good truth-tellers?" the defense lawyer began, pursuing his now standard line of attack.

"They're not very good truth-tellers initially, when they're scared," Quattrochi answered. "When we gain trust with them we find them to be highly reliable sources of information."

Stone tried another tack. He seemed genuinely surprised that girls like Felicia would readily admit to taking drugs and suffering sexual abuse but still balk at talking about working the streets for sex. "What would be the reason?" he asked.

It was a mistake. Lawyers, like much of the general public, might well assume that drugs and sexual abuse are worse than prostitution, but that's not the way the girls who are living it feel. Quattrochi seized on the lawyer's misstep and ran with it. "My experience is that the most shameful thing for these children to admit is prostitution," he explained. "It is an extraordinarily degrading thing, and they have a problem admitting that."

The defense lawyer should have cut his losses there, but he persisted. "They would be truthful about felonies, drug abuse, sex abuse, but they're going to clam up and they're not going to tell us about prostitution?" he asked with apparent skepticism.

"One of the big reasons is that they're afraid of the consequences that the pimp is going to dish out," Quattrochi replied. "Usually they're in fear of their own life."

"Some of them just lie, don't they?"

"Yeah, we encounter dishonesty," Quattrochi agreed but then pointed out that it was not a simple black-and-white issue. "Every lie has a purpose. So we're always trying to investigate what's the purpose of the lie. Typically, when we're talking prostitution, the purpose is self-protection and fear."

It was powerful testimony, and, more important, it was instructive. Gallagher hoped to build on that momentum when Detective De La Paz returned to the stand, this time with the jury present. To illustrate the fear and abuse Buggs used to dominate Felicia, the prosecutor presented two dozen photographs De La Paz had taken at the crime scene. De La Paz slowly described the pistol she found in Buggs's home, along with the three bullets next to it, the electrical cord used to tie Felicia up, and the sword with the broken handle.

Stone could not contest the photographic evidence. So he zeroed in on two clashing views of prostituted teens—criminals or victims. He asked De La Paz if she had ever told Felicia "that prostituting is a misdemeanor offense?"

"Well, not if you are compelled to prostitute," De La Paz replied. "If you are compelled to prostitute through force or any means, then I don't believe you are guilty of the misdemeanor."

"Would I be correct in saying that prostitution is a county-level misdemeanor offense?" Stone pushed, sticking to a strictly legal interpretation.

"Prostitution is an offense, yes," the detective answered, trying to keep the impatience out of her voice. "Again, I don't believe that the victim is guilty of the offense if they're compelled to prostitute. OK?"

"OK," Stone conceded.

The second day of the trial had allowed the prosecution to score some points by presenting a less stereotyped version of what the prostitution racket was all about. But as she left the stand, De La Paz was not sure the message was getting through. "I did not get a good feeling from the judge or the jury," she says.

The big test would come the next day, with the testimony from the two women who could speak directly to what had happened inside Buggs's home: Cheryl, his girlfriend and partner in the pimping business, and Felicia herself.

■ ■ ■

THE NEXT morning, all eyes turned to Felicia as she slowly made her way to the stand. She wore the white top and black slacks supplied by

De La Paz, and if she seemed a bit lethargic it was because she was a walking pharmacy: on Seroquel, a mood-stabilizing medication to treat bipolar disorder; Deprico, an antidepressant with a strong sedative action; Risperal, an antipsychotic for schizophrenia; and Prozac. It was a wonder the girl could talk, let alone testify about what she had been through.

She fidgeted nervously in front of the microphone. "You can sit back a little bit," Judge Magnis said to comfort her.

Once Felicia settled in, Gallagher proceeded to take Felicia through her early childhood, from the death of her father when she was three, her trip with her stepfather to the United States from Mexico when she was seven so they could join her mother, who was already working in Dallas, growing up as one of nine children, and dropping out of school by the ninth grade.

"When you were seven years old until you were eleven, did something happen between you and your stepdad?" Gallagher asked delicately.

"He molested me," the girl replied.

"Did you report that?"

"Yes."

"What happened?"

"He went to jail."

"Eventually he got out of jail, is that right?"

"Yes."

"Did he come back to your mom's house for a while?"

"Yes."

"When that happened, what did you do?"

"I ran away."

"And you've run away a bunch of times since then, haven't you?"

"Yes."

"Probably ten or twelve times?"

"Yes."

It took just sixty-four words and a couple of minutes to run through seven years of hell in a girl's life. Felicia, so inured to her own suffering and pumped up with drugs, told her story as blandly as if she were speaking of a trip to the store.

Next Gallagher had Felicia explain the fallout from her juvenile conviction for burglarizing a school with two boys. She explained that it meant that every time she ran away from her abusive home life, she would be in violation of her probation conditions. That was why she was afraid to return home after she had met Stephen Buggs, she told the jurors.

"What were you afraid would happen to you if you got arrested for [being a] runaway again?" Gallagher asked.

"That I would get locked up," Felicia said, which was precisely what had happened.

Gallagher wrapped up his portrait of Felicia by leading her through a description of the health problems that were finally diagnosed in detention and the long list of drugs she was taking. He ended with a query about her mental state. "You've had some problems in the past about hearing voices, is that right?"

"Yes," Felicia answered matter-of-factly, explaining that the "whispering" voices had stopped when she began taking her medication.

Having laid the groundwork for Felicia's vulnerability, Gallagher then moved on to the guts of his case—her recruitment by Buggs for prostitution and her kidnapping and assault. Felicia took the jurors back to the Greyhound bus terminal where she was hanging out with another fourteen-year-old runaway because it was "open twenty-four hours and we could stay there." She explained how they were approached by a man offering them a place to sleep, how she drove off with Buggs and eventually crashed at his home for a few days until he found her a job.

"What kind of work did he get you to do?" asked the prosecutor.

"In this strip club and prostitution."

"And did you make money when you were there?"

"Yes."

"And what did you do with the money?"

"I gave it to Peebo."

"And then where did you go after that?"

"I prostituted."

Her tale of despair was remarkable for its brevity and lack of emotion. In a few days, a fourteen-year-old had gone from runaway to strip-club dancer to prostitute.

Felicia described her task at various "escort services," where her job, she said bluntly, was "to get guys and have sex with them for money."

"Did Peebo put you on the street at some point?" the prosecutor continued.

"Yes," Felicia answered in her detached tone. "I was supposed to walk and try to find guys and have sex with them." She spelled out how Buggs arranged for her to bring her clients to a "special room" in a small apartment in East Dallas. The pimp conveniently provided the condoms.

"And once you had sex with the guy, what did you do with the money?"

"Gave it to Peebo," she repeated.

"So as far as you know, the only way that Stephen Buggs made money was by prostitution or girls dancing in strip clubs?"

"We object!" defense lawyer Stone burst in. "Calls for speculation on the part of this witness."

But the judge apparently felt the fourteen-year-old had seen enough action on the street to do more than speculate. "She can answer," he decided. "It's overruled."

"Yes," Felicia said with no hesitation.

Gallagher had gotten what he needed from the teenager to support two of the charges against Buggs—compelling prostitution and trafficking. Now he needed to sustain the accusation of aggravated kidnapping. He began by having Felicia run through the explosions of random violence she witnessed: Buggs hitting another of his women in the face with a shovel, throwing a chair at his girlfriend Cheryl, firing a gun in anger.

Then Gallagher took Felicia through her account of her own brutal beating and torture the night Buggs flew into a rage after he caught her talking to another pimp. "He started hitting me, punching me, and kicking me," the girl told the hushed courtroom.

"Did you try to run out of the living room?"

"No. I was just scared," Felicia said. In a monotone, she told of the Buddha statue Buggs threw at her, the two beer bottles he smashed over her head, and the gun he pointed at her head as he threatened to kill her. And of how he made her strip off her clothes, then grabbed some swords he kept on the wall. "He just started hitting me on my legs and arms and stuff. He made me lie down and then he grabbed a cigarette and he burned me."

"And at some point did anything happen with the cover of the sword?" Gallagher asked, referring to the metal sheath over the blade.

"Yes."

"What did he do?"

"He stuck it up me."

"Did he put it in your vagina?"

"Yes."

"And did he stick it all the way up inside you?"

"Yes."

"How many times did that happen?"

"I don't remember."

"Did it hurt really bad?"

"Yes."

"At some point, were you afraid you were going to die?"

"Yes."

No tears. No emotion. Just a dry recital of pain by a girl who had become all too accustomed to abuse. Felicia went on to recount how she was bound and hog-tied, stuffed in the closet, and forced to urinate as she lay on the bathroom floor. "Do you see in the courtroom today the person who caused you to be in that closet tied up, the person who hit you with the sword?" asked Gallagher.

"Yes," Felicia said firmly.

"Where is he sitting?"

"Right there," said the teenager, pointing at her former pimp. Buggs glared back, squirming noticeably.

To end his direct examination, Gallagher delicately tried to undercut the counterattack that he knew would come from Stone by having the girl directly address her lie about being involved in prostitution. He took her back to her first meeting with the Carrollton police officer who had asked if she had ever turned any tricks.

"You told her no, right?"

"Yes."

"Essentially, you lied to her."

"Yes."

"Why did you lie?"

"Because I was embarrassed." Buggs had also given her explicit orders not to say anything about him, she added.

Gallagher then asked why Felicia had failed to disclose her past to the various doctors and counselors in the juvenile system who subsequently treated her. "Have you at times told them that there was no sex and no prostitution?"

"I don't remember."

"Is that something that you are proud of?"

"No."

"Does it make you feel—what?"

"Embarrassed," said Felicia.

With that, the district attorney was done. It was not a high point to end on, but it typified Felicia's long day on the stand, with uncomfortably frank but disconcertingly low-key responses. Byron Fassett and Cathy De La Paz had been concerned all along about what jurors expected a child victim to look and act like. "People wanted to look for the fourteen-year-old middle-class girl with blond hair and blue eyes who would be emotionally distraught on the stand and completely devastated," Fassett says.

"Instead, she was very stoic up there," adds De La Paz. "What jurors didn't understand is that if you have been crying since childhood, you can only cry so much."

How much worse would things get that day, they both wondered. What damage would Buggs's lawyer try to do?

∎ ∎ ∎

IT WAS 12:40 in the afternoon. Felicia had been on the stand for almost four hours, and now she had to face her pimp's defense attorney. T. Price Stone knew this was his last chance. In many ways his only chance. He had spent most of the trial trying to turn the tables and put Felicia on trial instead of his client. Now he had to take her on face-to-face.

He walked up to the witness stand and quietly asked about her life at school, no doubt to put her at ease. But he quickly moved into the more sordid details of her past. He began by trying to minimize her stepfather's sexual assault. "You talked to the police and what-have-you, and he was arrested?" the lawyer said.

"Yes," Felicia confirmed.

"Those cases were eventually resolved, is that right? A Class C misdemeanor," Stone said, implying the weak sentence perhaps reflected a weak accusation.

Gallagher leaped to his feet. "Objection!" he cried. "He's trying to attack her credibility. She had no control over the disposition of the offenses. It's nothing to do with her." The judge agreed.

Stone moved on to ask her about other "family problems," her testy relationship with her mother and her constant running away from home. He queried her about her frequent use of false IDs and her abuse of drugs and alcohol. Then came his central attack, namely, her erratic confessions of her prostitution history. To underscore his argument, he entered the videotape of Felicia's statement to the Carrollton police officer as defense Exhibit 1. "At some point, [she] asked you very specifically about any kind of prostituting you'd been doing," Stone said. "You told her there had not been any prostitution?"

"Yes."

Then why, Stone wanted to know, did Felicia tell Cathy De La Paz something different? "You gave a written statement saying that you had in fact prostituted yourself—would it be fair—five or six times?"

"Yes. No, I don't, I don't know," Felicia hesitated. "Just sometimes."

If he was going to get his client acquitted, Stone would have to paint Felicia as a compliant if not a consensual player in the prostitution business. He zeroed in effectively on the biggest public misconception about children caught up in the sex trade—that they do it by "choice." He focused on Felicia's confinement in Bugg's home.

"Were you in any way restricted to that house? Could you go out the front door and do what you wanted to do?" Stone asked, voicing a question that might well occur to anyone who did not fully understand the emotional and psychological grip a pimp could wield over a child.

"No," replied Felicia.

"You couldn't?" Stone continued, with feigned surprise. "You couldn't leave the house?"

Felicia shook her head. "What prevented you from leaving the house?" Stone prodded.

"I don't know," said the girl. "They just—him, I guess. Just couldn't walk out and say 'Bye, I'm leaving.' I don't know. Just scared."

"But you certainly had walked out of various other places and said 'Good-bye, I'm leaving,' hadn't you?" Buggs's lawyer asked.

"Yes," Felicia agreed, but then added, "Since he hit me, I was kind of scared."

A few minutes later, Stone returned to the same line of attack. This time Felicia cracked. "You can leave, is that correct?" he asked.

"Yes, I guess, yes."

"You could open the front door—"

"Well, I don't know," Felicia hesitated. "If he would have let me."

"Did he stay awake twenty-four hours a day, seven days a week?" Stone pushed.

"No, he wasn't always there," the girl conceded.

"I mean it was your choice to go out the front door and go back with your mother, would that be fair?" Stone asked.

"Yes."

"In fact, finally that's what you did, isn't it true?"

"When I had the first chance, yes, I left," Felicia said.

Finally Stone went on to grill Felicia about her allegations of the assault, a harder story to discredit because of the photographs. "Do you know how long you were in this closet?" Stone began.

"No."

"One day, two days, three days? You've said various times," Stone pushed. "Would it be fair to say you don't really know?"

"I don't—I don't remember."

Stone asked about the beer bottles that had been smashed on her head. "Did they cut you? Did you bleed?"

"I don't remember," Felicia repeated. "But I know my head hurt."

"Your head hurt. Did it bleed any? Do you remember having a bunch of blood around?" Stone asked.

"No, it wasn't much blood. I can't see my head. I don't know," said the confused girl. "I was tied up. I don't remember."

It was the best Stone could do. He told the judge he was done.

Gallagher was eager to get his exhausted witness off the stand. "Your Honor, we have no questions for this witness," he said. "May she be excused?"

It was just after 2:00 P.M. Felicia's ordeal on the stand had lasted six hours. Detective Cathy De La Paz had been watching the jurors, and she was worried. Several of them had not paid much attention to the girl, instead looking around distractedly during her testimony. "There was just not that level of respect," De La Paz says. "And I thought, *This is not good.*"

■ ■ ■

AFTER JUST a ten-minute recess, the trial resumed with the testimony of the only other witness to Felicia's beating—Cheryl, Buggs's "bottom girl" who helped him run his pimping operation. The twenty-six-year-old had been with Buggs since she was twenty-one, stripping at a club while also prostituting for him.

"This is hard for you, isn't it?" Gallagher asked about her decision to testify against her former boss and partner.

"Yes, it is," Cheryl replied.

"You've had feelings for Mr. Buggs for some time, is that right?" the prosecutor asked.

"Yes, I do," Cheryl replied. "Yes, I have."

Gallagher explained to jurors that Cheryl was charged as a codefendant with aggravated kidnapping, compelling prostitution, and human trafficking and got her to confirm that he had not promised her any "specific sentence for your cooperation."* Gallagher had to clear that out of the way because as Buggs's accomplice, Cheryl was the one person who could verify Felicia's story of the beating and torture.

She spared no detail as Gallagher led her through what Buggs did that night—the bottles he smashed over Felicia's head, the cigarette burns, the hog-tying with electrical cord, the pistol-whipping, the swords he slapped against her limbs and forced into her private parts. The prosecutor showed her Exhibit 18, the photograph of Felicia's cigarette burns. "Where was she when he did that?" he asked.

"She was laying on the floor," Cheryl said. "She was getting beat up."

"Beat up how bad?"

"Real bad."

Gallagher handed her Exhibit 48, the picture of the sheath for the sword.

"He pushed it up her pussy," came the simple words from the witness stand.

"Deep inside her?"

"He just told her to keep pushing it up her."

Cheryl confirmed that Felicia's ordeal went on for two hours. "I sat there and I watched this happen in the living room."

"Couldn't you jump in and stop him?" Gallagher asked.

"I was afraid he would turn on me next," was the only thing she could say.

She described Felicia's injuries, her eyes swollen shut and the cuts, welts, and burns, and she said that the next morning Buggs asked her to clean the girl up and nurse her back to health.

"Why did he want to do that?" asked the prosecutor.

"To get her back to work."

"You say 'get her back to work.' Does that mean turning tricks as a prostitute, dancing naked in a bar?"

---

* After the trial, Cheryl pleaded guilty to trafficking and received a ten-year probationary sentence in addition to the time she had already served in jail.

"Yeah. Same thing."

Cheryl told the jurors that she didn't want the battered girl to go outside "looking like an elephant woman."

Gallagher asked her why.

"Then someone might have called the police," Cheryl replied. "I feel like it was some big nightmare."

"Big nightmare for who?" Gallagher pushed.

"For all of us."

"Maybe more for Felicia than anybody, huh?" said Gallagher pointedly.

On that caustic note, the court adjourned on the afternoon of May 10.

■ ■ ■

ON FRIDAY morning, the state's final witness was Frank Kenneth Balagot, the forensic biologist who performed the DNA testing on the evidence seized at Buggs's house. He could not have been more definitive. Blood traces on the electrical cord Buggs used to hog-tie the girl "matched the DNA profile" of Felicia, he said.

How unique was the match, Gallagher wanted to know.

One in 1.72 trillion, the expert replied, more than two hundred times the population of the earth. "If you have two hundred earths all lined up together, you don't expect to see one person in all of those two hundred earths with that genetic profile," Balagot said. Suggestive traces of blood on the blade of the sword were not enough to perform tests, he testified, but the DNA he pulled from the bloodstains on the handle and the sheath of the sword also matched Felicia's DNA.

After three days of powerful testimony, Gallagher was confident he had done the best he could. He told the judge the State was ready to rest its case.

Now Stone and his client faced the most difficult decision a defense team has to make in a trial—whether to have the accused take the stand in his or her own defense. For the lawyer and Buggs, both options were fraught with perils. On the one hand, staying silent in the face of such serious allegations could make Buggs look guilty in the eyes of at least some jurors. On the other hand, putting Buggs in the witness stand would expose him to the prosecutor's sharp cross-examination.

Stone cautioned his client against testifying. "He had nothing to gain," the lawyer explains. "He had no good story to tell other than 'I didn't do it.'"

Despite his lawyer's advice, Buggs wanted to get up there. He wanted to be heard, and he had a pimp's overblown sense of his ability to sell his version of events to anyone who would listen. It was a page right out of Pimpin' Ken's book, *Pimpology*. Rule number 43 decrees that one "talk shit and eat spit." Or, as the author puts it, "Those on top have the gift of the gab. They know how to sell it." Defense lawyer Stone learned the hard way that a pimp's ego was a hard thing to ignore.

So, on the fourth day of the trial, Stone stood and announced to the court, "Your honor, at this time it is my understanding that my client does wish to testify."

The judge, taken aback because it was so rare for defendants to take the stand, wanted to give the accused pimp fair warning. "Mr. Buggs, do you understand that you have an absolute right not to testify?"

"Yes."

To be absolutely certain, Judge Magnis pushed again, explaining that if Buggs took the stand, "certain prior convictions and prior acts" could become admissible.

"I'm not worrying about prior," Buggs quipped, with the street-savvy sense of knowing what battles to fight when. "I'm worrying about now."

The judge, apparently still concerned, turned to Buggs's lawyer. "Mr. Stone, have you been over that with him?"

But Buggs interrupted before the lawyer could open his mouth. "He ain't been over nothing with me." It would not be the last time he would slam his own defense counsel.

The heavyset man lumbered to the witness stand and swore the oath. If the defense's tactic was to win over the hearts and minds of the jurors, it got off to a rocky start. An effort to present Buggs as a family man backfired. His brother, he said, was "somewhere in the jailhouse." He told the jurors he had four children by different women but was unsure of their ages. His thought his oldest daughter was twenty-six, while his youngest son "would be probably nine."

Things only got worse when Buggs outlined his lengthy criminal record. "I was really hustling," he admitted. "I had a bunch of cars off and on through my career of breaking the law, selling dope." He recounted a long list of offenses stretching back to 1989, stating that he had served time for everything from assault to drugs. He was not sure he remembered them all but added with pride that "I be making some good money. So everybody wants some of my money."

Stone noted that Buggs had use the word "hustle" many times in his testimony so far. "Does that include hustling prostitutes?" the lawyer asked.

"No prostitutes. The only time prostitutes came around me—this is real—they came around me for drugs. I sold dope," Buggs insisted.

"And then, I'm not an ugly fellow either," he said with a grin, apparently confident he could charm the jurors.

It was not the most sympathetic character portrait, but it was the best Stone was going to get. He moved on to the allegations of compelling prostitution. Buggs insisted his partner Cheryl never prostituted for him. "She sit here and told that lie," he said. "We wasn't no pimp and ho. Me and Cheryl was like husband and wife, slept together every night," he said. And he was a dutiful husband, Buggs told the jurors. If he hung out at her strip club, he said, it was "so she know where I am all the time." If she gave him money from her strip-club act, he explained, "that's what couples do."

As for Felicia, Buggs proclaimed: "She really had me fooled. This cool little old girl really had me feeling sorry for her. She had me thinking she was just this lost little old chick that needed some help."

Felicia claimed she was twenty-three, Buggs said, insisting that he "would never involve myself with a kid, period." Then he admitted, "I kind of like Felicia, you know. I liked my cake and ice cream at the same time."

Felicia exploited him, Buggs claimed, not the other way around. "She was freeloading me," he said. "Felicia ain't never sold her body for me."

Stone knew his client could deny prostituting girls, but it was harder to dismiss the photographic evidence of the beating. He led Buggs slowly to the night in question. "There's a heck of a ruckus, fight, whatever you want to call it," he began, offering a disingenuous description of a savage attack. "What happened?"

"I recall me slapping Felicia on the side of her head," Buggs replied, admitting he had been in a drunken rage. "But just beating on her for two hours, tying her up, throwing her in the closet. I don't know where they get all that from."

"Did you hit her with a bottle?" Stone asked.

"No, if I hit that girl with a Corona bottle, don't you know it would have split her head? If I hit her with my fist, I could probably fracture Felicia's face."

"Did you threaten her with a sword?"

"I don't remember hitting her with the little sword," he said, a careful choice of words, denying the memory, not the act itself.

"Why I got to pull a gun on her?" Buggs went on, trying to deflect the allegation that he had pistol-whipped her. "I could beat her up if I want to. She can't whip me. I didn't have to use no weapon on her."

Next, Stone had to raise the even more damaging testimony that his client had used the sword's casing to sexually assault Felicia. "Did you force her to put that sheath in her vagina or did you put it in there?"

"They put this stuff together," Buggs replied, alleging that Felicia, Cheryl, and the prosecutor were all conspiring against him, that it was all fabricated. "Why didn't they get no DNA off the thing in her vagina? That thing will cut up a girl coochie. That thing will tear you up inside."

It was not the most elegant of defenses, a mix of "I was too drunk to remember" and "I could have pounded the girl without swords or guns." But it was all Buggs had. His testimony was rambling and flamboyant—and he was not above hustling even when on the stand, telling jurors to check out one of his son's rapping CDs. "Y'all might have heard of it. If not, y'all might want to get it." He had bursts of uncontrolled anger, complaining at one point that the trial had been a circus, and he fingered prosecutor Gallagher as the grand manipulator. "Old Picasso over there painted a pretty good picture." When he decried all the "bull crap" from other witnesses, the judge admonished him to "watch the language you use."

But instead Buggs turned his ire on the judge. As his testimony drew to a close, he stopped answering his lawyer's questions and pointed to the judge to complain about his rulings. "Judge been doing us like this the whole time. I know he don't want me to talk."

"Mr. Buggs, Mr. Buggs, Mr. Buggs, please listen to the questions," Stone begged. "Please answer them."

"Everybody works with the state," Buggs said, ignoring his lawyer.

"Mr. Buggs, please—" Stone sputtered, but then he simply gave up. "Your honor, at this time we pass the witness."

As prosecutor Tim Gallagher stood to begin his cross-examination, he knew he could be brief. He figured the pimp had done enough damage to himself. Gallagher introduced letters Buggs had written to Cheryl while she was in jail. "Do you recall writing to her about the night Felicia got beat up and talking to her about 'losing your head'?"

"No, you got to refresh me on that," the defendant said. Gallagher approached the witness stand and showed him the letter. "Now do you recall?" the prosecutor pushed.

"It don't say I done nothing," Buggs insisted after he reviewed his own writing. "I say 'Baby, I was drunk.' I say I *might have* blacked out."

"Did you write to Cheryl about not being able to 'remember no blood when we were into it'?"

"Because there wasn't no blood. I say 'I don't remember no blood,'" Buggs replied. "Me and Felicia had a little old altercation."

It was all over except for the closing arguments.

■ ■ ■

STONE MUST have sensed his client had done little good for his cause by taking the stand. In his summation, therefore, he reverted to the tactic he had used throughout the trial—shifting the focus and the blame onto Felicia.

He played on the errors the authorities had made, asking rhetorically that if Felicia's injuries were so severe, "what hospital did the Carrollton Police Department call and send her to?" He noted that she had admitted burglarizing a school, running away from a juvenile center, forging IDs, using drugs, and being involved in prostitution, though on that last crime he was quick to add, "So she says." By his count, Felicia's prostitution claims were "running fifty-fifty"—she denied she had been forced into prostitution to at least half the people who interviewed her.

Boldly, and much to Buggs's chagrin, Stone basically conceded his client had beaten Felicia but insisted it never rose to the level of kidnapping. "I'm going to submit to you there was assault, absolutely, clearly, no question," he said. "Shouldn't have happened. That's not kidnapping." How, he asked, could Buggs be charged with kidnapping if Felicia was in his GlenCliff house where, for good or bad, she had decided to live? "If that is aggravated kidnapping, Lord knows most of us are probably guilty of it with our kids, maybe sometimes our spouses," he argued.

"Folks, when do you stop being a victim?" he continued. "How many felonies, how many misdemeanors, how many pimps do you have to have before you are no longer a victim? How long do you stay a victim? When do you become part of the situation?"

It was a classic tool in sexual abuse cases: the "she deserved it" defense. Stone was doing his job, defending his client as best as he could, and that meant appealing to the not-so-hidden contempt many people feel for prostitutes as well as their pimps. "Folks, there are no good people in this case, I'll tell you that," he told the jury. "The people in this—Felicia, Cheryl, Peebo—we don't give any good marks to any of them.

"It will take courage, but I'm going to tell you we don't have a kidnapping," he concluded. "That's what y'all are here for is that courage."

If Stone was aiming low, dragging the accuser and the accused through the same muck, then Gallagher would aim high. The prosecutor opted for eloquence over exposition, fire over facts. He wanted to engage the jurors, to make them see it was not just Stephen Buggs on trial but the entire justice system. That it was not just Felicia in the witness stand but the thousands of girls whose plight society had ignored.

"Members of the jury, let's start with courage," Gallagher began, picking up where Stone had left off. "Think about courage from the witness stand. Who exhibited courage when they sat on this stand and told what they told? Did it take more courage for Felicia, a sixteen-year-old teenager, to get up there and talk about what happened to her and what she had been through, or did it take more courage for Mr. Buggs to get up here and do his spiel? If you're going to judge people by courage, then I think Felicia wins that.

"What's the worst thing you can call a teenage girl?" he asked the jury. "You can call her a dope head. You could call her a lot of things, but the worst thing you could call her is a whore. How would you feel if your daughters were called that, or your sisters? So you can imagine how hard it is for a girl to talk about what's happened to her.

"Do I condemn the Carrollton Police Department for not sending Felicia to Parkland [Hospital] to be evaluated?" Gallagher said to counter Stone's inference that her injuries were perhaps not that serious. "Yes, I do. Do I condemn the juvenile jail for not sending her? Yes, I do. But then that gives you some insight on what we have to deal with, the attitude we have to fight not only with the police department, the juvenile justice system, but with jury members as well, to keep people from calling girls like Felicia just another little whore. Because that's not what she is. She's a human being."

It was as powerful a plea as could be made, touching not just at the core of Felicia's case but at the hidden crime of child prostitution. It transformed her from nobody's problem to everybody's problem. But Gallagher still had to convict the man on trial for her abuse, so he got down to the nuts and bolts of the law. He told the jury that, under Texas law, kidnapping did not have to include snatching someone off the streets and holding them for ransom. "Kidnapping occurs when a person is restrained and physical violence or force is issued to effect that restraint," he explained. "She was bound and thrown in a closet. She was beaten to a bloody pulp. So she was kidnapped."

"In our lives we get choices," he continued, returning to his wider theme of responsibility. "We get to choose how we affect each other. Mr. Buggs had those choices when he saw Felicia. He had a runaway, mentally ill child. He could choose to take her to the Salvation Army, to take her to a church. Instead Mr. Buggs chose to take her out and use her for himself. He placed Felicia on her back, turning tricks, making dollar after dollar for himself while he sat on his backside and counted the money."

The prosecutor concluded by subtly shifting the responsibility from Buggs to the jurors. "He controlled her and manipulated her. And she was the perfect victim. Certainly Mr. Buggs thought that no one would believe her. Now who stands for a person like Felicia? What resort does she have? If you and I don't, nobody else will.

"What I am going to ask you to do is do something. Help me stand up for Felicia. Go back there and find Stephen Buggs guilty."

■ ■ ■

IT WAS Friday, 5:30 P.M. The jurors would take the weekend for their deliberations. Would they believe a heavily medicated teenager, a chronic runaway who herself had been on the wrong side of the law more often than not?

Stephen Buggs certainly hoped not. He was shocked that the police had ever bothered to arrest him over his "little cutie-pie," as he called Felicia, and he had never imagined doing serious jail time because of her. Now he was forced to spend yet another weekend behind bars, not knowing if the new week would bring freedom or the start of a much longer sentence. Felicia spent the weekend back at the juvenile center, still serving time for her probation violation.

On Monday morning, the jurors filed back into the courtroom. Case number F06-86343, the *State of Texas v. Stephen Buggs*, was nearing its finale. Buggs glanced nervously at the twelve citizens about to pronounce his fate. The foreman slowly read out the verdict on the first count: "We, the jury, find the defendant guilty of compelling prostitution as charged in the indictment." It was the same verdict for the other two counts—trafficking and aggravated kidnapping.

For the first time in her life, Felicia had won. Stephen Buggs had gambled and lost—big time. The only question now was how much. Under Texas law, the minimum he faced was twenty-five years on each count, to be served concurrently. But the jury could impose a sentence three times that severe.

Buggs's bad day in court was just beginning.

Judge Rick Magnis immediately began the punishment phase of the hearing, starting with "enhancements." The jury was reminded of Buggs's self-confessed criminal history going back sixteen years. But now they got to hear the full details of other crimes.

Before meeting Cheryl, Buggs had been in a nine-year common-law marriage with another woman. She took the stand to describe how he beat her "on a regular basis." That got him some jail time, but it did little good. After she came into some money after a lawsuit, she bought him a Rolex watch for his birthday. "But he said he wanted a brand-new Mercedes," she testified. "He started hitting me while I was driving, and he hit me so many times in the face that I was bleeding. I had to stop the car." Her eight-year-old son was in the backseat begging Buggs to stop. When the three finally returned home, the older man turned on the boy, forcing him to stand outside naked in the backyard and then, in a rage, taking a bite out of the child's cheek. When the boy, now eleven years old, came up to testify, the judge allowed him to leave the witness stand and walk past the jurors to show them he still had the scar of the bite marks on his left cheek years later.

The jurors gaped in horror. They seemed more moved by the boy's brief appearance than by the hours of Felicia's testimony. But as she watched the jurors' reaction, Cathy De La Paz felt it may have done the girl some good. "It gave Felicia credibility, because it gave credibility to the fact that this guy is a monster," she says.

To counter the stories, Buggs had no choice but to take the stand yet again. Bitter now that he knew he was going to prison, his performance had none of the playful humor he had attempted in his first round, just the anger of a deflated hustler. He lashed out at the judge and jurors. "Y'all made a bad verdict, y'all made a very, very, very bad verdict. I never kidnapped no one, restrained no one. I never made nobody prostitute. I never trafficked no one."

"It's your contention that everybody is lying but you, is that right?" prosecutor Gallagher asked him under cross-examination.

"No, I told the truth about everything I've said," Buggs replied.

"I guess one point is that all the people that testified seem to be women and children," Gallagher shot back. "Is that your style? You just intimidate and beat women and children?"

"That ain't my style," the once powerful pimp insisted, now reduced to venting his anger on the stand. "That ain't."

From the back of the courtroom, Byron Fassett could only smile. Pimps rarely testified, and when they did they did not tend to put on such an unabashed spectacle. "I had the time of my life watching him testify," he says. "I would have paid to watch that."

Fassett soon had much more to smile about. It took one hour and four minutes for the jury to return with their decision: seventy-five years for each count of compelling prostitution and trafficking and sixty years for aggravated assault, to be served concurrently.

"The look on Buggs's face was one of the most gratifying things I have ever seen," says Fassett. The pimp was going to spend the rest of his life behind bars because of a girl he had dismissed as "just another little ho."

If Stephen Buggs had ever bothered to pick up Pimpin' Ken's famous guidebook, he should have read it to the end. "The truth is that most people in this game end up in prison, on drugs, or dead," Ken wrote in *Pimpology*.

Buggs already scored two out of three, and he would most certainly be dead before he ever finished his sentence.

■ ■ ■

FELICIA MANAGED to come out of the entire affair with some sense of dignity. "She was so proud of herself," says Stephanie Lovelace, the probation officer who saw Felicia shortly after she testified.

"I told him off," the girl said about her former tormentor. "I looked right at him and I told him. I felt really good."

Ever critical, Byron Fassett gave himself and his team only a "high B plus" for the case. "We could always do a little bit better," the sergeant says. He was being overly harsh. They had taken a particularly nasty pimp off the streets forever. But Fassett had long since stopped being just a police officer. Getting convictions was great, but he cared much more about the fate of girls the High Risk Victims unit was trying to rescue.

Fassett and De La Paz remained deeply troubled by what Felicia had had to suffer on the stand, the withering questions she had endured and the barely contained contempt. "I don't know that we're not revictimizing her," Fassett says.

Moreover, he was convinced the jury had convicted Buggs not out of any deep empathy for Felicia but because they hated him. Was it worth it? Was there another way? Fassett resolved that he would do everything in his power to avoid subjecting another girl to that kind of humiliation.*

He had little doubt it was the pictures of Felicia's bruising, the broken sword they found at the crime scene, and Felicia's DNA on the implements of torture that had helped sway the jury. What made Felicia's case so rare was not the extent of the brutality she suffered but the exceptional evidence that existed to prove that it had happened. So Fassett vowed that his team would prepare a child prostitution case as if it were a murder—assume the victim is dead, that she cannot speak, much less testify, so that the evidence must be found elsewhere. "We have to work these cases like a homicide," he says. "We have to find the evidence to tell her life story for her."

What troubled Fassett even more was that Buggs had very nearly got away with it. It took the intervention of a specialized team of Dallas police officers trained and sensitized to deal with victims of child prostitution to believe Felicia in the first place and spring into action

---

* In part to avoid having to put Felicia through the ordeal of two more trials, the authorities accepted reduced pleas from two of the other minor players in her case. In August 2007, Bobby Hall pleaded guilty to a felony charge of unlawful restraint of a minor and got sentenced to two years of probation. A month later, Demarcus "Marvelous" Jones, who faced two counts of compelling prostitution, accepted the same plea and sentence.

to retrieve the evidence, fighting the courts and the juvenile system almost every step of the way. "In any other city, she would have fallen through the cracks," says De La Paz, and she is right. Felicia would have easily been ignored by an uncaring system. Indeed, her pimp counted on the system to come through for him once again.

"Did he think she would ever tell?" Fassett asks. "No. Did he think anyone would listen to her? No. Did he think anyone would ever pay attention? No. And you know what? He was almost right. He came close, real close.

"My question is, how many other Felicias are out there?"

There had to be a better way to find justice for girls like Felicia and Maria. One crusading judge in Las Vegas, where so many of America's prostituted children started or ended up, thought he might have part of the solution.

PART THREE

"Girls Are Not for Sale"

· 12 ·

Courtroom 18

"HEY, JUDGE, I'm back," the teenager cries out with a familiarity unusual in a court of law. But this is an unusual court. She waves to the man in black robes and then tries, not altogether successfully, to assure him, "And I'm doing better."

Christina wears her long brown hair pulled back in a ponytail. She has a fresh face with high cheekbones and a high-wattage smile that no doubt has served her well on the streets. Just one month shy of her eighteenth birthday, she is still a child in the eyes of the law.

She is also a prostituted youth.

She strides confidently to the defendants' table. "I'm guilty, always," she blurts out with a laugh.

Judge William Voy smiles back. "Christina has lots of issues," he says to the small crowd of officials in the court, "but dishonesty isn't one of them."

The public defender, the prosecutor, the probation officer, and the social worker all nod, for they know Christina all too well. She is what they call a "frequent flyer." This is her third appearance before the judge. But she'll get something here she and other girls caught up in the life of prostitution rarely find anywhere, much less in a court of law—respect.

Welcome to Courtroom 18 in Las Vegas's overcrowded Family and Youth Justice Center.

"These kids don't really belong in the juvenile justice system, but they don't fit anywhere else," Judge Voy explains. "They're victims, and they deserve to be treated as such."

In the eyes of the justice system, and in the eyes of many of the girls themselves, they are not victims. In most cities across America, underage girls being prostituted are either ignored or, worse, crushed by the system. Many who get arrested by police carry fake IDs nobody bothers to check, and they are bailed out as "adults" by their pimps within hours. If they do get identified as minors, almost anywhere else in the country except Las Vegas they are prosecuted as criminals or treated as troublesome repeat offenders.

Not in Vegas. Not anymore.

The atmosphere in Voy's courtroom is deliberately relaxed. Alongside the requisite American flag, there are posters on the wall with mottos that mix dreams with discipline. THERE IS NO END TO THE AMOUNT OF THINGS YOU CAN ACCOMPLISH says one under the image of a whale leaping high out of the water. NO! NO DRUGS! NO EXCUSES! says another. The only nod to courtroom decorum is a handwritten sign with the warning NO GUM CHEWING ALLOWED. The prosecutors and the public defenders have bought into Judge Voy's strategy, and they generally shy away from the usual courtroom confrontations. But that does not make the emotions any less raw or the failures of the justice and social services systems to help these girls any less tragic.

As a child, Christina was bounced from one foster home to another after her mother left her with an older brother one Thanksgiving Day and never returned. By fourteen, she started prostituting and abusing drugs. By seventeen, Christina was on probation after yet another arrest, but she managed to break the ankle bracelet monitoring her movements and fled her latest foster family.

"Texas, Oklahoma, Arkansas, California," she tells the judge, rattling off her recent journeys. "I had fake ID. When I got stopped, they didn't see any warrants out on me."

"How did you travel?" Judge Voy asks. Christina tenses, knowing that he really wants to know how she paid for her trips. For the first time, the teenager's smile disappears. She trembles and begins to sob. "I want to change, Judge. I was prostituting.

"I just hate my life. I was so unhappy. All those strangers, it was just killing me," she says as the words pour out along with the tears. "I could get married and be like everyone else. I know I am so smart."

She explains that, after several weeks on the road, she called a former foster mom who sent her enough money to pay for the bus fare home. Once back in Vegas, Christina turned herself in.

So far Christina has managed to escape the beatings, stabbings, and, all too frequently, the murders the young girls on the streets face. Judge Voy worries her luck may not hold. But he also knows his time to help her is running out. After her birthday, the law will consider her an adult.

"There is no easy solution to all this. We're just trying," he mutters to no one in particular.

"If I can walk the streets fourteen hours a day, I can hold a job, maybe even become a manager," Christina says with a pluckiness few in the court dispute.

"Let's see if we can get you a job," the judge agrees. He asks the court social worker to keep an eye on Christina.

"Oh, don't worry," Christina assures the judge. "She always tracks me down."

Seated in the back of the courtroom, Marisela Quintero grins. The social worker knows Christina has always been a handful in the past, and it won't be any different this time.

The judge tells Christina he will keep her out of jail and extend her probation for another nine months on the condition that she finds a job and gets some counseling. He sets Christina's next appearance in court for June 18—one day after she turns eighteen.

"Sounds good," she says with another laugh.

"I'm glad you're safe," the judge says.

"Me, too," she replies.

Legally about to become an adult woman but still very much a child, Christina waves again to the judge as she exits his court through a rear door that leads to the juvenile detention center where she is being held. By the afternoon, she will be free. Everyone—the judge, the prosecutor, her public defender lawyer—hopes that this time she will make it.

One case down, a dozen more broken lives to try to fix that morning.

...

LIKE MANY good ideas, Judge Voy's special youth prostitution court was not created overnight. It came in crisis and chaos; if any city in the country needed such a court it was Las Vegas, the epicenter of child prostitution in America. The local justice system could have ignored these girls much like most jurisdictions have in the rest of the country. But that didn't happen thanks to an unlikely alliance between Judge Voy and two women on opposite sides of the judicial barricades—a determined public defender and an open-minded prosecutor.

Initially, the two women seemed destined to be on a collision course. Susan Roske heads the Office of the Juvenile Public Defender; Chief Deputy District Attorney Teresa Lowry runs the Juvenile Division's team of prosecutors. Both women took remarkably similar journeys to get to their present positions. Both grew up in Vegas, and both were social workers. Roske handled foster children files, while Lowry focused on child abuse cases. In law school, their paths started to diverge. As a student, Roske began working in the public defender's office and never left. Twenty-six years later, she still calls it "the perfect match" for her passion and principles. Lowry, on the other hand, got her law degree with the single-minded intention to work in the special victims unit of the DA's office. She spent several years in the adult criminal division, prosecuting pimps and other sexual predators, before taking over the juvenile division.

When both women took charge of their respective posts in the Las Vegas juvenile justice system, they were standing in the eye of the child prostitution storm. Because of the pioneering work of the vice squad's STOP program, more girls in the sex industry were being rescued off the streets than in any other city. But that also meant more girls were being locked up in the juvenile detention center while police worked on their cases. Prosecutor Lowry did not see much choice. "How else can we protect these girls?" she asks. "How can we make them safe?"

Public defender Roske saw it in a dramatically different light. "These children are victims of human trafficking and we're charging them with committing a crime," she says, bristling with anger. "That's protecting them? Aren't we harming them more than we're helping them?"

The controversy spilled into the open in the spring of 2005, when Roske made a frank if somewhat indelicate comparison between police and pimps in a *Las Vegas Sun* article. "We see these vice officers victimizing these girls all over again just like the pimps," Roske was quoted as saying. "They sweet-talk them, they give them all this attention, and then they discard them afterward."

The remarks did not win her any new friends among the police. "I would strongly disagree that we just throw these girls away when we get what we want," says Aaron Stanton, who had worked to break Maria and Sandy away from Knowledge's pimping empire. "We care about their well-being, we care about their lives."

But the dustup at least had the advantage of thrusting the issue into the open. Roske and Lowry used the attention to start a public dialogue. Over the years of courtroom battles, they had come to know and respect each other. They shared a passion for the law and for the children they were seeing in court. "She's a public defender. I'm a DA. We're regularly on opposite sides of the courtroom against each other litigating," Lowry explains. "But we came together on this issue because we both believe very strongly in helping these girls and trying to make changes."

It was unusual for such a deep partnership to develop between a district attorney and a public defender. So much so that when, at a national juvenile justice conference in New Orleans, Roske and Lowry were busy chatting in the hallways with obvious friendliness, it raised more than a few eyebrows.

"If this is such a novelty, we thought, 'Why don't we work with it and start seeing if we can raise some interest in this issue?'" says Roske.

Adds Lowry, "Susan and I decided to use that dynamic to get people's attention."

They began what they only half jokingly referred to as "our little road show," speaking to community groups, law enforcement gatherings, the media—anyone who would listen to their pleas for action.

Their timing was fortuitous. William Voy, a hardworking and driven judge, had transferred from the divorce and civil division to the juvenile section in 2004 and was growing increasingly frustrated by what he saw. An overburdened assembly line of youth court justice was trying to cope with an unending flood of minors facing charges that ranged from shoplifting to sexual assaults. In the ensuing chaos, prostituted youth were getting lost in the shuffle. They would appear before a rotating series of judges, public defenders, and prosecutors, few of whom had the time to handle these girls, much less any clear policies or understanding of what to do.

"We have to figure out how to deal with these kids, because I'm caught in the middle," Voy told Lowry and Roske.

They convened a meeting and invited the probation officers, social workers, and vice detectives who dealt with the girls. It was a bold attempt at judicial bridge building among people more used to being foes than friends. Cops don't usually trust defense lawyers and vice versa; social workers are busy trying to care for the same children the prosecutors are sometimes trying to put behind bars.

But they found there was more than enough common ground. "Do we view these girls as delinquents or as victims?" Voy asked the group. Everyone agreed the children were really victims, even if they had broken the law. "Well, we need to try to treat them that way," Voy said.

In September 2005, Voy began to set aside his Wednesday morning court sessions exclusively for children arrested on prostitution-related offenses. Lowry and Roske appointed seasoned lawyers to handle these cases and develop an expertise, and the probation office and the social work agencies followed suit. Instead of an endless rotation of court personnel handling a child's file with little knowledge or experience, a small cadre of caring professionals came together. The vice cops coordinated their work with the courts and the lawyers. Every-one was trying to get on the same page when it came to each case. "We've come a long way from where we started, working for the good of the girls," says Vegas cop Aaron Stanton.

It was simple yet revolutionary. For the first time in America, young people forced into commercial sexual exploitation were getting the special attention they needed inside the justice system. In its first three years of operation, from 2005 until 2008, more than three hundred girls filed through Voy's special court. They came from all races and classes. About half were white like Christina; half were black or His-panic. They were middle class, working class, and poor. Their aver-age age was sixteen, but close to two dozen were fourteen and under. Several were as young as twelve. Voy did not coddle them; he did not go soft on them just because he believed they were victims. Some got sent to Caliente, a tough state reformatory north of Vegas. Some got sent to group homes. Others got probation or counseling.

But they all got heard. Often for the first time in these girls' lives, somebody was prepared to listen to their stories, their hopes, their fears, and their dreams. Voy's youth court boasted an impressively low reoffender rate: only 12 percent of the girls who appeared before him were charged again for prostitution-type offenses. That's proof, says Judge Voy, that treating these young women with the dignity victims deserve can work.

Sometimes.

Reserving one morning a week in a crowded court calendar for the girls was the easy part. Figuring out how to help them would be much harder.

■ ■ ■

WHEN JUDGE Voy entered Courtroom 18 one morning in the spring of 2009, he was thirty minutes late, as usual.

"I just came back from the doctor, that's why I'm late," he said by way of explanation. "He recommends I cut certain things out of my life."

"Like?" asked the prosecutor, falling for the bait.

"Lawyers," the judge chuckled. And another morning marathon was underway.

Despite the easy banter, there were still the natural tensions that arose when you put a prosecutor, a defense lawyer, and a judge in the same room with tough cases and tough defendants. Roske and Lowry might agree on principles, but in practice the public defenders and prosecutors still saw things through different lenses.

The defense lawyers complained the girls were still being treated too harshly. In Las Vegas, it was standard juvenile court policy that all offenders brought before a judge be shackled with leg irons and handcuffs tied to a chain around their waist. That made sense for an eighteen-year-old gang member charged with a drive-by shooting, but it seemed unfair for a petite fifteen-year-old girl.

"We shackle them and bring them into court in handcuffs and then try to convince them they are victims?" protested chief public defender Roske. Judge Voy was able to convince the courts to remove the leg irons for the girls, but the handcuffs, tied to a chain around the waist, remained. With just one overworked bailiff to handle all the traffic in the court, the authorities insisted that's the best they could do.

The prosecutors, for their part, believed that sometimes the girls were getting off too leniently. Amity Dorman, one of the regular prosecutors assigned to Voy's court, felt that, however sad their individual stories might be, many girls could not be trusted to tell the truth. "Prostitution is based on secrets, lies, getting people to buy what you're selling," she points out. Dorman recalled the case of one recalcitrant girl. "No matter what we did, she was always back out there on the streets. She had been given every chance," she says. "At some point, she ceased to be a victim. She has to take accountability for the path she chose." Voy eventually sentenced the girl to a jail term in the Caliente reformatory.

Dorman at first found it hard to give up the winner-takes-all mentality that pervades the confrontational justice system. "In most courtrooms, you have to win at all costs. How many trials did you win is what everyone asks. I used to keep a tally of my track record," she says. But what was remarkable about Voy's court was how it forced all the players to put aside their long-held assumptions and practices. "You walk in here Wednesday mornings and you have to completely change your mentality," Dorman says. "You can't treat these girls as traditional repeat offenders. You have to understand what makes them want to keep going back to the streets. Here, my job is to seek justice—and sometimes justice doesn't have the traditional meaning that people attach to it."

Seeking justice every Wednesday morning meant the judge, the lawyers, and a battery of probation officers and social workers tried their best to figure out what to do with a bewildering array of teenage girls who could be angry, speedy, sulking, or smiling—sometimes all at once. In the space of roughly three hours in his courtroom, Voy, with jet black hair and a trim beard that is starting to gray, will be part father who sternly wags a finger at the wayward girls, part psychologist who tries to figure out what's behind their behavior, and part cop who looks for the bad guys exploiting the girls—a difficult juggling act that Voy handles with practiced aplomb.

The "easy calls," as he puts it, are the nervous newcomers. "They're the ones who have never been involved in this before," Voy explains. "They think this is kind of cool, they get in way over their heads, and then realize, 'Oh my God, what do I do?'"

Newcomers like Susan, a small seventeen-year-old with auburn hair who shuffled hesitantly into Voy's courtroom one morning, a bright yellow detention center–issued sweatshirt over her blue sweatpants. "Do you know what a trial is?" the judge began.

"Yes," she answered softly.

"And you're not having one?"

"Not having one, yes," she repeated in a monotone. "I'm pleading guilty."

"Did your lawyer tell you I could send you to Caliente?" Judge Voy asked sternly, referring to the state reformatory.

"Yes."

When police had arrested Susan thirteen days earlier, they found out she was a runaway from Cedar City, a small town just across the state border in Utah.

"She came to the big city," said the probation officer with a sympathy that comes from hearing the same story all too often, "and she met the wrong people."

Judge Voy nodded his head. More than 60 percent of the children paraded in front of his bench are from out of state, girls like Susan with big dreams and little sense of the perils that await them. Voy wanted to see if he could scare her into not becoming another statistic. "This is not glamorous like you see on TV," he lectured her. "A lot of girls get beat up or get diseases or die. This is not something you want to repeat."

"No, never," Susan said, her lips quivering. "I want to go back home."

"See what happens to a seventeen-year-old lost in the big city," Voy said to the courtroom crowd. He turned to Susan's mother, who sat next to her daughter, nervously fingering a heart pendant on her necklace.

"Do you think this was enough of a lesson for her?"

"Yes," she answered.

The judge shifted his gaze back to Susan. "I don't want to read about you in the newspaper."

Even when they are arrested for soliciting, girls like Susan will often plead down to a lesser offense such as loitering, breaking curfew, or giving false information to police. The guilty plea gives the youth court the jurisdiction it needs to have some control over the girl through the probation period while at the same time removing the stain of prostitution from her juvenile record.

Voy sentenced Susan to six months' probation with the condition that she stay with her mother and be ready to help police and the prosecution if they need her to go after her pimp. "Go back to what you were doing before you got into this mess," he said. "Fair enough?"

"Yes," Susan answered, sighing with relief. The judge ordered her to return to his court at the end of her probation and promised he'd go one step further to help her. "I will withdraw the charge then, dismiss the case, and you will have a clean record," he assured her.

As the mother and daughter left the courtroom, Judge Voy allowed himself a small smile. He was fairly confident that at least one girl had been saved this morning.

■ ■ ■

IN AN otherwise grim court calendar full of abuse and neglect, there would be other stories of hope and redemption. An eighteen-year-old named Latisha showed up in court with her two parents. Unlike the other girls, who came straight from the detention center in regulation sweatpants and tops, she was wearing a white blouse and slacks. On the run from the law for two years, she had contacted the public defender's office the week before to try to clear her name.

Latisha told the judge she was first arrested at the Bellagio casino when she was sixteen. She had a series of other run-ins with the law throughout 2007, then she bolted and missed her court appearances. But in the intervening period, Latisha somehow managed to get off the streets. Now, with a steady job at a health care company, she was worried a criminal record could harm her career.

Prosecutor Amity Dorman told the court a fugitive should not be rewarded for disappearing for two years. But Voy leaned toward being more charitable.

"How come that part of your life stopped?" he asked, trying to gauge the sincerity and depth of Latisha's reform.

"I just realized that is not the right path to take," she answered, explaining that she liked the security of a steady paycheck.

"But if you don't have a job and you need the money, could you go back to that?" Voy pushed.

"No, I'd be scared," Latisha said.

"Is that the only reason?"

"No, that's not even in my mind now. Even if I was to lose my job, that's not the person I am now. I feel better about myself."

Judge Voy nodded approvingly, apparently convinced of Latisha's resolve. He ruled to close her file and wipe out her record. A grateful Latisha hugged her parents and headed out the door, back to her job and, she hoped, to the rest of her life.

Shania, the next girl to walk in—this time in handcuffs and in the detention center uniform—was much like Latisha must have been when she was sixteen, a girl on the precipice. And Voy hoped to catch her before she fell too far. Shania stood before the judge, her silky black hair falling elegantly to her shoulders. Her father, a long-distance trucker, huddled nervously behind her. Her grandmother sat next to the girl, her purse plopped on her lap and a stern smile fixed on her face.

Shania had been caught a few weeks earlier breaking curfew. (Children under eighteen are not allowed out past 10:00 P.M. on weekdays and midnight on weekends unless accompanied by an adult in Las Vegas; on the Strip itself curfew begins at 9:00 P.M.) She compounded her error by lying about her age to the cops, which earned her a second charge of giving false information.

Voy listened intently as the probation officer gave her report. Shania had been getting into more and more trouble in the past two years despite attempts by her grandmother to rein her in during her father's lengthy absences.

"What do you think?" Voy said, turning toward the father.

"I want to take her home with me," the man replied. "I'm going to have to find me another job. I'll flip burgers if I have to."

"You're willing to make that kind of commitment?" Voy asked.

"I have to," Shania's dad answered with calm determination. "She's my daughter."

Voy set his eyes firmly on the nervous girl. "What about you?" he asked, peering down from his dais. "Are you going to stay put? We have to put an end to this, you acting twenty-five when you're fifteen. What do you think we're doing here?"

"Trying to get me to go home and do the right thing," Shania answered in a barely audible murmur.

"You gave false information to the police," Voy said, reading from the police file on his desk. "Do you think I even care about that part? Why do you think we're spending all this time here?"

"Me being safe," Shania said.

"Yeah, we want you to be safe and successful," the judge agreed. "We're not trying to punish you. I'm trying to make sure you have a chance to grow up."

Voy sentenced Shania to a twelve-month probation term, under the condition that she live with her father and enter counseling. He warned her that if she ran away again and was arrested, he would ship her to the Caliente youth jail.

"All right, we'll keep her safe," her dad promised. Shania's grandmother hugged the girl as she was led back to the detention center to gather her belongings. The older woman caressed her granddaughter's cheeks softly with the back of her hand.

Voy seemed heartened by the display of family affection. "I'm glad the vice guys found her before someone else did," he said as he folded her file away and reached for the next one on his desk.

■ ■ ■

GIRLS LIKE Shania and Latisha, who wanted help and had supportive families to back them up, were not the cases that caused Judge Voy grief. It was the defiant ones whose problems were tough to resolve, the girls who didn't think they needed any assistance or were too confused or frightened to ask. "It's the girls who have been in the life for a while who are the hardest to help," Voy says. "Unfortunately they've been abused and neglected and sexually exploited even before they even got into it, and now the pimp has a firm grip on them. That is a very complicated problem to unravel. What works for one kid is not going work for the other. There is no easy answer."

When Cindy, a short fifteen-year-old with dirty blond hair, shuffled into the courtroom, she tried hard to look like a grown-up. But the red-rimmed eyes still wet from tears gave her away as the frightened teenager she still was. Her mother, who sat at the small table set aside for the young offenders, handed her a tissue. Cindy took it grudgingly. It was hard to tell if Cindy was more upset at what she had done or at being caught.

She had a previous record for assault and battery. This was her first arrest for loitering on a street known for prostitution not far from the Vegas Strip. "She told me she was going to a friend's house, but she has been lying to me," her mother said, her voice catching in her throat. "I have told her what she can get into. I think she needs to be taught a lesson."

"Cindy, what do you think?" the judge asked.

"Walking in here was a big wake-up call for me," she said. "I was really scared. I know what I did was wrong."

"Why, Cindy, why?" the judge pushed.

"I don't know."

"What she's doing is dangerous," her mother interjected. "She could end up dead. No matter what I said, she did it anyways. What am I to do? I thought she was dead when I got the call from the cops."

But there was a problem with the arrest. The public defender argued the case was weak. Cindy was just standing on the sidewalk looking at traffic, not legally loitering. The arresting officer had the right instincts, but he jumped the gun by making the arrest before she engaged in any overt act such as stopping a car or beginning to negotiate with a customer. Cindy herself later admitted to the cop that she was trying to prostitute herself.

Judge Voy tried to explain the legal dilemma to the worried mother. "Because she admits to doing it, that's not enough to support the charge, because there is no probable cause," he said.

Cindy's mother was desperate now. "This is out of control, and I am tired," she sighed. "I am tired of chasing her."

But the judge was adamant that legally his hands were tied. "There is no probable cause for the charge—I have to release her," he said. "If she comes back here we can put her in a place where she is safe."

He was worried—and for good reason.

Two hours later, Cindy was released and walked jauntily through the outside courtyard at the Clark County Family Courts. She looked comfortable in the clothes she wore the night she was arrested: a revealing black blouse tied at the back and tight short blue jeans, a small purse dangling from her wrist and a pair of silver stilettos on her feet. She lagged a few feet behind her mother, who ignored her.

Cindy would be back on the streets of Vegas in no time.

. . .

JUDGE VOY was just a judge, not a miracle worker. He had little power outside the four walls of Courtroom 18. Much as he wanted to give the girls who appeared before him a chance to start a new life, he had little to offer them once he they left his courtroom.

At the high end of the punishment scale, Voy could put a girl behind bars at the juvenile state prison at Caliente. But that was a harsh solution reserved only for repeat offenders or girls charged with additional, more serious offenses such as theft or assault. Between the extremes of releasing a girl back on the streets or keeping her behind bars, a more palatable option for girls like Cindy was to find a group home or rehab center. But no such center that specializes in helping prostituted children exists in Las Vegas.

Even if Voy and the court's social workers could find a bed in a shelter for a girl, there was a good chance she would soon run. That's what happened with Christina, the cheerful, ponytailed eighteen-year-old who promised Judge Voy she would find a job and counseling. The afternoon after her court appearance, as she was preparing to leave the detention center, she met with court social worker Marisela Quintero.

"I just want someone to be there for me," Christina said. "Someone to give me affection and love."

Quintero was impressed by Christina's determination. "I think that she genuinely wants to change," she says. "Christina is really open about everything that's happened to her. You don't see too much of that with the girls." But Quintero also knew how hard it was for the girls who leave Voy's court to make it. "A lot of the girls have been sexually abused, they have a history of running away, and they don't have a big support system," she notes.

The social worker put Christina in touch with an evangelical group in Las Vegas called Hookers for Jesus, led by a former prostitute. Christina seemed to take to the church's message of spiritual reawakening and began attending their sessions. But every time she went back to her foster home, she would hang out with drug dealers and prostitutes. She missed her follow-up court date in front of Judge Voy two weeks later. Quintero drove around the streets of Vegas looking for her but had no luck.

Christina, she suspected, was back in the game.

"I'm tired of running," Christina had told her social worker. "I'm tired of working the streets. I just want help."

Help was something in short supply in the streets of Las Vegas. If a decent refuge for the hundreds of girls walking through his court did not exist, then Judge Voy, along with prosecutor Teresa Lowry and public defender Susan Roske, would have come up with a bold plan. They had built a special courtroom for the girls. Why not try to build a safe recovery home for them as well?

· 13 ·

No Safe Haven

FOR ALL Judge Voy's efforts, his innovative court was just a small cog in a justice wheel that turned excruciatingly slowly when it came to helping young girls forced into prostitution. Voy and his Las Vegas colleagues faced the same dilemma as people across the country who worked with children forced into prostitution: what do you do with a young girl after she has been picked up or arrested?

You can have caring cops in Las Vegas or Dallas or Atlantic City on the lookout for young girls being exploited on the streets or in the casinos. You can have a caring judge in Vegas trying to give them a chance to start a new life. But where do you place girls in a justice system that does not seem to care for them?

The answers divided erstwhile allies, pitting cops and prosecutors against caregivers and community activists. This was not a dispute between tough law-and-order types who felt you should jail these young girls and throw away the key versus liberal do-gooders who felt they were just angels who had done no wrong. Everyone agreed these girls were troubled, often uncooperative victims who needed help, not criminals who deserved punishment. But how to deliver that help was the subject of sharp disagreement.

Law enforcement tended to favor keeping the girls safe and secure in locked facilities, usually juvenile detention centers. That, they insist, was the only way of keeping them from their pimps and giving them a chance to break out of the cycle of abuse. The cops saw detention not so much as punishment as a sort of psychological detox center. "You have to have time to break that bond of trust they have with their abuser, so that you can do undo all the damage that has been done," says Aaron Stanton of the Las Vegas police. "There is no other way to do it."

But it was still jail. "You are sending a mixed message to these girls by locking them up," complains Rachel Lloyd, whose GEMS organization in New York City ran one of the country's most successful programs for prostituted children. "I have seen enough girls that have been in a detention facility for months and that didn't break the bond. Detention in and of itself does not guarantee an interruption of the trauma bond. Giving somebody therapeutic support and helping them work through what got them into this life—that breaks the bond."

Lloyd and other activists favored shelters, transition houses, and community programs that treated the girls as the victims they were and empowered them to fight back. But that approach, however admirable, had its own problems. There were very few spaces. GEMS, the only residential shelter in the northeast United States for girls trying to escape prostitution, helped more than 250 girls a year, mostly through various outreach programs; it had thirteen beds for girls to stay on any kind of permanent basis. In Minnesota, Vednita Carter's Breaking Free group also helped hundreds of minors but offered another fifteen beds at most. The Las Vegas authorities tried to send as many girls as they could to Children of the Night in California. One of the oldest and best-financed shelters in the country, it offered an on-site school and recreational outings but still had only about two dozen beds. Indeed, throughout the entire United States there were perhaps a half-dozen such rehab programs with no more than fifty beds to serve several hundred thousand children at risk. "It is scandalous that we don't have the facilities for these girls that we are supposed to help," admits Judge Voy.

But even if there were more centers, the cops were not convinced they were the right answer. Most centers practiced an open-door policy, and a determined girl could bolt and make her way back to the streets. As in all recovery and addiction programs, the ones who are ready to change stick it out. The rest run.

Locked-down detention or open-door rehab? It was a perplexing problem, with strong arguments by people on both sides who cared deeply for these girls. Judge Voy wondered, if both sides were right, maybe he could split the difference and find a solution in the middle.

...

THE CLARK County Detention Center stands across the street from Desert Pines golf center, about a dozen miles from the Las Vegas Strip. One way or the other, this is where almost all the girls picked up by the Metro police on prostitution-related offenses, or any girl waiting for a decision in Judge Voy's court, end up. Some are there for days, others for weeks or months.

It was here that Sandy, the fourteen-year-old from the poor West Side district who was recruited into Knowledge's network, was detained during her numerous arrests. And it was here that Maria spent a month back in December 2003 when she was arrested while working for Knowledge. "It was better than Rikers," she notes, referring to the notorious New York City adult prison, "but it was still jail."

There are 192 beds in the facility, but with close to 230 juvenile inmates on most days, there is a lot of doubling up. Twenty-four beds are set aside for girls, but usually about thirty girls are crammed into the two wings reserved for them. "Bed" is a generous description of the cement blocks that are molded into the walls in each small cell, which has yellow walls, a white floor, a stainless steel toilet, and a sink. That is it—no mirrors, no shelves, no table or chair. Just a gray foam mattress to toss on top of the block and a pile of clothes and sheets folded in the corner.

The only personal touch is the crayoned artwork some of the girls have posted outside their cells, each drawing a testimony to a dark past or a hoped-for future: stick figures of a child, a house with a fence, a heart shape, or a sun. ABUSE THRIVES IN SECRECY says one. ALWAYS BE A FIRST-RATE VERSION OF YOURSELF INSTEAD OF A SECOND-RATE VERSION OF SOMEBODY ELSE says another.

Each girl's name is handwritten on a card that is placed in a little slot in the cell door. The cells are kept open during most of the day, as girls circulate in a central open area that has a TV mounted on the wall and a few shelves filled with textbooks and teen novels. There are two small classrooms for their daily studies; a teacher comes in regularly for the basic high school–level courses all the girls are required to take.

Here the girls are subdued and reserved, their youthful faces fresh-scrubbed and their hair clean and loose. Their nails are unvarnished and their ears, necks, and hands are free of jewelry—a stark contrast from their heavily made-up appearance when they were working the streets. They all wear loose sweatpants and T-shirts, brown for the new arrivals, then orange, and finally gray for those who have been around for a couple of weeks and behaved well. Underneath their clothes, they make do with paper panties, an indignity imposed for sanitary and budget reasons.

KEEP TRUE TO THE DREAMS OF YOUR YOUTH reads a banner in the middle of the cell block. And while the dedicated staff tries its hardest to make the girls feel comfortable and safe, it is hard not to see them for what they are—prisoners in a justice system not built for prostituted children. "It's about handcuffs. It's about barbed wire," admits chief juvenile prosecutor Teresa Lowry. "It's about jails."

Within days of their arrest, the girls will get their first hearing before Judge Voy and then, depending on what he decides, be returned to the detention center until a more suitable place or solution has been found for them. But police and prosecutors can also go to court to get a "material witness" hold on a girl they are convinced has information she is not willing to disclose on a pimp or, conversely, on a girl who has given information but might be a flight risk if she is released.

"What other victims in society do we lock up? It's just mind-boggling," says an outraged Susan Roske, the chief public defender. "They're being held as criminals. They sleep in cells. They're hand-cuffed. That's totally traumatizing to these girls. The system just hardens them, and we reenforce in their minds that they're not victims because we're not treating them like victims."

Needless to say, the Las Vegas police don't see it that way. "They're not suspects, they're not criminals, but what happens with juvenile prostitutes is that they don't realize they are a danger to themselves," argues vice cop Gil Shannon. "We are putting them in a situation where they are being protected from the pimp and from whatever abuse made them run from home. A girl needs to be in a safe place until we can find a realistic alternative for her and her future."

As unpleasant as a stay in a juvenile jail cell may be, the Vegas cops insist that breaking the bonds with a pimp takes time. "When she's locked up she makes good decisions, but when outside, she's easily malleable," says Woody Fieselman. "That's the way it is with a lot of these girls."

Some of the girls who began the hard road back to a normal life after a long cooling off period in detention would agree. When Maria was arrested in Las Vegas back in 2003, Judge Voy was still two years away from creating his special court, so she never got the benefit of his attention. But looking back at it now, she dates the beginning of her turnaround to her long stay at the juvenile center and the constant meetings with Fieselman and Stanton. "It was hard to break me," she admits. "It took them a month before I talked." She was badly shaken when the cops showed her what they like to call "the death book," a collection of unsettling pictures of prostituted youths killed by drugs, johns, or pimps. "There was a picture of a girl in chains, getting dragged to her death," Maria says. "It woke me up."

Stanton had similar success with another teenager named Jill, whose lengthy detention helped wake her up, too. Blond, blue-eyed, with a striking figure at five feet, seven inches (even when she wasn't wearing her fluorescent green shoes with six-inch heels), Jill had a natural beauty that made her a big attraction on the Strip. She had grown up in a white working-class neighborhood of Vegas where the glittering lights of the casinos in the distant skyline were about as close as she got to the city's pomp and parties. Only eleven when her mother died, she was miserable at home with her father and soon began to hang with bad boys and run away from home. "I went downhill pretty quickly," she says, starting with marijuana and alcohol, then turning a few tricks for her boyfriend to make some cash.

Things turned serious when she met a Californian pimp named Demarcus "Smoke" Webb. "Smoke really trained me," Jill says. "He showed me the way you talk, the way you act, the way you dress. I thought it was really exciting and fun in the beginning." There were trips to Los Angeles, New York, and Boston, with fancy clothes and fine hotels. But there were also the increasingly regular beatings, the drugs, and the endless servicing of clients for her pimp. In one day alone in New York, she pulled in $1,950 for him.

Back in Vegas, she "chose up" with another pimp named Anthony "Tony" Carter. Business was steady, and even three arrests over a week in January 2005 didn't slow her down. By now seventeen, Jill looked older and had several fake IDs that allowed her to pass as an adult. Her luck ran out on November 20, when the Vegas cops busted her and correctly identified her as a juvenile. Stanton got the call and brought the extremely uncooperative Jill to the detention center. "She was a very intelligent girl; she knew how to manipulate people, and she would not give up anything," he says.

Through calls Jill made from jail and from bail records, Stanton was able to trace Carter and make an arrest. But Jill would not budge. "I had never told them the truth. I had never told them that Tony was my pimp," she says, the pride at deceiving the cops still apparent. "I stayed loyal the whole time."

For most of the month of December, Stanton and Fieselman met with Jill as she cooled her heels in the detention center. She was fishing for information as much as the cops were, always curious to know how their investigation of Carter was progressing. "She wanted to protect him, terribly," says Fieselman. "She didn't know how much we knew, and she didn't want to give away anything unless she was sure we already knew about it. It was like a chess game."

The cops kept pushing. "We're not only trying to get the information regarding the abuser," explains Stanton. "We're also trying to deprogram the girls from the lifestyle. We're trying to show them this isn't the best course to follow in life."

Jill admits she was torn. "What do I do?" she says. "I thought I loved Tony. I know now I didn't, but I was in love with the idea of loving him."

The stalemate lasted for a month. The day after Christmas, Jill found herself in a room with Stanton and Fieselman at the courthouse where Carter's preliminary hearing was set to begin. The cops brought in Jill's older sister for moral support. They hugged, cried, and laughed together.

"You need to tell the truth," Fieselman told Jill. "You need to start thinking for yourself. It's time for you to take charge."

Jill walked out, still giving no indication of what she would do.

The two cops looked at each other skeptically. "I don't know," Stanton muttered to his partner.

Fieselman winced. "I'd like to see how this turns out," he said.

It turned out well. For whatever reason, once she got on the stand, Jill told the truth for the first time. It came out in tears and sobs, but it came out.

"I was really proud of myself," says Jill.

So was Stanton. "It was amazing. I think as soon as she got on the stand, it all clicked," he says. "They get this feeling of liberation and power, and finally they're in control."

Detention and testifying seemed cathartic for Jill. When a girl won't give up her pimp, it's a clear indication she is not ready to make the break with a life on the tracks, Stanton notes. "When they do, they're beginning to say, 'I'm cutting my ties with him. I'm trying to start something new with my life.'"

Jill moved to her father's home in South Dakota and got a job as a waitress. "Back in Vegas, I was very lost," she says. "I just wanted somebody to love me. And that is what pimps do. They play that part, pretending to love you."

After the preliminary hearing, Jill promised to return for the trial scheduled for February 2006. When she did show up, much to the surprise and dismay of her former pimp, Anthony Carter folded and pleaded guilty. He was sentenced to five years in prison. Meanwhile, in San Francisco a federal grand jury indicted Demarcus Webb on two counts of taking girls across state lines for the purposes of prostitution. He was eventually sent away for eight years.

Jill had kept her word and returned to take the stand at Carter's trial. Many girls don't. Once released, they never show up for court, either too frightened or too much under the sway of their pimp—or both. That is why Deputy District Attorney Teresa Lowry and her prosecutors sometimes force an early preliminary hearing within fifteen days of a pimp's arrest while the girl is still in detention. That way they can get a girl's testimony on the record, where she can be cross-examined by the defendant's lawyer. Even if she subsequently flees, her testimony can be entered into evidence during trial.

Lowry used that tactic against a pimp named Andrew Meeks from Minnesota. He brought a seventeen-year-old to Vegas with him and then recruited two other local minors. He was arrested and charged with kidnapping, child abuse, and attempted statutory sexual seduction. The seventeen-year-old never showed up for the trial, but while she was in detention Lowry was able to get her testimony during a preliminary hearing. Meeks got life.

• • •

FOR THE Las Vegas police and prosecutors, the rescue of girls like Jill and the jailing of their pimps pointed to the strengths of a detention program.

The very success Vegas authorities had with some of the girls in custody, however, revealed a flaw in the process: the more a girl cooperated with police and prosecutors, the more likely she was to remain longer behind bars. A girl who shuts up and says nothing to identify her abuser may be released in days because police can't build a case against a pimp they don't know. Conversely, a girl who tells all may be held as a material witness. Gil Shannon acknowledges that some girls are warned by their pimps or by other minors who have been arrested, "Just don't say anything, they have to release you."

"We've had kids who have said, 'I promise I will cooperate. I've already spilled my guts, let me go home,'" says Susan Roske. "But she might be kept in custody until she testifies. And I have a problem with that." So the public defenders feel obliged to caution the newly arrested girls that if they cooperate with the vice cops and their pimp is arrested, there is a good chance they could be adding time to their own jail term. "They have a right to know," says Roske. "We are not there to help the police trick them into testifying."

Roske says her public defenders have a duty to respond to the expressed interest of their child clients, even if that might not always be in the child's best interest. "Our role is to pursue what she wants to do," says Roske. "If she says, 'No, I want to get out,' then it's our job to argue for her to get out. These kids need someone in the courtroom in their corner, someone who helps them express what their desires are, whether we agree or not."

But that in turn creates an ethical dilemma for the public defenders. They know that most of these girls are "runners." They've all successfully argued to get a client released only to have her run off and be back on the streets a few days later. "As a concerned adult you're just horrified at what these children are doing," Roske says. "I think if it was my daughter, I wouldn't want her to go back to their pimp again. I would want her to be locked up. It's a fine line we're walking."

Indeed, it was a fine and confusing line everyone was walking. Police and prosecutors who were troubled by locking up victims sometimes found they had no choice but to fight to keep some girls detained longer for their own protection; defense lawyers sometimes fought to get the girls released even if they knew they might be safer behind bars.

There had to a better way. Susan Roske and Teresa Lowry were determined to find one. Together with Judge Voy, they came up with what seemed like the perfect compromise between the harsh jail settings of a detention center and the open-door policy of group homes: a "safe house" to help girls break out of the life of prostitution. Such a secure residential facility would combine trained staff and locked doors with the look and feel of a comfortable group home in a residential neighborhood. No cells, no barbed wire—but no easy way for the girls to flee back to their pimps.

"It would be a home where the children will feel secure and would not be treated like criminals," explains Voy. "They will be cared for by social work and mental health professionals who understand the medical, social, and psychological needs of victimized children. Our ultimate goal with these kids is to prove to ourselves and to the community that there is a better way of dealing with child prostitution."

Voy and his team set up a nonprofit foundation with a fund-raising Web site. Community groups like the Junior League and the Frederick Douglass Foundation came on board. Shared Hope, the national antitrafficking lobby group, provided funding for a major study. Local architects volunteered their time to design a spacious, comfortable, yet secure home, right down to minor details. Doors to the rooms, for example, would open out, not in, as they do in most homes, to prevent an angry or misbehaving youth on the inside trying to block anyone from entering.

The 7,500-square-foot building would be able to shelter up to fourteen girls at a time, a good fit since about half of the thirty girls at the detention center at any given time are being held on prostitution-related offenses. Once the house was built, Lowry, Roske, and Voy planned to lobby the state legislature to enact a law that would allow the courts to declare a child "in need of protection." It would be similar to the rules that allow the state to take a child away from abusive parents, except in this case the child might be at risk not only from her pimp but also from herself. "These children are so brainwashed and so scared, they don't know who to trust," says Roske. "The safe house would get them in a frame of mind to deal with some very painful issues, to help them find for themselves what they want in life."

Roske, Lowry, and Voy figured they would have no trouble convincing the politicians to pass a law that had rare unanimous support from all sides. What they didn't count on were the bureaucratic and financial storms that would prevent them from even getting the home built. Early plans for the house were scuttled back in 2006 by the then director of the juvenile justice programs, who argued there were not enough girls to justify the expense and in any case most of the youths arrested were from out of state. That outraged the lawyers working in Voy's court. "Many of the girls may be from other jurisdictions, but they come to Las Vegas because it's Las Vegas," says public defender Jessica Murphy. "It's become our problem."

Voy, for his part, would not give up. He kept meeting with county and court officials, proposing everything from a liquor tax to a small levy on Las Vegas's ever-popular instant marriage licenses to help pay for his dream project. "It has been a battle," he says. "It has consumed so much of my energy and my attention. It is extremely frustrating, and it wears on you. But you just keep doing the best you can."

Three years later, Voy, Lowry and Roske were still lobbying furiously. But the delays cost them dearly. By 2009, the recession had hit the Las Vegas tourism industry with a wallop. City and court officials were even less willing to spend taxpayer dollars on helping a population like prostituted children that has no voice, little clout, and even less voter appeal. Recognizing Las Vegas as a center for child prostitution was also not exactly a great civic image booster.

"We already are a center for child prostitution," Voy says angrily. "Let's face the facts, we've got that label. But this is a nationwide problem. It's everywhere. At least in Las Vegas we are trying to do something to address the problem."

"A safe house just seems like a no-brainer," says an exasperated Teresa Lowry. "This is just the right thing to do."

But what is right and what is politically palatable in the world of child prostitution are two different things. In the meantime, all Judge Voy could do with many of the girls who came into Courtroom 18 was park them in the juvenile detention center and then release them on probation.

For at least one girl, that turned into a death sentence.

■ ■ ■

THE MOTEL 6 parking lot is just across the street from the MGM Grand, but it might as well be an ocean away. The glistening green and blue towers of the casino dominate the Vegas Strip, casting a shadow over the discount hotel on the corner of Koval and Tropicana. It's a popular intersection for prostitution, so there was little surprise when police officers arrested a seventeen-year-old girl there at 12:53 A.M. on Saturday, January 17, 2009.

Kathy was seventeen, a tall African American teenager with a round face, bushy hair, and expressive eyes. "She was a very bright young lady," one of her friends would later say on a Web-page tribute. "She had the most unforgettable laugh and smile." A high school photo shows her in blue jeans, a white T-shirt, and a pink jacket, beaming and hugging two friends in front of their lockers.

But on that night, Kathy was far from her small-town home on San Pablo Bay in California, about twenty-five miles northeast of San Francisco. Her dad was a trucker and not around much. She claimed her mother was often "strung out on drugs." A frequent runaway, she told the Vegas police a pimp had "sent me out here to learn the ropes."

Five days after her arrest, Kathy made her first of three appearances at Judge Voy's youth court. After she gave a false name to the authorities, they could find little background on her, and her case was held over for another week. Seven days in juvenile detention did not seem to improve Kathy's truth-telling abilities. On February 4, she pleaded guilty to giving false information to the police and then promptly lied to the judge by identifying herself as Lamina.

The probation officer explained that Lamina, when asked for parental contacts, twice gave a false name and number for her father. She also named two high schools she had supposedly attended, but neither had any records for her.

"Is she a spy working for the CIA?" the judge joked.

"It's a mystery," admitted the probation officer.

"So what do we do with this young lady?" Judge Voy asked. "I may have to send her to Caliente because I have nowhere else to send her. I'm not going to send her back to the same environment from which we plucked her out."

Voy ordered the girl detained another week. This time, shortly after leaving court, she confessed her real name to her probation officer.

"Thank you, finally," the judge told Kathy when he saw her again on February 4. With Kathy's full identity, the Las Vegas authorities were able to determine she was wanted on a bench warrant for violating probation back in California. The judge "held open" her case in Vegas for six months, meaning that if she returned to the city, she could be rearrested and brought before him again.

"All right, good luck," Judge Voy said.

Kathy shuffled out. It was 11:15 in the morning.

Ten days later she was dead, shot to death and dumped by the side of a railway track.

The plan had been for the Las Vegas probation department to put Kathy on a plane back to California, where probation officials would meet her at the airport. But, unbeknownst to the judge, a few days later the California authorities notified the Vegas officials that they would not be seeking extradition. As often happens, Las Vegas might arrest a minor wanted in another jurisdiction, but the local authorities there did not want to pay for her return.

The Vegas officials scrambled and managed to arrange for Kathy's mother to pick her up at the airport. She ran away from home again. On Valentine's Day, Kathy left a friend's home in Oakland between 1:00 A.M. and 3:00 A.M.—just about the same time she had been picked up exactly four weeks earlier at the Motel 6 in Las Vegas. Her body was found two days later, dumped near the train tracks not far from her hometown. "It was dark and just pouring rain, and she was wearing heels," said a detective on the scene.

The police had few leads. An angry pimp who suspected she had given his name to the cops? A trick gone wrong? Nobody knew.

Judge Voy sits in front of his computer in his office, replaying the video of Kathy's three appearances in front of him in the final weeks of her life. He looks for clues, for any indication of what questions he could have asked, what steps the court could have taken that would have kept Kathy from dying in the rain along the railway tracks.

But he comes up empty. If only he had his safe house for girls, perhaps there would have been a refuge for Kathy while they tried to work something out. "This is the kind of girl I would have been able to keep for thirty days in there," he explains. "We could have worked with her and maybe gotten through to her and got the pimp's name."

That's a lot of maybes. But the judge knows one thing for certain. "If Kathy had a safe place to stay," he says, "she would have been alive today."

· 14 ·

Unequal Laws

PROSTITUTED CHILDREN remain the orphans of America's justice system. They are either ignored or, when they do come in contact with law enforcement, harassed, arrested, and incarcerated while the adults who exploit them—the pimps and their customers—largely escape punishment.

It is rare for a politician, let alone a presidential candidate, to speak out forcefully on the issue. But in August 2008, when he was still several months away from claiming the White House, Barack Obama turned his oratory to the touchy subject of the domestic sex trade.

"What we have to do is to create better, more effective tools for prosecuting those who are engaging in human trafficking, and we have to do that within our country," he said. "Sadly, there are thousands who are trapped in various forms of enslavement, here in our country, oftentimes young women who are caught up in prostitution.... It is a debasement of our common humanity."

Change, as Obama is fond of saying, is needed. Eloquence is easy; effective action is harder. But there were growing challenges to the unequal laws that victimize prostituted youth instead of helping them. A former prostitute turned community leader in New York, a federal prosecutor in Kansas City, and an activist professor from Rhode Island would each in their own way make a difference in the way the law, and people, looked at America's forgotten children.

· · ·

THEY GATHERED on a sweltering June day in 2008 in a corner of
City Hall Park in lower Manhattan. Twenty-five teenage girls, half of
them white and half of them black. Some wore jeans, and some wore
shorts; some sandals, and others sneakers. But all of them wore hot
pink T-shirts with the slogan GIRLS ARE NOT FOR SALE.

Rachel Lloyd of GEMS had brought her girls onto the streets, no
longer as prostitutes but as protesters. It was the third annual Day to
End Sexual Exploitation of Children that GEMS had organized in
New York. In the decade since she created GEMS, Lloyd had built her
organization into not only a vibrant refuge and help center but also
a powerful political movement. Her girls were fighting not just to get
away from their pimps but to change the laws that treated them as
criminals instead of victims.

"People frown on us and look down on us," a former teen victim
turned activist told the crowd that had gathered to watch and listen.
"They only see a young girl on the street selling herself and they don't
know the story behind them."

"We're here to help them out and we're here to show them the right
way," explained another survivor. "We feel it is important they get the
support services they need rather than put them in jail for something
that wasn't their fault."

What bothered Lloyd—and a growing number of activists across
the country—were the inequalities built into the laws of the country.
The injustice began with the glaring contradiction between the age of
consent and the age of criminality. The age of consent for sex varied
in most states from sixteen to eighteen—with sixteen being the most
common—and yet nearly all states allowed children of just about any
age to be prosecuted for prostitution. So a fourteen-year-old who was
seduced by her high school teacher would be treated as a victim—
since by law she could not consent. But if that same fourteen-year-old
was paid for sex, she could be arrested and jailed, even if her pimp
forced her to hand over any money she had made. The situation made
little sense—girls whom the law said were too young to consent to sex
in the first place were judged old enough to be criminally responsible
when money changed hands.

The unfairness was aggravated once the girls were arrested because of the difference between how the system treated foreign and domestic victims of sex trafficking. In 2000, Congress passed the Trafficking Victims Protection Act, which in principle aimed to help all victims of labor and sex trafficking. But any funds authorized to nonprofit groups could only be spent to help foreign nationals. The U.S. government could issue "certification" letters to foreign victims of severe forms of trafficking, which gave them access to cash assistance, food stamps, and other benefits. But no special funding, no special programs, existed for American girls trapped in the same predicament.

The upshot was that, as strange as it might seem, a girl from Honduras found in the sex trade in New York City would get help, but a girl from Harlem more often than not got jail.

Rachel Lloyd wanted to challenge the unequal justice her girls faced. "We're talking about child sexual abuse," she said. "We're talking about children who are bought and sold by adults to adults. We shouldn't be criminalizing young people for something that was done to them." So Lloyd and GEMS set out to change those laws. They began with the state of New York, but the legal revolution they set in motion would eventually sweep across the nation.

For four years, Lloyd and the girls from GEMS made regular trips to the state capital of Albany to convince legislators to take action. Her organization and its allies were lobbying for passage of a new bill called the Safe Harbor for Exploited Youth Act, which would divert children who had been arrested for prostitution into counseling and treatment programs.

"For too long, these young people have been sexually exploited by pimps and predators and then exploited again by state law, which treated them as criminals instead of victims," said Assemblyman William Scarborough, a Democrat from Queens and the chief sponsor of the measure. The irony was not lost on the New York state politicians: while disgraced former governor Eliot Spitzer spent thousands of dollars on high-priced call girls, the state was jailing teenagers being trafficked on the streets by their pimps.

GEMS built up powerful media support. "Prosecutors tend to argue that the threat of being locked up is vital in getting children to name their pimps and face them in court.... But by treating sexually exploited children as criminals, the law victimizes them a second time," said the *New York Times* in a sharply worded editorial. *Newsday* noted, "Children can't legally consent to sex. That's recognized when they're trafficked across national borders and forced into sexual slavery. And it's recognized when they're abused by pedophiles. It should be no different when the child is American, the predator is a pimp and the pedophile is a 'John.'"

Despite the editorial endorsements, the safe harbor legislation also faced stiff opposition, notably from the administration of New York City mayor Michael R. Bloomberg. The mayor's criminal justice coordinator, John Feinblatt, condemned the bill for having "no teeth." In a *New York Post* article ominously titled "NY's Pro-Pimp Bill," he argued unless the girls were kept within the criminal justice system, they would find it too easy to run back to their pimps.

But on September 26, 2008, after four years of intense lobbying and pressure, GEMS won out: the Safe Harbor Act was signed into law in Albany. In New York State, at least, it ended the widespread practice of arresting, prosecuting, and incarcerating teenagers for prostitution. Now girls under sixteen years old would be viewed as "persons in need of supervision," shifting them away from the juvenile justice system into child welfare services. They would be offered social services and protection from their pimps. The act required the state to establish safe houses and to train law enforcement and others who came into contact with trafficked and exploited children.

"The bill sends a strong message to the rest of the nation," said Rachel Lloyd in an e-mail to GEMS supporters. "Commercial sexual exploitation and trafficking of children is a heinous crime against children, not one that is committed by them."

As in all political battles, there were compromises. The law applies only to girls fifteen years and under, not to older teenagers, even though New York State law sets the age of sexual consent at seventeen years old and federal legislation defines victims of sex trafficking as children if they are eighteen years old or younger. Nor does the Safe Harbor Act offer girls unconditional immunity from prosecution. If they refuse community services and fail to comply with a rehab program once they start it, a judge can send their cases back to the criminal justice system. Moreover, repeat offenders are not protected; the offer of social services instead of jail is good only for first-time offenders.

Lloyd knew that the success of the Safe Harbor Act would lie in its implementation. In an era of economic crisis and drastic government budget cuts, finances were uncertain; proper funding was required for the network of safe houses and community services needed to help the girls who were diverted from jail. But she took comfort in the fact that the debate over the law had forced the issue of the sexual exploitation of prostituted children into the open. "I felt we achieved a lot of our goals in terms of raising public awareness, getting legislators to change their perspective, getting the media coverage we did," she says. "At least we got people talking."

Indeed, the Safe Harbor Act reflected a new sensibility in the law and among lawmakers toward the treatment of prostituted children. By the end 2009, Congress had passed legislation that strongly equated modern commercial sexual exploitation with slavery. Congresswoman Carolyn B. Maloney (D-NY), the cofounder and cochair of the Human Trafficking Caucus, spearheaded the William Wilberforce Trafficking Victims Protection Reauthorization Act (TVPA), named appropriately after the nineteenth-century abolitionist who campaigned to end slavery. The TVPA, on the books since 2000, was hampered by uneven enforcement. Significantly, Maloney's version increased assistance to all victims, including U.S. citizens, helping chip away at the myth that trafficking of children was mainly a foreign, not a domestic, problem.

It was indicative of how far the political winds had shifted that a letter to the Obama administration's attorney general, urging swift action on the revamped TVPA, was signed not just by activists like Vednita Carter of Breaking Free and Rachel Lloyd of GEMS but also by evangelical Christians, Southern Baptists, and Gary Bauer, president of the conservative American Values organization. The wide coalition called for a "crackdown on sex traffickers with a range of federal, state, and local prosecutorial strategies."

More and more states were offering "safe harbors" for minors caught up in sex trafficking. Within days of the passage of the New York law, California announced prostituted youth would get treatment and counseling under new legislation that strengthened protections for victims of human trafficking. By 2010, Washington and Connecticut would follow suit. In Illinois, the Chicago Alliance Against Sexual Exploitation worked with the Cook County State's Attorney to change the law and offer social services, not criminal penalties, to minors forced into the sex trade. The Illinois Safe Children Act provided immunity from prosecution for prostituted children. The law also gave police more tools to crack down on sex traffickers, with everything from extended wiretapping authority to stiffer penalties for pimps and johns.

It was not always an easy battle. In Georgia, a Republican state senator named Renee Unterman took on her own party and many conservative voices to push for a new law that would offer prostituted children under sixteen rehabilitative service instead of jail. She pointed out the hypocrisy behind jailing children as prostitutes even though—by law—they were too young to consent to sex. Unterman also insisted that treating minors as victims, not criminals, was not just good social policy but good policing policy as well. "You put handcuffs on a twelve-year-old kid, put them in the back of a police car, they shut up just like that," she told the *Atlanta-Journal Constitution*. "But if you get them into therapy, they never have those handcuffs put on them—they're more apt to talk" about the real criminals who were pimping them.

Her opponents, mainly from conservative forces such as the Georgia Christian Coalition and Concerned Women for America of Georgia but also from some antitrafficking activists, argued the changes would eventually decriminalize prostitution and only embolden pimps. Unterman was attacked for helping "the profitable and growing pedophile industry," and her critics said many minors and adult transgressors could be "scared straight" by the threat of arrest and a criminal record. By the middle of 2010, the reform had stalled, and the debate raged on.

But at least, as Lloyd had said, people and politicians were talking about girls who had been ignored for so long.

■ ■ ■

JUST AS some of the laws—and politicians—were finally catching up to the reality of sex trafficking in America, the pimps had begun to move the young women under their control off streets and onto the Web.

For men on the prowl for anonymous sex, it was as simple as clicks for tricks. There were plenty of Web sites that served as thinly veiled prostitution meat markets, the names scarcely concealing their real intent: Bootycall, TopKitten, Eros. But Craigslist, the Web's largest classified ad service, remained the most popular means of peddling prostitution online. With an estimated 25 million users in 450 cities around the world, Craigslist advertised everything from work to washing machines to women. It was all done with a Web wink and a nod. Clicking on the "erotic services" link brought up a disclaimer releasing Craigslist from any liability. Another click led to a list of posts featuring naked or scantily clad young women; all claimed to be adults; many were obviously not.

"I like to fulfill fantasies," read one ad in the spring of 2007 from a supposed eighteen-year-old named Lushes in Atlantic City. "I'm lonely and need company." In fact, she was a fourteen-year-old from Allentown, Pennsylvania, lured, along with her sixteen-year-old sister, by a pimp from Pleasantville named Casson Coward and his partner, Kevin Mayfield. (The two were eventually arrested and jailed for lengthy prison terms after an investigation by Dan Garrabrant's FBI team in Atlantic City.)

Jill, the Las Vegas teen eventually rescued by vice cops Stanton and Fieselman, saw firsthand the popularity of Web prostitution across the country. In California, one of her pimps had her post her picture on Craigslist, charging two hundred dollars "for my complete service."

Within minutes the phone starting ringing. He then set up "appoint-ments" for her at the Executive Inn near the San Jose airport, and men kept filing in. "I don't remember how many people I saw that day," says Jill. When the pimp flew her to Boston to build up more Craigslist business there, she made eighteen hundred dollars for him in a single day.

The ease with which pimps were exploiting the Web enraged police, perhaps none more than Cook County sheriff Tom Dart. He was the top lawman in the second most populous county in the country (after only Los Angeles), a sprawling jurisdiction that included Chicago and 40 percent of the Illinois population. He no doubt had his hands full coping with the gang violence, drug busts, and the usual illegal may-hem that plagued the real world in Cook County, but Dart had made it his mission to go after what he saw as a burgeoning crime in the virtual world. In July 2007, his office arrested sixty people who adver-tised on Craigslist on prostitution charges. A year later, in June 2008, another seventy-six men and women were nabbed as undercover offi-cers made "dates" through the Craigslist's "erotic services" section. "Craigslist is the single largest source of prostitution in the nation," the blunt-talking sheriff told reporters.

That month Craigslist began posting a notice on its Web site warning users that human trafficking and child exploitation would be reported to police. But Dart and others dismissed the move as cos-metic. Then in November, in a deal with attorneys general from forty states, the company announced it would start charging a small fee for the "erotic services" ads and oblige advertisers to use a credit card for payment. In theory that could help the company or authorities track down users, but critics pointed out that Craigslist had a staff of less than fifty to monitor millions of ads and nothing stopped criminals from using stolen credit cards.

Sheriff Dart was unimpressed with Craigslist's claims that it was helping law enforcement. "Missing children, runaways, abused women, and women trafficked in from foreign countries are routinely forced to have sex with strangers because they're being pimped on Craigslist," he said at a news conference in March 2009 as he announced he was suing the company in federal court to get them to remove its "erotic services" section. His lawsuit cited an FBI operation that uncovered a trafficking ring with prostituted children in which pimps posted over 2,800 advertisements on the Web site. "It's abundantly clear what's going on with Craigslist and what's being advertised," the sheriff said. "All I'm asking them to do is either monitor it appropriately or stop it, and they have no interest in doing either."

Five weeks later a murder in Boston did even more damage to Craigslist than Dart's verbal and legal assaults. Julissa Brissman, a twenty-six-year-old from New York, had advertised herself as an "exotic masseuse" on Craigslist. When she met her client in a room at the Marriott Copley Hotel in Boston on April 14, 2009, she had no idea he would be the last person she would ever see. Philip Markoff, a former medical student, was arrested after Brissman's bloodied corpse was discovered in the room. He pleaded not guilty but was nonetheless dubbed the Craigslist Killer after it emerged he had allegedly robbed another woman and assaulted a third victim he met online. Markoff was set to stand trial on charges of first-degree murder, but in August 2010 he committed suicide in his jail cell by putting a plastic bag over his head.

The media firestorm that ensued forced Craigslist to buckle yet again. On May 13, 2009, the company announced it was closing its "erotic services" and replacing it with an adult section that, it vowed, would be closely watched by employees for any illegal activity. But the criticism—and criminal charges—showed no signs of dying down. A week later, seven alleged members of a prostitution ring who operated through classified ads on the Web site were arrested in New York. "Until Craigslist gets serious about putting real protections in place, it will continue to be an environment where criminal operations thrive with impunity," said New York State attorney general Andrew Cuomo. The only good news for the battered company came in the fall, when a federal judge in Chicago threw out Sheriff Tom Dart's lawsuit, arguing that the Web users who posted the ads, not Craigslist, were responsible for any illegal prostitution services sold through the site. Indeed, the Communications Decency Act of 1996 largely absolved Web site owners from any responsibility for content posted by users.

Craigslist maintained all along it had done nothing wrong. "Like the yellow pages, newspapers, and virtually every other classified service, we provide a separate category for legal erotic services to advertise," it said on its Web page, noting that all profits from the sex advertisements go to charity.

"I would not accept money from Craigslist," Rachel Lloyd told the *New York Times*, which reported that it was far from clear how and when Craigslist would hand out any of its cash to charities. "That money has come from pimps and traffickers who have sold many of the girls who will then walk into my door."

In May 2010, Lloyd sent an open letter to Craigslist CEO Jim Buckmaster, telling him of an eleven-year-old girl GEMS had rescued: she had been sold through his Web site as "HOT N SEXXY FOR U," along with her fourteen-year-old and sixteen-year-old sisters. Buckmaster responded by insisting his company was doing everything it could to stop the "unspeakable crime" of child prostitution.

But the pressure kept mounting. In July, a coalition of eighty-five human rights and antitrafficking groups staged a noisy protest outside Craigslist headquarters in San Francisco. "By providing traffickers and johns with a virtual red light district, Craigslist is aiding, abetting, and enormously profiting from sex trafficking," said one of the organizers, Norma Ramos, executive director of the Coalition Against Trafficking in Women (CATW).

And those profits were skyrocketing. The Advanced Interactive Media Group reported that Craigslist would increase its revenue 22 percent in 2010, largely thanks to a $36.3 million boost in its sex ad income. It didn't help Craigslist's image when those earnings projections came out shortly after the FBI arrested more than a dozen members of the Gambino Mafia crime family on multiple charges, including prostituting girls between the ages of fifteen and nineteen on Craigslist.

"The Craigslist brothel business seems booming—belying its promise to fight prostitution," said Connecticut attorney general Richard

Blumenthal, who, along with top law officials from sixteen other states, sent a letter to Craigslist in August 2010 demanding the company put an end to "the scourge of illegal prostitution, and the suffering of the women and children" being facilitated on its Web site.

In September, the Web company seemed to buckle, blocking its "adult services" ads with a black CENSORED box and eventually announcing it was permanently shutting down the sex-related advertising section of its sites.

Activists were proud they had won the battle but knew the Web remained an increasingly popular and more dangerous venue for sex trafficking. "On the street there was always a measure of protection in numbers, as the girls would look out for each other," says Vednita Carter of Breaking Free. "But on the Internet, they're isolated. Alone. They have no one to talk to but their pimp and the clients.

"It's a lot more dangerous for them."

■ ■ ■

THE INTERNET not only made it easier for pimps to sell girls; it made it a lot more convenient for anonymous johns to buy them. Yet law enforcement has been remarkably reluctant to crack down on the men who purchase sex, be it on the dark corners of the Internet or the street corners of almost every American city.

When the vice squad in Woburn, Massachusetts, made a sweep of local hotels in early 2008, it arrested several women but let their customers go. "It's embarrassing enough for them" is how one police detective explained his empathy for the johns to the media. "We're just trying to stop the problem, not create them."

As if the problem could be solved without stopping the men who help cause it in the first place. If even the low estimate of three hundred thousand children caught up in commercial sexual exploitation is accurate, given the frequency of the "tricks" they have to turn every week there must be millions of johns paying for sex with underage victims every year. Yet if pimps are often glorified in popular culture and prostitutes scorned, johns seem to benefit from public sympathy, if not pity.

"A lot of people think they are lonely guys and whatever happens behind closed doors is consensual and none of our business," says Donna M. Hughes, who heads the Women's Studies Program at the University of Rhode Island and has carried out extensive research on prostitution and trafficking. "But they aren't pathetic, lonely guys."

That was borne out by extensive interviews with 113 men who bought sex in the Chicago area carried out by Rachel Durchslag and the Chicago Alliance Against Sexual Exploitation (CAASE). The majority were married or in a stable relationship; about 79 percent had some college education or a college degree; 62 percent made more than forty thousand dollars a year.

What they craved was not just sex but control, power, and freedom to do as they wanted. Forty-three percent of johns interviewed by CAASE stated that "if the man pays the women for sex, she should do anything he asks." And the consequence of that attitude was often violence. Eighty percent of the women Donna Hughes surveyed in one study said they were physically assaulted by their clients; 86 percent were sexually assaulted.

The police in Woburn and other cities who turned a blind eye to the men buying sex with minors had it backward: the johns generate the demand for young girls; the girls do not create the johns. "If there's a buyer, there has to be a product," insists Linda Smith, the founding president of Shared Hope, the organization dedicated to fighting human sex trafficking. "If we all agree that selling a child or buying a child is wrong, then why is there is no attempt to solve the demand side?"

Smith was driven to create her organization when, as a congresswoman from Washington State, she visited some of the world's worst brothels near Mumbai, India. Her organization went on to set up "villages of hope" for children rescued from trafficking in several countries, including India, South Africa, and Jamaica. But, unlike other antitrafficking groups that only looked abroad, Shared Hope also lobbied for tougher laws and investigated the state of child prostitution in several major cities in America.

In a searing report funded by the U.S. Department of State on the trafficking business, Shared Hope concluded that "demand for younger girls is increasing" because children "present the vision of innocence and vulnerability sought by buyers." But those buyers were largely escaping punishment. "We have found that a man buying a child for sex is rarely arrested," says Smith. "When arrested, rarely is he sentenced to the tough penalties deserving of a child rapist."

The statistics bear that out. In 2005, a congressional survey found that for every six women arrested in New York City for commercial sex acts, only one male purchaser was charged. In Boston, the gap was even greater, at eleven to one. In Chicago, 89 percent of the prostitution arrests in one heavy crime area were of women, while only 10 percent were of johns.

In lieu of jail time, more than forty cities across the country offered "john schools" for men arrested for soliciting. To avoid criminal prosecution, the men paid a fine and agreed to attend what was usually a daylong session of education and exposure to the real human toll of their actions. Though sometimes derided by critics as get-out-of-jail-free cards that offered nothing more than a vocal slap on the wrist, the john schools could be powerful wake-up calls, especially when run by dedicated community activists and no-nonsense cops. Kathleen Mitchell through her DIGNITY program in Phoenix, Vednita Carter of Breaking Free in St. Paul, and law enforcement professionals like Byron Fassett in Dallas and the FBI's Dan Garrabrant in Atlantic City were all very adept in shaking up the men obliged to attend the john schools. They brought in young women who had survived the trafficking business to give disturbing testimonials of what it felt like to be at the other end of the transaction the men cared little about. A study done for the Department of Justice in 2008 looked at the arrest records of 198 men and found that those who completed a serious john school were 30 percent less likely to reoffend than men who did not attend such a program.

If reeducation did not work, there was always shaming. City police in Springfield, Massachusetts, started sending the local media the names and pictures of men arrested for soliciting. Minneapolis police went one step further. The department had a Web page with mug shots of convicted johns. On the interstate highway that cuts through the Twin Cities, the police posted a large, unnerving message on an electronic billboard: PICKING UP A PROSTITUTE? YOUR PHOTO WILL BE POSTED ONLINE. Below the warning was the easy-to-remember Web site of shame: www.JohnsPics.org.

Perhaps no city went further than Atlanta in confronting child prostitution and the men who encourage it. A survey done by the Atlanta Women's Foundation and the Juvenile Justice Fund in May 2008 found that 272 girls in the city were exploited on the streets or over the Internet every month—more girls harmed by prostitution in one month, they noted, than were killed in car accidents in a year. Mayor Shirley Franklin had the courage to publicly disclose that she had been sexually abused at the age of ten by the father of a girlfriend. "This can happen to anyone," she told the media when she unveiled her city's "Dear John" campaign. "Not only can it happen; it does happen to a lot of children."

Franklin put her words and face at the center of a very public education campaign that used posters, videos, and advertisements to send a direct message to the clients of the child sex industry:

> Dear John:
> You have been abusing our kids, prostituting them, and throwing them on the street when you're done. When you buy sex from our kids, you hurt them, you hurt our families, and you hurt our city.
> It's over John.
> No more.
> Not in Our City.

Still, for all the benefits of naming and shaming campaigns, there remained the glaring inequality that saw large numbers of women yet few men going to jail for the crime of prostitution. Charges against johns, much less convictions, were rare and largely limited to city or state courts where the sentences were light. On the federal level, the Trafficking Victims Protection Act made it a serious felony to engage in "the recruitment, harboring, transportation, provision, or obtaining of a person for the purpose of a commercial sex act." It was the word "obtaining" that gave authorities the clout to go after the men who buy children, not just the pimps who harbor, transport, and provide them.

But for nine years since the law was enacted in 2000, there had not been a single attempt to prosecute a john under federal trafficking statutes. There were multiple excuses: it was not a priority; it was difficult to gather evidence; it was likely some jurors might be reluctant to convict men who were doing what society has tolerated for centuries and what no doubt some male jurors themselves had done.

Cynthia Cordes wasn't buying any of that. An aggressive prosecutor who had joined the U.S. attorney's office for the western district of Missouri in 2004, her specialty was human trafficking and child exploitation. Her other specialty was winning: she had secured convictions in every one of her federal prosecutions. In the spring of 2006, her office set up the Human Trafficking Rescue Project, a joint task force with local, state, and federal law enforcement—not without some misgivings on the part of skeptical police officers and prosecutors. This was Kansas City, after all, not New York or Vegas. "I heard a lot of people say, 'I don't think there is human trafficking here,'" says Cordes. "But I felt that's just because we were not looking for it."

She was right. In the following three years, the task force uncovered seven major cases of trafficking and prosecuted seventeen defendants. Cordes proved to be an innovative prosecutor. The law usually required some kind of interstate activity to occur before federal antitrafficking statutes—and the heftier penalties that come with them—could kick in, though the definition was wide enough to include everything from the pimp's making out-of-state cell phones to providing condoms. But in the task force's first trafficking case, the pimp never used cell phones and did not even supply condoms to the two twelve-year-olds and the fourteen-year-old he was running on the streets.

Cordes was stuck, but not for long. She found an old case in which the Supreme Court had ruled farmers colluding to set the price of wheat in one state could be charged federally, because such price-fixing has an influence across state borders as well. She made the case that fixing the price of selling girls on the street was the same thing—

and the judge agreed. Her innovative legal theory helped set a precedent for federal prosecutions across the country. Equally important, the pimp got nine years.

Cordes was not satisfied. The joint police task force was busting pimps and rescuing children, but the customers eager to pay for young prostituted girls were getting away. "These guys were getting a pass," says Cordes, "and it bothered me."

Late in 2008, she asked police to find prosecutable cases against johns. But they were slow in coming. Cordes understood some of the challenges. Many of the men were onetime customers—the tourists, traveling businessmen, or wayward husbands from across town—and not regular clients. The pimps were hardly willing to identify the regular customers they did know, and the girls were not in a position to remember many details about the never-ending lineup of men they were forced to serve. In any case, minors forced into prostitution were not likely to go running to the police to report on their johns, much less testify against them. Even if the police arrested a john, proving he knew a girl was under eighteen could be problematic, as a pimp often dresses a girl in clothes and makeup to make her look like an adult.

Cordes was frustrated with the slow pace of building strong cases against the buyers. "I wasn't very patient about it," she admits. So she came up with a plan that she hoped would overcome a lot of the obstacles: a sting operation.

They called it Operation Guardian Angel. Working with the Special Victims Unit of the Independence, Missouri, police and the FBI, Cordes helped set up a clever undercover ruse. In January 2009 and again in March, the police placed ads on Craigslist and in a local magazine. Replete with spelling mistakes to add authenticity, the ads left little to the imagination:

> YOUNG FUN!!! While there mommas away these girls will play.
> My girlfriend is out of town her daughters are ready to play with
> you. Be the first for thes little girls. $young$$younger$$$youngest.

"We intentionally made them explicit so that a defendant couldn't say that he clicked on an ad thinking it was an adult being offered," Cordes says. "We wanted to make it clear this would be somebody looking for a minor."

The team drew up several versions of the ads to run consecutively, expecting the provocative solicitations would be taken down by a newly chastened Craigslist that had promised to clean up its act.

"They never took them down," says Cordes. "I was just shocked."

She was equally shocked by the response. With minutes men started responding; there were hundreds of queries in all.

"Sadly, the sting was easier than I thought," she says. "On the one hand, you want your undercover operation to be successful. But on the other hand, there was a part of me that hoped that this whole thing would fail and that no one would respond to the ads. It was very disheartening to see what was really going on."

Undercover cops began fielding the requests by e-mail and phone, asking the men what age they preferred for the prostituted children they were paying for. Prospective clients were given directions to a house in the south end of Kansas City that had children's toys scattered in the front yard—and plenty of police audio- and video-recording equipment hidden everywhere else. In the end, seven men went every step of the way from the initial contact e-mails and phone negotiations over prices to showing up at the door. Once the clients paid cash for what they thought would be a prostituted child, they were arrested.

The sting netted a cross section of the all-too-ordinary men who prey on children for sex, from an insurance executive and a car dealership's finance manager to a truck driver and a U.S. Navy recruiter. According to court papers, the thirty-two-year-old navy man allegedly used his government-owned computer and cell phone to arrange the transaction and was decked out in uniform when he knocked on the door. He paid sixty dollars to have sex with an eleven-year-old girl and threw in an extra twenty dollars for the privilege of not using a condom.

The elaborate ruse gave the prosecutor, Cordes, plenty of electronic evidence and e-mail records to build a solid case of attempted interstate trafficking of children. With the facts not in dispute, defense lawyers were left to argue that the sting was entrapment and "outrageous government conduct." They insisted that the federal antitrafficking statutes were not designed to target customers. But the judge threw out the motions, noting that "innovation and creativity" on the part of prosecutors was not a defense for criminal conduct.

Cordes took that as a compliment. She was even more pleased when all seven defendants eventually pleaded guilty. Almost all of them got sentences ranging from ten to fifteen years, depending on whether they had asked for sex with a girl under fourteen years of age or older. Cordes's perfect score—her 100 percent conviction rate—was preserved.

More important, her team had secured the nation's first-ever charges under the Trafficking Victims Protection Act against alleged customers of child prostitution. It had been a long time coming, but finally, the message was getting out: buying children for sex will buy you a lot of time behind bars in a federal prison. Word of Cordes's success spread. There were inquiries from other jurisdictions eager to copy the idea from as far away as Arizona and South Dakota.

"We had chosen the name Guardian Angel for a reason, because we are protecting children," explains Cordes. "The men who responded to those ads and showed up at that house would be abusing a real child that night if they had not fallen for our sting."

That's why the Kansas City team planned a new series of undercover operations in 2010.

■ ■ ■

FOR SOME people, there was not too much prostitution in America but too little. Or at least too little legalized prostitution.

Las Vegas mayor Oscar Goodman, for one, had floated the idea of extending some form of the sanctioned brothel system that existed elsewhere in Nevada to his city. In 2007, Goodman told *New York Times* columnist Bob Herbert that a series of "magnificent brothels" could bring "tremendous" benefits to Vegas. Herbert, who pointed out that before becoming mayor, Goodman—as a criminal attorney—had defended some of the city's best-known mobsters, slammed Vegas for its "systematic, institutionalized degradation" of women. Goodman was not happy with the *Times* writer. "I'll take a baseball bat and break his head if he ever comes here," he shot back in the local press.

In January 2009, at one of his weekly news conferences, the mayor brought up his pet project yet again. While conceding there were legitimate moral objections to prostitution, he stressed there were also good reasons to regulate the trade. "I've met with folks from that industry who make a very compelling argument that it could generate $200 million a year in tax dollars and that would buy a lot of textbooks, pay for a lot of teachers," he said. He suggested such a regime could also be beneficial to the women themselves, once brothel owners set up a "program for employees where they could get education, they could receive child care instead of leaving their kids in a latchkey situation, classes on self-esteem, those kinds of things."*

Though few others tried to make brothels sound like Club Med with daycare, Goodman was not alone in promoting legalization of prostitution as a plus for women. Given the harsh treatment women often face at the hands of their pimps and the demonstrable prejudice of the law in punishing women and not their exploiters, it was understandable that some feminist organizations and sex workers rights groups saw decriminalizing prostitution as a solution. Legalizing the sex trade, they argued, would bring it out of the shadows and free women of all ages from fear of their pimps and police. It would erase the stigma of the trade, they said, and end the degradation of its willing practitioners. One of the loudest voices for legalization came from COYOTE (Call Off Your Tired Ethics), which went so far as to call for the laws against pimping to be replaced with "labor laws dealing with working conditions in... managed prostitution businesses."

---

* Instead of talking to "folks from the industry" the mayor would have done better to read the extensive study by Melissa Farley, *Prostitution & Trafficking in Nevada*. The founder of the Prostitute Research and Education Foundation uncovered violence, coercion, and abuse in her investigation. "Wherever a thriving sex industry exists, children as well as adults are sexually exploited in prostitution," she warned.

As positive examples abroad, advocates of legalizing the sex trade point to the Netherlands, where prostitution has been regulated for some time, and, more recently, to New Zealand, where since 2009 brothels can operate once they are court registered and certified and up to four women can set up a "collective" to sell their services.

But many other activists and academics insisted that decriminalizing prostitution would only make things worse, especially for its youngest victims. There was a subtle but important distinction between the two positions. Rachel Lloyd and other leaders were fighting hard to decriminalize the actions and behavior of children forced into prostitution; they did not want young girls to be treated like criminals. But that was quite different from legalizing the entire sex trafficking business.

"Prostitution is not a sin, it is a social injustice," said Norma Ramos of the Coalition Against Trafficking in Women, in a powerful polemic in the *New York Times*. "Legalization leads to an expansion of the sexploitation industry and protects no one. You don't tax a human rights abuse; you abolish it."

Instead, Ramos and other antitrafficking advocates push for what they call a human rights approach as practiced in Sweden: protect the women, but go after the real criminal. In 1999 Sweden made it legal to sell your own body for sex but criminalized selling someone else's body or buying sex. Instead of being viewed with contempt, the trafficked women in Sweden are treated as the victims they are. Prostitution, says the Swedish government, "is officially acknowledged as a form of exploitation of women and children." Sweden set up drug abuse programs and other services to encourage women to leave the business. According to one survey, the law cut in half the number of women forced to prostitute themselves on the street and slashed the number of customers by 80 percent.

Iceland and Norway soon followed Sweden's example. Under a new law that went into effect in 2009, Norwegians caught paying for sex face a stiff fine or six months in jail—and up to three years in prison if their victims are children. But the women involved in the trade get access to free education as well as drug and alcohol recovery programs.

It is the reverse of what happens in America, where more often than not the woman lands in jail while her pimp and the john walk away.

■ ■ ■

BACK IN the United States, the debate over legalizing prostitution came to a head in 2009 in—of all places—Rhode Island. Most Americans associate legal brothels with freewheeling Nevada, not the nation's smallest state. Few realize that, while prostitution is legal in only a few parts of Nevada, indoor prostitution was sanctioned by law throughout Rhode Island for close to three decades.

In the late 1970s, Rhode Island was facing a double-barreled assault on its prostitution laws. On one front, residents in the West End of Providence were frustrated not only with the increase in the sex trade on their streets but also with the slow judicial process. Charged as a felony, prostitution cases—if they ever made it to court—were subject to lengthy trials and appeals. Meanwhile, the prostitutes' rights group COYOTE had brought a sex discrimination lawsuit against the state, arguing that criminalizing prostitution between consenting adults violated their right to privacy and was enforced unfairly because many more women than men were arrested.

In May 1980, the state's General Assembly passed a law that reduced street prostitution from a felony to a misdemeanor for loitering; the dubious logic was that this would lead to simpler and speedier judicial remedies. Then, in a nod to the pending COYOTE legal case, the lawmakers in effect also made prostitution legal as long as it was carried out indoors.

"If prostitution was occurring indoors, it was invisible to the community," wrote Melanie Shapiro in her definitive study of the legal battle, an honors thesis under the direction of the University of Rhode Island's Donna Hughes.

But it didn't stay invisible. The state went from four strip clubs in the 1990s to forty-one known establishments that offered prostitution a decade later. Twenty prostitution venues opened up between 2003 and 2008 and then ten more in 2009 alone.

"What happened was that progressively the bottom had fallen out of any kind of police response to the problem," says Hughes, who watched with dismay as prostitution exploded in her own backyard. Police could arrest people on the street for loitering, but they could not pursue any investigations against pimps, johns, or women inside any home, hotel, or business because prostitution indoors was not against the law. They tried to go after so-called massage parlors for operating without a permit to carry out massages, but then business owners got away from any licensing requirements by simply changing the status of their operations to "spas." Young girls, many from nearby Massachusetts, were being trafficked in to service the booming demand as strip clubs and brothels expanded. In June 2009, a sixteen-year-old Boston girl was found in an apartment "bleeding and incoherent" by a South Providence police officer, her purse filled with condoms. She told police she had been punched in the face by her forty-year-old "boyfriend," an escaped convict who had forced her to work at a local strip club.

For Hughes, Rhode Island was graphic evidence of what happens when prostitution is legalized. This was not an academic debate for her. She had seen the suffering caused by sexual violence when she volunteered at a rape crisis and domestic abuse center in the 1980s while working on her own doctoral thesis. "You get to see the real pain, the real harm that is being done," she says. "It is not an abstract argument. It's not a theory. You're dealing with concrete damage that has been done to people, and that was the underlying motivation of my work."

As an academic and as an activist, Hughes had campaigned against sex trafficking around the world. Now it was time to try to make things right at home. Along with her graduate student Melanie Shapiro and a handful of other volunteers, she set up an informal alliance called Citizens Against Trafficking (CAT). With no budget and a simple Web site, they kept up a relentless barrage of advocacy and education to mobilize public opinion and force the state legislature to change the laws.

It was not going to be easy. They faced a well-financed sex industry—according to the *Providence Journal*, the ten most prominent strip clubs reported $11.1 million in sales in 2008—that had the clout to hire a former senator and the husband of a state Supreme Court justice as its chief lobbyist. Several powerful politicians opposed any toughening of the laws against prostitution. If anything, they pushed the other way; at one point, the Senate proposed a bill that would have repealed all antipimping offenses in the law.

But Hughes and her small band of concerned citizens kept up the pressure. In one CAT newsletter, Shapiro documented the violent crime that accompanied the sex industry's expansion into the state: Jeffrey Mailhot, called the Rhode Island Ripper, a regular patron at a popular strip club who killed three prostituted women between 2003 and 2004; Philip Markoff, the infamous Craigslist Killer, who prior to his arrest for that murder had assaulted a Rhode Island stripper; Troy Friggs, a local pimp convicted of murder after he sent out a young woman to work the streets for him and then beat her two-year-old son to death. In another bulletin, Shapiro and Hughes listed all the known brothels in Rhode Island by Senate district, prompting voters to complain to their elected officials. "Without effective law enforcement, the sex industry is expanding rapidly, creating a haven for sex traffickers," warned Hughes in one of her many online opinion pieces. "Far from a libertarian utopia, decriminalizing prostitution has fostered coercion, exploitation, and abuse."

Slowly, CAT and other antitrafficking groups built up the momentum for change. There were rallies, church meetings, petitions, and legislative hearings. There was embarrassing national media attention from CNN and Fox News when it came to light that teenagers could perform at strip clubs in Rhode Island provided they were sixteen, had work permits, and got home by 11:30 P.M. on school nights.

One determined politician, State Representative Joanne Giannini, kept up a relentless battle to get decent laws enacted. Finally, in November 2009, the state assembly passed three pieces of legislation that pushed Rhode Island from an embarrassing model to an exemplary one in terms of handling sex trafficking. Promoting prostitution—indoors and outdoors—was once more made illegal in the state. Pimps and landlords who knowingly allowed prostitution on their property would face one to five years in jail and fines up to five thousand dollars for the first offense, with the punishment for subsequent offences rising to ten years behind bars and a ten-thousand-dollar fine. Minors were banned from working in "adult entertainment" businesses under any circumstances.

But the new law also went further than legislation in most other states in trying to protect rather than penalize the women caught up in the sex trade. The package enabled the prosecution of sex trafficking of minors without needing to prove that "coercion" was used. It also prohibited the victims of sex trafficking from being convicted of prostitution offenses—an important "affirmative defense" as Donna Hughes called it, a provision that she had fought hard to include in the new laws.

"The next step is that the citizens have to make sure there is political will to enforce the law," a triumphant Hughes told reporters. "We will see the effects of this bill when they start arresting the sex predators, the pimps, traffickers, and 'johns.'"

That's the way it always has been. A law is only as good as the people behind it—the police, the prosecutors, and the public.

■ ■ ■

IT WAS not the kind of crowd the tourists in Las Vegas were expecting to see. No flashy dressers, skimpily dressed starlets, or celebrities stepping out of stretch limos. Instead, on a warm Friday evening in June 2009, one hundred protestors sang prayers, chanted slogans, and carried signs that said NOT IN OUR CITY and END DEMAND.

They were marching in one of several rallies Shared Hope had organized in cities across the country that serve as hubs for sex trafficking. In a direct jab at the culture of tolerance toward johns, several placards screamed out provocatively: DO YOU KNOW WHERE YOUR HUSBAND IS?

Linda Smith vowed to keep on marching and campaigning until America woke up to the trafficking nightmare going on to its own girls, on its own streets. In her home state of Washington, a new law meant johns—who previously got away with small fines and a few weeks in jail at most—now faced a five-thousand-dollar penalty and as much as two to twelve years in jail.

Smith compared the movement today to efforts a few decades earlier to bring to light another form of abuse that was also shrouded in silence, shame, and public ignorance: domestic violence.

"Back then, we made sure that people knew what was happening in families, behind closed doors, to wives and mothers and children," she says. "Today, we're trying to bring the same attention to these girls.

"As long as people don't know, they don't cry out for change."

15

Finding Their Own Voice

WHATEVER LAWS and reforms were being tested in the courts or debated by politicians, in the end child prostitution was a crime that would have to be solved where it started—in the streets.

A handful of activist leaders across the country, often former prostitutes themselves, were trying to make a difference where the young girls were being recruited in the first place. Kathleen Mitchell with DIGNITY in Phoenix, Vednita Carter of Breaking Free in St. Paul, and Rachel Lloyd and her GEMS team in New York were going where the cops and courts could not. They were using street outreach patrols, diversion programs to replace prison time, intensive group therapy sessions, and long-term housing to offer prostituted women a hand and a hope.

It was painstaking and often frustrating work trying to help one girl at a time and watching too many others slip through the cracks. But they kept on going and kept on building on their successes. Because it wasn't about rescuing helpless lost souls. It was about nurturing and empowering young girls.

■ ■ ■

ON THE streets of Phoenix, the women walking the tracks call it the Ho Van; the DIGNITY workers who ride in it are nicknamed Captain Save-a-Ho.

The scratched and dented white Toyota looks like many of the other vehicles cruising the roads on this hot April night in Phoenix. By midnight, it is still sixty-nine degrees and business is brisk. The only indication of the van's special mission is a red bumper sticker with a quote from Pope Paul VI: IF YOU WANT PEACE, FIGHT FOR JUSTICE.

Inside the van, two women prepare for another long night of outreach work through the underbelly of the city. Michelle is barely five feet tall, with short black hair. "But I stand much taller in my attitude," she is quick to note. Cindy has shoulder-length brown hair and sports a pair of red-framed glasses. Both women are survivors, out of the life and sober for some years now. Both wear yellow T-shirts with the DIGNITY emblem that Kathleen Mitchell created a decade ago: a starfish and the motto "It matters to this one," inspired by the story of the young girl who tried to rescue every starfish she found on the beach.

Mitchell saw her work blossom into a citywide program run by Catholic Charities that reached hundreds of women. Though a grandmother now and retired, Mitchell still made regular visits to local juvenile detention centers and jails until her last days on the job to talk to the young girls about her own struggle for redemption and respect.

"When you started talking about prostitution, their ears would prick up," she says. But in that kind of public group setting, only a few girls would overcome their shame and admit that they had been selling their bodies. "Afterwards, though, others would run back to their cells and you could hear them sobbing hysterically," Mitchell says. "I would hold many a young kid and rock them until they were through crying."

"It's going to be OK," she would tell the girl in her arms. "This isn't something you have to do. When you get out of here, we're here for you."

To make sure help is there for hundreds of other girls and young women, the DIGNITY van patrols the streets four nights a week, sometimes racking up more than a hundred miles a shift as the team crisscrosses the sprawling Phoenix cityscape. Cindy and Michelle stock the van with small bags of food that include a can of Chef Boyardee, a cup of fruit salad, and some Pringles, along with health and sanitary products and leaflets with information about the DIGNITY program.

For their own safety and that of the girls, they avoid approaching any women if their pimps or johns are nearby.

At the corner of Fifty-first and McDowell they spot a petite and very pretty girl with long braided hair and a small gold stud in her right nostril. It's not just the late hour that gives her away but also her attire, a tight shirt and blue-checkered shorts not much bigger than a belt. Michelle rolls down the window to introduce herself as the DIGNITY van pulls up alongside the girl.

"What's your name?" Michelle asks breezily.

"Chocolate," the girl replies with a cautious smile. She says she just got into town from Riverside, California. She gives her age as twenty, but there is a telltale hesitation before she answers.

Michelle explains what DIGNITY is all about. "A lot of the staff are survivors ourselves, so we know what it is like trying to get out," she says. "You end up with nothing. You walk out with exactly what you walked in with—and that's absolutely nothing."

Chocolate, still too fresh in the game to even contemplate getting out, nods politely.

"If and when you decide this is not your life's goal, call us," Michelle presses on and hands her the literature on DIGNITY. "This is a number you can call twenty-four hours a day. Make sure you hide this because if your man finds it, he's going to take it and rip it up. So memorize this number right here, please."

Chocolate seems genuinely touched that someone would even care that much about her. "I'm not ready to get out, but thank you for sharing this with me," she shouts as she walks away into the noisy traffic.

"I know," yells Michelle. "When you *are* ready, call us."

Michelle is used to resistance from the young women just starting out on the tracks. "They've still bought into the life," she says. "They're still in love with their pimp." At the Jimmy Jack fast-food joint on West Van Buren, two skimpily dressed teenagers ignore the DIGNITY van as they rush to the takeout window. But a withered woman approaches Cindy's rolled-down window. Roxanne says she is forty-eight, but her stringy brown hair, pallid eyes, and sunken cheeks make her look at least a decade older. She is the face of what the young girls will become if they don't get out in time.

"I've been trying to get out," Roxanne says. "I do heroin."

"We know how hard it is," Cindy acknowledges as she explains DIGNITY's housing and rehab program. "If you go to detox and get sober, we'll come pick you up."

Roxanne gratefully takes the food and water the DIGNITY women offer, plus a bus pass. "I will be calling you sometime," she says as she shuffles away under the neon fast-food sign.

Before the night is out, Michelle and Cindy will come across a dozen women. Some are veterans like Roxanne, with wasted bodies and weathered faces. Feather and Chastity—one Native American, the other white, both in their forties with missing teeth and drug-scarred veins along their arms—wave at the white van they know all too well. Another woman, a corpulent African American in her thirties, claims she is just walking to her boyfriend's house but promises to pass on the DIGNITY literature to "some friends I know" who might need it. As she walks away, she steals a glance at the pamphlet and keeps reading.

The young girls on the street, on the other hand, remain more suspicious and standoffish. Two of them refuse to stop for the van as they scurry across a parking lot, dragging a small suitcase on wheels behind them. Another teen in a miniskirt and maxi makeup blurts out defensively, "I'm not a prostitute!" before the DIGNITY women even have a chance to introduce themselves, much less explain who their program is trying to help.

At 10:54 P.M., back on the corner of Fifty-first and McDowell, Cindy and Michelle catch sight of Chocolate crossing the street. It has been ninety minutes since their encounter, but already she looks tired and worn. They calculate the teenager has had time to turn at least three tricks.

Their last stop that night is on an isolated stretch of Van Buren. Chrissie, a girl they recognize from previous patrols, stands listlessly on the sidewalk. She gives her age as twenty-one but looks no older than seventeen, with short blond hair, blue shorts cut just below the knees, and a clean white T-shirt. Her face twitches constantly, the unmistakable sign of a meth habit. She smiles wanly as she takes the food and water.

Then she walks away as the headlights of the next car break through the dark of the Phoenix night.

■ ■ ■

IF ANY of the women Michelle and Cindy meet that night get arrested, they might have a chance of avoiding jail if they opt for a special diversion program DIGNITY has set up in cooperation with the City of Phoenix prosecutor's office.

"I am a former prostitute, a former drug addict," Lois Lucas, one of the program's caseworkers, tells the women who sign up. "I have been to jail. I have made a lot of bad choices. This program helped me change my life."

Maybe, she hopes, it will change some of their lives.

The Diversion program is not a permanent get-out-of-jail-free card. It is only offered on the first or second arrest; a third prostitution bust in Phoenix leads to automatic jail time. Not that Lucas thinks that jail would be a bad thing for some of the women. She makes it clear from the start that she wants to challenge the women, not coddle them. "I don't like to see people go to jail," she says. "But I didn't die in jail. Sometimes that is what you need, to be locked up repeatedly before you decide that you don't want to do this anymore."

For about ten weeks, the women attend two sessions a week. The first focuses on addiction, not just to drugs but to money and men; the second emphasizes life skills. Then the women also have to go through an intensive thirty-six hours of courses in a single week. Health professionals come in to explain sexually transmitted diseases and offer free testing. Prosecutors talk about the law, vice cops give graphic examples of abuse and violence, and survivors and DIGNITY graduates come back to offer inspiration and a way out.

It's those peers—the ones like Lois Lucas who have made it out—who form the core of the program, says Diversion coordinator Cathy Bauer. "We're trying to instill hope," she says. "We're trying to help the women to believe, perhaps for the first time, that they can accomplish the changes they want to make in their lives."

A woman who "graduates" from the Diversion program gets her arrest taken off the books. But caseworker Lucas always hopes that for those participants who stick through it the program will mean more than simply wiping their records clean. "While you are in this program, you are going to learn a lot about yourself and we are going to plant a seed," she tells them. "What happens is up to you. Your choice."

It took Imogene a decade to make the right choice, but the seed DIGNITY planted finally helped turn her life around. She grew up in a rough section of Phoenix, the kind of neighborhood where gangbangers and dope dealers ruled the streets, where geography and class played as much of a role in pushing a young girl into prostitution as anything else. "I have known girls who have been beaten in front of homes with water hoses," she says. "They've been pistol-whipped. Thrown out of windows." Imogene's mother, a single parent who worked long hours as a nurse, had no money to pay a babysitter to care for her three children when they were not in school. "I had to put them in God's hands," her mother says.

That wasn't enough to protect Imogene from an uncle who abused her when she was only six. The frightened girl kept the abuse secret from her mother for years. At thirteen, an older cousin lured her to some local pimps who drugged her and kept her in a room for two days as clients filed in. All she remembers is the door opening and closing as she lay on the bed in a stupor. "They ran a train on me," she says.

By her late teens, Imogene was an accomplished street survivor. "I was young and fast, and I liked my little clothes," she admits. She managed to escape an arrest for prostitution until she was nineteen. That run-in with the law gave her a first chance at the DIGNITY Diversion program, but she blew it and never completed the course. Instead she headed for more trouble. She had four children by the time she was in her early twenties, all by different fathers. A burglary conviction for tying up a trick and stealing his money earned her several years in a California jail, leaving her mother stuck with raising the grandchildren. Once out of prison, Imogene violated her probation by leaving the state and coming back to Arizona to see her children.

In principle that should have meant more jail time for Imogene and probably a revolving door of pimps and prisons. But the authorities cut her some slack. They gave her one last shot at the DIGNITY Diversion plan and a chance to clear her prostitution record, which was still on the books. A chance, too, to clear up her life.

In November 2008, when she was twenty-nine, Imogene restarted the Diversion program she had abandoned as a headstrong nineteen-year-old. "I knew that I had done wrong, that I had messed up, but I was still in denial," she says. She was struck by Lois Lucas's firm but forgiving stance. "Anywhere else, people would point fingers at me. I still felt ashamed," Imogene says. "Here I was able to open up and speak about my pain. If I had something to say, I said it. They let me know that if you are feeling it, how can it be wrong to let it out if that is what you feel. And that really made a difference to me."

Imogene had grasped the central lesson that DIGNITY tried to teach the women who came through its doors, that what they had done did not define who they are. Or as Imogene put it, "They made me feel that I could be who I was and deal with my past at the same time."

Today, Imogene proudly shows off pictures of her four beautiful girls, all decked out with ribbons in their hair and prim and proper white dresses. She rubs her large belly—a fifth child, also a girl, is on the way. She worries about patterns repeating themselves. She never knew her father, none of the men who fathered her children are around, and her own daughters are growing up on the same tough streets that dragged her into trouble. "A lot of things I did in the DIGNITY program will help me talk to my kids," she says. "Because I know that I will have to tell my kids one day what I've been through. They are going to ask me. And I want to let them know that this is what can happen to them."

More than six hundred young women like Imogene have successfully completed the Diversion program since 2004. Only 11 percent of the women who finished fell back into prostitution.

. . .

THE TEDDY bears are everywhere. Near one bed, a plush brown one clutches a sign that reads LOVE MY VALENTINE. A pink bear sits on a second bed, and next to the third bed lies a big white one sporting a red kerchief.

It's as if the women are trying to hold onto the children of whom they have long lost custody. Or perhaps they are trying to clutch onto a safe childhood they never had.

The room is on the second floor of a cottage on a quiet residential street nestled near the foothills of the Phoenix Mountain Reserve. There are ten beds in all here and five more at another location, part of DIGNITY's residential program that offers a few lucky women shelter for up to a year and a chance to rebuild their lives. Along with street outreach and the Diversion program, it's the third pillar in DIGNITY's support system.

In the small garden out back, birds chirp next to a brown swing surrounded by white flowers and a small brick wall. The women call it their "meditation place." On the kitchen table there is a jar of jelly beans and a tray of fresh oranges. A wooden mobile over the door has an engraved message: YOU CAN DO ANYTHING YOU WANT.

Despite these outward signs of tranquility, the DIGNITY house, like its sister Diversion program, is no vacation spot. It is tough to get in and just as tough to stay. Prospective residents must agree to a year-long commitment and a strict lifestyle contract. There are no drugs, no alcohol, and no intimate relationships allowed while in the program. For the first month, the women cannot even have telephone contact with friends or family. "This is a time for them to work solely on themselves and their issues," says Rachel Irby, the program's manager. "The whole purpose of the first thirty days is to stabilize the women." Irby knows about the need for stability; after watching her mother unravel in a spiral of alcohol and prostitution, she devoted her life to working in the toughest arenas of community work, from juvenile detention centers to rehab programs.

Most of the residents are battling some form of drug addiction. In their first ninety days of residency, they have to attend ninety meetings of Alcoholics Anonymous or a similar twelve-step program. But the program recognizes they face other dependencies. "They have this other addiction where they freeze themselves off, so they learn not to feel," says program founder Kathleen Mitchell. "Because they can't feel and continue the life that they are living. It's called protective denial—and if you don't do that, you won't survive out there." That's why the women at the halfway house also attend weekly sessions of a Prostitutes Anonymous program. Just as the addict seeks refuge and escape in a drug, prostituted women are dependent on their pimps, desperate for the love and affection they feel they lack, and suffering from low self-esteem and even self-loathing.

After their first month, residents have to go job hunting. Most have no social security cards or even birth certificates, so the DIGNITY team gets them the proper paperwork and helps them prepare job resumes. In return, the women pay 30 percent of their income from work for rent and contribute one hundred dollars a month for food.

The discipline and demanding schedule pay off. Since the DIG-NITY shelter opened its doors in 1996, over 130 women have found a haven there, while a remarkable 82 percent of them were drug-free and out of prostitution a year after leaving the program. You can see the success in women like Dawn, a veteran of more than two decades on the street who now works as a case manager at the shelter. At thirty-nine she still bears the traces of the beauty that prompted one man to tell her when she was a teenager that she was "sitting on a gold mine." Her light auburn hair falls just past her shoulders. She has a sharp nose and chin, fine eyebrows, and large gold rings dangling from her ears.

The man with his eye on Dawn's "gold mine" was her mother's boyfriend. When she complained to her mother that he was sexually molesting her, it was Dawn who got tossed out of the house. She survived in small-town Illinois with a string of gigs at strip clubs and turning tricks for weed. By her early twenties she had degenerated into what she calls a "bag whore," selling herself cheap for a hit of coke and a place to sleep.

Kathleen Mitchell's faith in her and DIGNITY's strict program saved her; now Dawn is returning the favor, hoping her experience will give her enough "street cred" to impress the newer residents at the halfway house. "Unless you actually walked down that street with me and did what I did, I was not going to listen to you," she says, understanding how recovering prostitutes feel. "I went from the very top of the game to selling my ass for less than ten bucks of heroin. But I picked myself up. So there is hope."

DIGNITY estimates it gives hope to about nine hundred women a year through its street outreach, Diversion, and residential programs. At least one-third of those are minors, though the percentage is probably higher because that figure includes only the girls who openly admit they are eighteen or under. The staff members make regular visits to the local juvenile detention center and county jail to speak to the girls there. The "Ho Van" continues to encounter frightened teens on the street. But there is no place to house any of the prostituted children who want help; at the moment, the halfway home is for adult women only.

The DIGNITY team drew up a detailed plan for a special safe home just for children, but it's an expensive undertaking that has to be licensed and staffed twenty-four hours a day. As DIGNITY waits for funds, so do Phoenix police officers who find the number of prostituted minors on the streets is mounting steadily. "The police desperately want us to open a house for children," says Rachel Irby. "They promise us they can keep the beds full year round."

Saving the youngest "starfish" would fulfill a long-held dream for Kathleen Mitchell, but others would have to take charge of making it a reality. Almost twenty years after she created the DIGNITY program in the Durango County Jail, Mitchell officially retired in June 2007. "It's truly been a miracle to watch these women transform their lives," she said when Catholic Charities made the formal announcement.

But Mitchell was not the kind of woman to retire from a fight. She moved back to the Twin Cities of Minneapolis–St. Paul, where she grew up, and found yet another outlet for her energies and expertise— helping an old friend and colleague, Vednita Carter, run one of the most successful rehab programs for prostituted children in the country.

. . .

IN THE distance, sunlight reflects off the white dome of the State Capitol building in St. Paul, illuminating it in a yellow glow. But just a mile away, on the desolate stretches of University Avenue, the colors lean more to gray and brown. Here in the rough-and-tumble neighborhood historically known as Frogtown, the small homes fronted by clumps of scrub grass are separated by car repair shops and cheap Asian restaurants. At night, the streets and alleys turn into well-traveled tracks for prostitutes of all ages.

Four evergreens stand like sentinels outside a faded gray and white clapboard house with a small bay window and a shaded porch. There is no sign on the door, but most of the women walking the streets of the Twin Cities know that this is the headquarters and drop-in center of Breaking Free, Vednita Carter's activist group that is dedicated to unshackling what she likes to call the "invisible chains" of prostitution.

The black wrought-iron grate on the front door keeps clanging with the constant traffic of people going in and out. Inside the cramped first-floor offices, the phone on the receptionist's desk never stops ringing. On the wall near the door there is a poster for an "endangered runaway" named Rachel, a sixteen-year-old suspected of being in the area. Pictures of demonstrations and rallies against local pimps and their nightclub party events are pinned up on a billboard.

About 30 percent of Breaking Free's clientele are court-ordered cases, women directed here in lieu of jail. The rest are walk-ins or referrals from the city's teeming drug treatment clinics and battered women's shelters. "This community here is mostly African American," Carter says, sitting behind a cluttered desk in an office filled with books, awards, and antitrafficking posters. "The FBI reports that African American women and children have the highest statistics for prostitution. We are the first target."

In an office across the hall, Kathleen Mitchell, who met Carter back in the 1990s when they were both starting out as activists, is busy typing e-mails. She helps lead group counseling sessions here for the young women while still finding time to keep in touch with her DIGNITY team back in Phoenix and a network of supporters across the country.

Surviving on money from foundations and government grants, Breaking Free may have only five full-time staff members, but it supplements their efforts with energy from more than eighty volunteers who come from all walks of life. They are teachers and social workers, members of churches and small business owners. A neighborhood baker has just dropped off two cartons filled with loaves of bread and buns. Two women from a church group come by with a box of new and used purses to hand out to the women.

Breaking Free can barely keep up with the demands on its services. Forty percent of the women of all ages who were coming through their door were homeless, but there were fewer and fewer beds for them. The serious recession that started in 2009 led to government cutbacks in already threadbare services. "They've been closing youth shelters in Minnesota because there's no money," she says. "That just means more girls are likely to get involved in prostitution."

So Breaking Free struggles to cope as best it can. It runs the House of Hope halfway home; a second, longer-term residence; a street outreach program to give food and information to women working the tracks; a monthly "john school" to educate men arrested for solicitation; and, at its core, the busy drop-in center on University Avenue. The women come from all over and at all hours of the day. They come for a bite to eat, some new clothes, some fresh toiletries, and, for those who are ready, some counseling and a chance to escape a life of selling their bodies. Breaking Free is not in the charity business. It's in the change business.

"Most women enter this program in a state of extreme crisis, often lacking basic needs such as shelter and food and in need of immediate medical attention," explains Carter, who has lost none of her political fire. "Once the emergency conditions are dealt with, the women begin a twelve-week intensive education group to examine prostitution as a slave-based system and issues related to addiction and recovery."

They call it the "Sisters of Survival," or SOS for short. Breaking Free runs several SOS groups a week at its drop-in center and at various women's shelters and drug rehab programs across the city. Kathleen Mitchell leads one of the weekly Tuesday sessions. "I'm not here to tell you what to do," she tells the half-dozen young women sitting around the table one summer afternoon in a small meeting room at the Breaking Free headquarters. "I'm going to give you some options, and whether you take that or not is going to be up to you."

Vednita Carter decides to sit in on this session, cradling in her arms the newborn baby of one of the girls in attendance, a nineteen-year-old named Fanny. The teenage mother has a sharp and vibrant face framed by thin, elegant eyebrows.

"I was with another girl," she begins, describing how she got lured into prostitution. "She had a walk-in closet full of clothes and all these diamonds. She always had at least $2,500 in her purse."

Her eyes open wide as she reenacts for the women how she gazed into the cash-filled purse of the prostitute trying to recruit Fanny for her pimp. "How do I jump in?" she recalls asking. "How do I get a piece of that?"

"Yeah, show me how I can get that too!" pipes in Cynthia, another young girl sitting across the table. "I grew up in a suburban home. I was sick of living this preppy, goody-goody life. I just snapped. I figured if I was going to have sex, might as well get paid and not do it for free."

Several other women nod, recognizing themselves in Cynthia's story. "But then one day I woke up and said, 'This is disgusting,'" she continues. "You get so addicted, it's hard to stop."

Mitchell interjects gently. "But you two have something going here," she says, pointing to Cynthia and Fanny. "You're strong women, you're getting out early. There is nothing weak about either of you."

Fanny's face grows dark. "They don't tell you at first what you're really getting into," she says. "It's really easy to recruit somebody by just glorifying it."

Carter chooses this moment to join the discussion, telling the young women how she was recruited into the stripping and sex industry as a naïve girl back in the early seventies. "The ads said 'Dancers needed.' I didn't read anything about stripping," she says. "If they had put in that detail maybe I would have thought differently about it.

"But we're never told the truth. And there is a reason for that—this is a multibillion industry," she continues, her voice gathering the force of conviction. "If you tell women you are going to be screwing somebody seven to ten times a day, any way he wants it, any way he likes it, that's ugly. That's evil. If maybe we heard that, it might make a fourteen- or a fifteen-year-old think differently.

"But you never hear it like it really is," Breaking Free's founder concludes, still holding Fanny's infant in her arms. "It's all about telling lies. It's a big money-making industry."

That evening, Joy Friedman, Breaking Free's program manager, takes over for a longer-running SOS group for those who are close to finishing their twelve-week course. It's a more intense, no-holds-barred session with women who have grown comfortable talking about their past lives and future hopes. A big, garrulous survivor of seven years on the mean streets of St. Paul, Friedman booms out her message with the force of a drill sergeant. "You can't give up. It took a powerful woman to endure what you did, the murders, the beat downs," she declares. "That's what it's going to take, that same attitude to pull yourself out of this garbage. What are you willing to give up for the betterment of yourself? This is about you deserving better."

While it was true girls did not "choose" to become prostitutes, it was also true that once they sought help and understood the alternatives before them, they did have tough choices to make. They could break free.

There are eight women around the table on this evening: one Hispanic, three African Americans, and four Caucasians. Six of them say they started turning tricks in their teens, four of them as young as thirteen and fourteen. "After a while you realize that I'm out here earning all this money and my pimp gets it all," says Becky. She and her sister, both teenagers, were reported as runaways from nearby Forest Lake when officers found them working for a hustler in St. Paul. Instead of charging them, the vice cops, who work closely with Breaking Free, brought them here for counseling and support. "I was just blessed by getting busted," says the younger sister, Trish. But Becky's voice catches when she talks about "the hurt that it caused my family, having to lose the ones that you love." Now they are both struggling to stay straight in a world that does not take kindly to ex-prostitutes.

"It's hard out there trying to get a job with a criminal record," says Cecilia, a Hispanic woman with a thick mane of curly hair. She talks about filling out job applications and waiting for the call back that never comes, until the phone rings and she sees that it's one of her "regulars," a former customer. "You know what he wants, you know what you can get from him, and sometimes you rationalize," she admits. "You say to yourself, 'I need that money to put food on the table.'"

The other women smile in sympathy and solidarity. They talk about the difficulty in finding housing and share tips on the best places to look, through the names of sympathetic landlords provided by the local AA group, or through private listings rather than corporate rental agencies that conduct more rigorous background checks.

"It's scary when you try to let go of your past," Friedman tries to assure them. "The panic sets in. Not knowing what to expect can be a barrier to people crossing over to a new life. But you have got to get out of the old to live in the new. You can't live in both worlds."

The discussion turns to how they were drawn into the world of prostitution in the first place. "The excitement, to be somebody," says one. "You watch TV and it's glamorized," says another. "In the strip bars, that's what you get caught up," adds a third.

But whatever excitement and glamour there is soon dies. "This is the saddest thing that's ever going to happen to anybody, let me tell you," says Sally, a black woman with short, straight hair. The room falls silent for a moment as each woman seems to retreat into her memories of pain and loss.

"You think you're going to get that Gucci bag, but all you end up with is a free case of gonorrhea," says Cecilia to an appreciative outburst of loud laughter and clapping. "They don't tell you the bad side."

Andrea, a pretty twenty-one-year-old in blue hospital scrubs with blond hair neatly pinned back, nods in agreement. "Yeah, the dirty nasty tricks," she says. After beginning to turn tricks in her teens, she had her first child two months shy of her sixteenth birthday and her second just two weeks before she turned nineteen. Now expecting her third child, she has come to the meeting straight from her training as a medical assistant. She hopes to graduate in a few months and then study to become a registered nurse, and she carries herself—and her growing belly—with the confidence of someone who has begun to put the pieces of her life back together. But tonight something bothers her.

She looks at Friedman hesitatingly. "How old do you have to be to come here?" she asks.

"I've had a twelve-year-old walk into my office," the program manager replies.

"Because I'm worried about my sister," Andrea says. "She's sexually active, and she's doing a lot of things I did before I got into prostitution." She tells the group that Cassandra, her fourteen-year-old sibling, has started running away from home, flirts with older men in chat rooms on the Web, and once even arranged for a man in his forties to pick her up after school. "She's on the same road that I was on," Andrea continues. "I learned the hard way. And I don't want her to make the same mistakes."

Under gentle prodding from Friedman, Andrea reveals her troubled family background. A mother addicted to crack. Six children spread across four different foster homes. A stepfather who sexually assaulted her from the first through the sixth grade. Although she told her mother what was happening, she wasn't believed.

"How did that make you feel?" Friedman asks.

"Horrible," admits Andrea. "She wasn't a mother when she needed to be. I was angry. I kind of blocked it out."

Andrea recounts how she kept silent until she discovered her stepfather was also sexually abusing another younger sister. Then she told a school counselor. Friedman asks Andrea if she has tried to find out if Cassandra was also a victim.

"No," Andrea answers firmly. "She's so much like me I'm scared to ask her."

"Why?" Friedman pushes. "Are you scared she'll tell you the truth?"

"Yeah."

"And you don't want to know because you weren't there to protect her?"

"It frightens me," Andrea admits. "Because I know what I've been through."

"But did you make it out?" Friedman asks, seeing a way to turn this around.

"Yeah."

"And you're doing OK today," Friedman continues. "So maybe we can intercept her now before she starts going completely buck wild, before she ends up where you did."

"But she's also at that age when she's so hardheaded," Andrea insists. "So do I let her just go and wait until that point before I need to intervene?"

"OK, but what if that point is now?" Friedman pushes back firmly. "If she doesn't feel she has a place to talk, people are going to feed on her shame and tap into it because she has no place to let it out. If she is so much like you, you might be the safest person for her to trust. Because you've been through it."

Andrea nods and tells the group how much Breaking Free has meant for her. "Meeting other people and hearing their stories, hearing what other women have gone through," she says as she looks at each woman around the table. Then she says the words that seem to sum up how many of her newfound sisters of survival feel: "Just knowing I wasn't alone."

■ ■ ■

FOUR TIMES a year, about seventy women who found the courage and the wisdom to successfully complete the Sisters of Survival program invite friends and family (and even the occasional probation officer or cop) to a graduation ceremony at the local Martin Luther King Center or a nearby church. Complete with black caps, gowns, and diplomas, it's a special evening for many.

"A lot of the girls have never graduated from anything," says Joy Friedman. "It's a really beautiful thing to see."

Leslie is one of the graduates of Sisters of Survival who soaked up everything Breaking Free has to offer and managed to turn her life around in record time. In little over a year, she went from being busted in a major dope and prostitution ring to finding refuge and redemption.

At five feet, six inches, with shoulder-length curly blond hair and brown eyes, she is, by her own admission, "what every guy wanted." Her story is much like that of many middle-class girls pushed into prostitution by circumstance and crisis. Her mother died when she was ten, and her father, while loving, was very strict. In the summer before her senior year at high school, she started smoking dope. Soon she was using meth. By spring she was snorting coke but still somehow managed to graduate; within a week of finishing high school, she moved out of her father's house and into the crack scene. After running out of money and drug dens to crash in that fall, she met a handsome forty-year-old man who offered her a place to stay in exchange for prostitution. She took it. "I chose the bed and the food and the shower every day," she says.

Posting ads on Craigslist and other Web sites, Leslie pulled in a thousand dollars a night for her pimp. "I got extremely intrigued by how much money I could make," she says. "I still wanted to be addicted to something."

Her pimp let her operate out of a hotel room instead of on a street corner. She had a car, a house, a cat, and a dog—enough to fool herself into thinking life was good. But her pimp was also a big-time drug dealer, and when he got busted in a major federal raid in the spring of 2008, she was taken down as well because the house where he stored many of his drugs was in her name. The cops told the frightened girl she faced twenty years in prison. Instead she struck a deal and agreed to testify before a grand jury. She knew that turning against her pimp ran the risk of getting her killed, but that chance sounded better than the certainty of being locked up in prison until she was forty.

"I don't know how to live on my own without prostitution," she admitted to the cops. They took her to Breaking Free. As luck would have it, a space had opened up in the House of Hope, the halfway home that was dedicated to the memory of Sergeant Jerry Vick, the vice cop who worked so hard to get young girls off the streets of

St. Paul. It was that stability of a safe place to live combined with the shake-up she got at the sometimes grueling sessions of the Sisters of Survival that helped Leslie turn her life around.

Leslie fancied herself superior to the women forced to walk the tracks because she was living what she thought was the more pampered existence of a high-priced call girl. "I was doing it 'the right way,'" she says. But the Breaking Free counselors managed to shatter those illusions. It was, she says, "one of those 'holy crap' moments," an epiphany that cut through the lies she had been telling herself. "They had to pry some of this stuff out and show me what my life was really like, because you get so brainwashed," Leslie says.

In the spring of 2009, she started her first semester at Metro State University while holding down a job as a front desk clerk at a local hotel. It's a long way from where she started, but she clings to the security that comes with living in housing provided by Breaking Free. She pays a portion of her rent from her earnings, but she also knows if she loses her job, she won't be evicted. If she were living on her own, she might be tempted to make ends meet the easy way.

"If I run out of money, I know how to get it fast—and I'm good at it," says the young woman who has been out of the sex trade for just a year.

Leslie has broken free, but she understands there was always the temptation to slip back into the life she once knew, the constant tug-of-war between both worlds.

■ ■ ■

"WHY AM I still in love with my pimp?" the girl in the counseling group asks plaintively. "I know he's wrong."

"I'm his investment, his way of making money," says another. "I didn't have options."

Rachel Lloyd, the founder and leader of GEMS, tries to give options to the teenagers gathered around her in a circle, who are caught in the struggle all girls fleeing prostitution face, between their past and their future. She wants them to look forward, not back. "Who are you going to be in your life?" she asks. "You know you're destined for something better, even if it gets blurred at times. God didn't put you on this earth to work the track."

The scene is from a remarkable documentary, *Very Young Girls*, which chronicles the struggles of a handful of exploited teenagers who came to GEMS for help. Working closely with Lloyd, a film crew followed her on the streets, in group counseling sessions, in tearful one-on-one sessions with girls trying to break away from their pimps. "Our primary competition is pimps," Lloyd says. "One hundred and ten percent of their time is devoted to recruiting and brainwashing and getting these girls back."

With favorable reviews in the *New York Times* and other prestige publications along with wide distribution by Showtime and NetFlix, *Very Young Girls* went a long way to breaking the public's stereotypes about prostitution and the girls caught in its web. It did so without sugarcoating the problem. The scenes of the girls' street life were gritty and unrelenting. A few of the girls, desperate for money or affection, slip back into prostitution. A girl named Shaquana tells of barely surviving her two years on the street, starting at age fourteen. The film shows the aftermath of a horrible beating she suffers, her face blue and swollen. Shaquana finds not just shelter and solace with GEMS but a new mission in life, becoming—much like a younger Lloyd did after her dangerous years in the life—an outreach worker trying to help other girls. The movie and the political campaign GEMS built around it were typical of Lloyd's in-your-face approach to politics and publicity. "If we just framed it as 'rescuing children,' people would give us more money," she says. "I could put pictures of little scared blond kids on our Web page. But this isn't about rescuing a child from a bad situation. This is about what we, as a culture and a society, are creating; why can this be perpetuated within our society?"

In fact, Lloyd was bothered by the very term "rescue." "We stop short of using the word," she explains. "Sure, initially in a practical sense there may be an element of rescuing a child from a pimp. But if you stay there, if you treat the girls as so damaged and traumatized, they're always ashamed about what happened to them. They never learn the power of their own voice."

Helping young girls find the power of their own voice is what GEMS is all about. Lloyd calls it survivor leadership, and it is what sets GEMS apart from many other community or charity groups. "Sure, we all need clothing and housing and the basic necessities," says Lloyd. "But what's important is not to stop there. What's important is to make sure that this is about empowerment."

You can see that power when the GEMS girls take to the streets for their outreach program, talking to other young girls in detention centers, group homes, and jails. "It gives them a face behind the story," says one of the GEMS survivors, explaining the impact she can have when talking to a girl who might otherwise ignore any advice about the dangers of prostitution. "We know the game and how it's played. We know how they talk, how the pimp manipulates their mind."

You could sense that power when the GEMS girls rallied every year in the streets of New York for the annual Day to End Sexual Exploitation of Children and fought hard for the passage of the Safe Harbor Act, which inspired legal changes across the nation. "They were at the forefront of advocacy for the law," Lloyd says with an almost motherly pride. "If it wasn't for their testimony and their perseverance we would be nowhere on this."

Lloyd's commitment to empowering her GEMS team grew out of her experience as a survivor. As she started to get more involved in the anti-trafficking movement, people would come up to her after a speech or a presentation at a conference to comment, almost with surprise, on how "articulate" she was. Lloyd bristled at the backhanded compliment. "There were these stereotypes and misconceptions out there about survivors that we were kind of doomed to always be victims," she says.

For Lloyd, empowerment was not simply a beneficial aftereffect of helping young girls rebuild their lives; it was central to that recovery. "You begin to feel stronger and bolder," she says. "Your voice is important, what happened to you is important. You begin to discover that you have talents and abilities, and you begin to feel like a whole person. The sexual exploitation you experienced becomes integrated into your whole personhood, but it doesn't define you. That's a big step toward your freedom."

GEMS's message and its methods were drawing attention and requests for aid across the country. Lloyd was contacted by organizations and people looking for training and assistance in San Diego, San Bernardino, Miami, Tampa, Indiana, Ohio, Portland, Oakland, Connecticut, and Philadelphia. To build on its success, GEMS set up a "Council of Daughters" with such luminaries as Hollywood star Halle Berry and singer Beyoncé Knowles as a "national network of women and girls working to protect and empower girls who have been victims of commercial sex exploitation." The Council would aim to strengthen laws to protect victims, fight for services, and bring the issue to schools, offices, and places of worship. In July 2009, the campaign got a huge boost when Beyoncé welcomed GEMS girls backstage at her New Jersey concert. Sinead O'Connor planned to record a song to help the cause. Halle Berry pitched in with a passionate letter to try to raise awareness—and money—for the cause:

> Today in New York City, a girl will flee an abusive home, only to be approached by a pimp-trafficker who will promise her love and protection. He will not deliver on these promises. Instead, he will assault and degrade her, and later sell her repeatedly to johns.
>
> I have never met this girl, but she is my daughter.
>
> In Chicago, a girl will have her picture taken and posted on a popular social networking site, a virtual marketplace for johns interested in buying very young girls. Her pimp will force her to meet these johns in motels and brothels and apartments around the city, and will punish her mercilessly if she refuses.
>
> She is my daughter.

The girls of the street were no longer just somebody's daughters. They were everyone's daughters.

16

Making the Invisible Visible

THE PHONES never stop ringing. Children desperate for help, desperate for shelter, desperate for someone to talk to them.

At the National Runaway Switchboard (NRS) in Chicago, the oldest hotline of its kind in the world, volunteers field more than one hundred thousand calls a year. The NRS serves as the federally designated national communication system for homeless and runaway youth. The phones are staffed twenty-four hours a day, 365 days a year. The toll-free number is posted in bus terminals, homeless shelters, and schools across the country. And because even runaways can be plugged into the Web, the NRS has also built a presence online with Facebook, MySpace, and Twitter.

The runaway switchboard keeps the names of callers confidential, but it logs and categorizes every one. The statistics tell a disturbing tale, not just because the number of calls is up dramatically but also because the children on the other end of the line are increasingly in danger.

For starters, they're staying out on the streets longer. In 2010, the biggest increase in calls—a 37 percent jump—came from children who had been away from home for longer than six months. They are also getting younger. While most are still between fifteen and seventeen years old, the number of crisis calls from the very young—children under twelve—increased 89 percent since 2000. A runaway child does not have a lot of ways to survive on the streets. Panhandling will only get you so far; stealing has its own dangers. But the one thing a desperate girl on the run can sell is her own body. The NRS found that since 2000 there has been a 30 percent increase in the number of callers who confessed they had turned to the sex industry to survive.

The economic meltdown in America that began in 2009 and lingered into 2010 and beyond only made things worse. Desperate times make desperate people even more vulnerable, and the recession hit youth already at risk with a triple wave of woes. For girls trying to cling to some kind of life in already troubled families, there were more stresses, crises, and abuse at home as unemployment climbed. For runaways looking for alternatives before being forced into prostitution, there were fewer jobs. And for those already trapped in the life, the massive slashing of federal and state budgets wreaked havoc on what few resources existed to assist them. Little wonder then that over the past three years the NRS experienced a 200 percent increase in callers who identified the economy as the key factor in their plea for help. Calls from homeless youth doubled in 2010, and the number of "throwaway" children—kicked out of their homes or abandoned—rose by 21 percent.

"They are afraid, they are in trouble, they are traumatized," says Jennifer DiNicola, the NRS call center manager. She recalls a fourteen-year-old who phoned to report that she and her seventeen-year-old sister had been lured to a massage parlor after they ran away from their Texas home. In those kinds of cases, DiNicola trains her staff to delicately tackle the question of forced prostitution with the children at the other end of the line, without judging them.

"It's not open, it's hinted at," says Joanna Wozniak, a busy dancer with the Joffrey Ballet troupe who finds several hours each week to work the phones as a volunteer. "You can feel it in their voices."

One of the calls she took around noon on a spring day came from a seventeen-year-old girl who ran away from her Indiana home because her father's new girlfriend didn't like her. There was a hint that she was running from something worse.

"I can't go back home," she pleaded. "I can't."

Wozniak rifled through the thirteen thousand resources for runaways the NRS has collected in its database and found a shelter not too far from the girl.

"What if I go and they don't have a bed?" the teenager asked in a shaky voice.

"We'll find you something," Wozniak tried to assure her. "Call back, and we'll work on it until it is solved."

There would be another two to four hundred calls like that at the National Runaway Switchboard before the day was over.

. . .

BYRON FASSETT was one of the first cops to realize, as far back as the early 1990s, that the police had to understand the crisis of runaways if they wanted to stop juvenile prostitution. Now, almost two decades later, the Dallas police sergeant was finally beginning to see change across the country.

On the third floor of police headquarters where his High Risk Victims and Trafficking team is stationed, Fassett keeps a small hand-drawn card. The crayon coloring on the paper is jumbled and bright, a maze of blues and reds and yellows. Inside, in childlike writing, Felicia had written a simple message to the Dallas cops who saved her: *Please don't forget me.*

Not that Fassett and Detective Cathy De La Paz are likely to forget one of their most grueling cases. Two years after her pimp, Stephen Buggs, was sentenced to seventy-five years in prison for kidnapping and assaulting her, Felicia is coping as best she can. She left Texas to stay with an older sister who was, she complained, "too strict." The cops thought a strict but loving family was just was Felicia needed. She told them she had dreams of becoming a teacher, and within a year she had earned her GED, the General Educational Development test that is the equivalent of a high school diploma. "She's doing well," says De La Paz, who keeps in touch with the girl by e-mail.

But Fassett wanted to ensure that his team had learned from the ordeal Felicia endured during the trial. He told his officers to mount cases of such convincing weight that the pimps' victims would be subject to as few court appearances as possible.

That's what they did for Janet, a sixteen-year-old with long strawberry-blond hair. With both parents dead from drug overdoses, she had been forced to live with her grandparents until she ran away from abuse at the hands of her grandfather. By sixteen she was being prostituted out of hotels by a pimp named Anthony Dawn. Picked up by local police one day on the street with serious injuries to her face, she eventually admitted Dawn had beaten her. Using her testimony, recorded phone calls, and other evidence, Fassett's squad built an airtight case. Twice during court hearings, the defense lawyer told the judge he had recommended that his client plead guilty rather than go to trial because there was no way he could win the case. It was music to a cop's ear.

The convictions of pimps like Buggs and Dawn were becoming common practice in Dallas because Fassett had built a system to respond to and respect the girls on the street. According to prosecutor Tim Gallagher, who had been promoted to chief of the Organized Crime Division since prosecuting Buggs, his office was winning cases against more than 90 percent of the pimps arrested.

"Word is out on the streets for pimps that Dallas has become a tough place to work," says De La Paz.

What made her and Fassett even prouder was that three-quarters of the prostituted children rescued by the HRVT teams were identified not through vice arrests but from regular patrol officers. In other words, a new attitude was taking hold in the rank-and-file.

"We wanted to ingrain the protection of these kids into the system," Fassett says. Every Monday for three hours, he and De La Paz speak to a different group of officers as part of the department's official training program. It will take them two years to reach every person on the force.

But already they are seeing results. After the end of a particularly long shift, Fassett and De La Paz were about to leave police headquarters when the phone rang. A patrol officer was concerned. That morning, he had been on the scene when the police found the body of a young heroin addict in an abandoned warehouse. The homicide detectives had ruled it a drug overdose, but the beat cop was not so sure. He recognized the victim's name; she had been a runaway on the High Risk Victims list. "Her clothes were a mess; it just didn't look right," he told Fassett.

It was late, but Fassett and De La Paz called the police morgue only to find that a rushed autopsy had already been done and her body had been shipped out for the funeral. "Get it back," Fassett said. "We need to reexamine her for sexual assault."

Sure enough, a reexamination found contusions on the girl's knees and head, anal lacerations, vaginal tears, and foreign DNA. She had been savagely raped.

The HRVT team began reconstructing the last twelve hours of her life. The trail led to two young neighborhood thugs who had been feeding her drugs in exchange for sex. Their trial is pending. All because an alert beat cop saw signs of child prostitution.

"They don't call them 'whores' anymore," says De La Paz. "We have changed the face of the problem in the eyes of officers."

All their years of bucking the system, of fighting the prejudices and stereotypes, of getting the message out to the police ranks, are paying off. Says Fassett with the relief and the pride of a battle well fought: "We have built up an army one person at a time."

And that army may be growing across the country. In September 2010, Congress began debating the Domestic Minor Sex Trafficking Deterrence and Victims Support Act, introduced with the support of both Republicans and Democrats. Drawing inspiration from Fassett's program and Rachel Lloyd's successful battle to implement a Safe Harbor Act in New York State, the bill called sex trafficking "one of the most lucrative areas" for modern criminal gangs. Noting that "children who have run away multiple times are at much higher risk" of being exploited by pimps, the bill obliged the government to change the National Crime Information Center database—the main collection of crime data in the country—so that each child reported missing more than three times in a year would be automatically designated as an "endangered juvenile." It authorized $50 million in spending for

the changes, as well as for shelters and other treatment programs.*
The seeds that Fassett had planted years ago in Dallas now stood a
chance of spreading nationwide. "I'm amazed that what started out
in our police department as only a 'what if'—what if we treated these
runaways differently?—has translated into this much action," he says.
"When people tell me all the reasons they cannot do something, I tell
them this demonstrates that one or two regular cops *can* bring about
big change with just a single idea."

Determined to spread his message beyond the streets of Dallas,
Byron Fassett lectures at training conferences whenever he gets the
opportunity. At the annual Crimes Against Children Conference—
the largest child safety gathering for law enforcement in the country,
conveniently held in Dallas every year—several hundred people pack
his four-hour sessions to hear his story. They are FBI agents from large
cities and sheriffs from small towns, probation officers and prosecutors, social workers and child psychologists. With his Texas drawl
and shoot-from-the-hip criticism of police and court bureaucracy, Fassett has them laughing at the justice system's follies and crying at the
plight of girls like Felicia. He berates and pleads with them to wake
up to the crisis in their streets.

"We have to beat the pimp," he declares. "He has invested a tremendous amount of time and money in this girl. We have to want to
get this girl out of this life more than he wants to get the money out
of her. And that's a high threshold."

• • •

NO CITY has set a higher threshold for rescuing prostituted children than Las Vegas, but then no city has as many children to rescue.
According to statistics released by the police in the summer of 2009,

---

* Elsewhere, there were other signs that runaways were finally getting the attention they
deserved as potential recruits for prostitution. The National Conference of State Legis-
latures was considering new legislation on runaways to recommend to lawmakers that
would oblige people who work with children to report any youth believed to be involved in
prostitution. The American Bar Association, through its "Youth at Risk" program, called
for more money to track runaways and get them the services they need.

half of the pimps arrested in Vegas that year had underage girls in their stable. In the previous two years, the Vegas vice squad had arrested or detained nearly four hundred girls under the age of eighteen.

That battle takes its toll; many vice cops burn out after a few years of late-night calls and gut-wrenching encounters with the forgotten and abandoned children of the streets. Detective Don "Woody" Fieselman remembers his heart sinking when he saw the purse, one of many jammed into two storage drawers at the booking desk of the Las Vegas juvenile detention center where personal belongings of the arrested girls are kept. It was a sparkly little bag in gold and white, with a name tag attached by the property clerks. It belonged to Sandy, the fourteen-year-old who had been briefly recruited into Knowledge's pimping network.

"Son of a bitch," he muttered. "She's back in the game."

The purse gave off the dank smell of fake leather. Inside, Fieselman found a few condoms and a business card for a "CEO" of an "entertainment company"—in other words, her pimp. "You have hope for all these girls," Fieselman says. "She had a chance." Maybe she still had a chance to get out of the game. But if Sandy was going to be rescued again, other cops had to do it. In April 2008, Fieselman quit the vice unit after four and a half years and moved on to the outlaw biker squad. His partner Aaron Stanton left vice as well, after five years, going on to investigate political corruption.

Still, their tour of duty in vice was longer than most. And while good cops could leave vice and the streets, the streets and vice never left good cops.

"If you do it well, you have to be passionate about it," says Fieselman. "And if you are passionate about it, you stick with it for life."

Both he and Stanton stay in touch with several of the girls they once arrested. Fieselman gets e-mails from a girl named Debbie, who was fourteen when she started on the tracks and became addicted to heroin, just to let him know she has been "safe and sober" for the past year. He also sees one seventeen-year-old from New York regularly every time she flies down to testify against her former pimp. "He is really supportive," says Yolanda, who was lured to Las Vegas but got arrested before she got very far into the life. "To have a police detective talk with me with respect the way that he did, I appreciated that a lot."

"We care that they're out of the game and doing good things," says Fieselman's former partner Stanton. He stays in contact with Jill, the reluctant teenage witness whose long spell in detention helped finally turn her against her pimp. From her new home in Idaho, she keeps him up-to-date on her new life

At twenty-one she had a baby she put up for adoption because she didn't think she could raise the child by herself. It's an open adoption, so she gets to see the infant on a regular basis. She enrolled in business classes in college, hoping to get an accounting degree. A different horizon for the girl who once could not see past the neon lights of the Vegas Strip. "I am really excited," Jill says. "I turned my life around."

■ ■ ■

THOSE LIGHTS were still burning bright at 5:00 A.M. one Thursday in June when Gil Shannon started his patrol. Shannon was the exception—the Vegas vice cop who stuck it out. After more than a decade in vice, the sergeant, who for several years ran the vice unit's juvenile investigative team, was now back on the front lines, in charge of the undercover enforcement teams. Shannon walked through the casinos with an undercover female agent as they covered the center of the Strip. Another team worked the north end. "There are days when we walk miles," Shannon says.

In a red baseball cap, casual shirt, long shorts, and sneakers, he looked like a tourist, which was precisely the idea. It was the end of another long night of partying, and there was still plenty of action. Near the slot machines at one casino, he spotted a young woman in a slinky black sleeveless top, tight jean shorts, and white shoes. Her shoulder was tattooed with a red rose.

Shannon struck up a conversation, and within minutes the woman offered to join him in a hotel room upstairs for four hundred dollars. Shannon pulled out his badge, identified himself as an undercover cop, and brought the woman to booking at the casino security offices.

But he took time on the way to try some education. He pulled out a condom from her purse and pointed to the warning label that stated the prophylactic reduces but does not eliminate the risk of sexually transmitted diseases. "Do you know we've had five hundred girls here in Vegas with HIV?" he asked. The young woman, who was not used to any man, much less a cop, expressing concern about her health, simply shook her head in resignation.

After a couple more hours of cruising the casinos, Shannon and his enforcement teams moved to their vehicles, patrolling some of the better-known tracks off the Strip: Tropicana Boulevard, Fremont, Paradise, and Boulder Highway. Shannon was on the same route the previous Saturday when he spotted a petite girl walking on the sidewalk, talking on her cell phone. The other cops with him were not sure she was "working," but Shannon had a hunch. As he drove by and rolled down his window, she turned her head expectantly, ready for her next customer.

"Want a lift?" he asked.

She scurried into the car. She was in the eighth grade, she told him. Karen was her name, just two days out of school on summer vacation. And she immediately started talking sex, running down her price list. Even a veteran of the streets like Shannon was jarred to hear a fourteen-year-old talk so blandly about selling her body. When Shannon revealed he was a cop and took her to the detention center, Karen was emotionless.

In Judge William Voy's court the following Wednesday, Karen acted more like the child she was, playing with the handcuffs and chains around her waist, cracking her knuckles, and pouting so hard, her expression was like a baby's before it lets out a wail.

The eighth-grader already had a long arrest record for petty larceny and drugs. Her mother was a heavy drug user, her siblings were in foster care, and she had run away from her group home.

"Mom's not much interested in us," she told Voy.

"You giving up on her?" the judge asked.

"Yeah," the girl replied in a voice that suddenly made her sound a lot older than she looked.

"We're in limbo here," he said to the lawyers and probation officers in the courtroom. He was referring to Karen's case, but he could have just as well been talking about the entire status of juvenile justice in Las Vegas. He opted to detain Karen until the social workers finished their assessment, and there was talk of sending her to a youth care facility just outside Omaha, Nebraska. It was 1,500 miles away and offered no special program for prostituted children, but it was better than nothing.

Closer to home, the judge has not given up on building a rehab center for juveniles right in Vegas. Some help came in June 2009 when Nevada passed a special law allowing the courts to freeze the assets of pimps convicted of trafficking children, including their cars, homes, and safety deposit boxes. More than half the forfeitures would go to the district attorney's office to help prosecute other pimps, but 40 percent of the funds were to be directed toward the safe house Voy wants to build. It was a welcome gesture but still far from the stable funding he needs to make his dream of a secure sanctuary a reality.

Voy got another boost that July when Katie Couric and a CBS TV crew shined a national spotlight on "the lost girls" of Las Vegas and his crusade. "We are failing these children because we're failing to recognize the problem," Voy told her. But he also pointed out that at least Las Vegas has the courage to confront the problem many other cities are ignoring. "We get one jurisdiction that deals with the problem effectively, they just move them somewhere else. You need a concerted nationwide effort—you need national attention to this."

Voy showed the news anchor the lot on the outskirts of the city where he hoped to build his safe house. But it still stood empty, a refuge for prostituted children hardly a priority in a city that tries to sell itself as America's capital of sex and sin.

And there were always more girls to take care of. The number of juveniles who had come through Courtroom 18 since Voy opened his special court back in 2005 had topped four hundred. One Wednesday morning a pretty African American girl stood before him, her hair highlighted with a few streaks of blond and tied back in a small ponytail with a red elastic. It was the only sign of playfulness in the otherwise grim face and listless body of the fifteen-year-old repeat offender.

A drug user, she had been on the streets and in detention on and off now for months. Her latest arrest was for assault and battery. Her mother talked to the judge vaguely about "conflict at home." She had been bounced around from one home to another, living with an aunt in California, then staying with a cousin in Vegas. Perhaps her sister in Arkansas could take her in, her mother suggested.

"We'll have to look at some options," the judge said grimly, knowing there were few at hand. He set another court date and sent her back to juvenile detention.

"She does not listen to me," her mother complained. "She runs away."

A wayward daughter, perhaps, but it's her daughter nonetheless.

"Bye, honey," the mother said, hugging her child. The daughter sobbed quietly as she was led away.

The mother turned to Judge Voy. "She doesn't need to be here," she said.

"Jail?" the judge asked.

"No," she replied as she headed for the door. "Vegas."

■ ■ ■

LAS VEGAS was one of the cities targeted in June 2008 when, to mark the fifth anniversary of the creation of the Innocence Lost program, the FBI coordinated a national sting operation. Operation Cross Country led to the arrest of 356 people and the rescue of twenty-one children.

By October of that year, Operation Cross Country II had spread to twenty-nine cities, with 642 arrested and forty-nine children recovered, some as young as thirteen. In Las Vegas alone, FBI agents and local vice squad officers arrested forty-nine people and rescued a seventeen-year-old girl trapped in a child prostitution ring. Then in February 2009, another six hundred people were arrested nationwide and an additional forty-nine children rescued in the operation's third wave. In October 2009, Operation Cross Country IV led to the recovery of another fifty-two children.

"We have moved from backstreet alleys to criminal enterprises that treat children as another commodity for sale," said FBI Director Robert S. Mueller III. "Child exploitation has become a growth industry." The *Los Angeles Times* editorialized that the FBI sweeps "should end the illusion that this terrible crime happens only in other countries.... Trafficking [is] a homegrown problem, not a faraway phenomenon."

Yet there remained a reluctance to confront the scale of the problem—or even to try to estimate its size. When Congress authorized a massive $64.4 million spending bill to help children abused by sex offenders in December 2009, only $5 million was set aside for prostitution victims. The Department of Justice, meanwhile, had still failed to conduct a nationwide study on the domestic sex trafficking, even though Congress specifically authorized such a study in 2005.

"We're looking at resistance within the department, which never requested the funds to conduct the study," said Donna Hughes of the University of Rhode Island. "If they did, we might be close to having an idea of just how big the illegal commercial-sex industry is in the U.S. and the number of women and children victimized by it."

As always, it would fall to the foot soldiers to keep fighting, with or without the proper resources. At FBI headquarters in Washington, agents continued to expand the work Eileen Jacob started when she helped set up the Innocence Lost project back in 2003. Jacob had moved on to Jacksonville, Florida, but she had lost little of her passion to go after sex traffickers. In one recent case she investigated, a twenty-nine-year-old pimp named Marvin Leigh Madkins had recruited two teenage girls, fifteen and sixteen years of age, from Virginia with promises of an extravagant vacation in Florida. Once in Jacksonville, he forced them to service many customers a night, often recruited through Craigslist. A tip from a hotel security guard put Jacob on Madkins's trail. Both girls had the courage to take the stand against their former pimp in court. Prosecuted under the stiff federal trafficking statutes, Madkins in late 2009 was sentenced to fifty years behind bars.

"People still don't get the dynamics of why a child goes into prostitution," says Jacob, stressing the importance of training and education—not just for law enforcement but for teachers, school counselors, and other front-line workers. "When they understand what's at stake and how these girls don't have a choice, it's like seeing a lightbulb go off in people's heads."

A bright young FBI analyst named Jamie Konstas was one of those following in Jacob's footsteps at FBI headquarters. She helped put together the Innocence Lost database, designed to collect and track intelligence on pimps and their victims. It contained more than seventeen thousand entries from law enforcement agencies around the country, including not just arrest and conviction records but also biographical information, aliases, and physical descriptions.

The national database was accessible to any officer cleared to use the FBI's virtual private network, which is known as LEO (Law Enforcement Online)—a handy resource for local police trying to cope with a crime that crossed state and even national boundaries. Pimps migrated where the money went, from city to city. They trained their young victims to use different IDs. Konstas cites one case where a thirteen-year-old was arrested five times in different cities before police at last identified her as a juvenile.

"In many cases, we are all seeing the same people, we just don't know it," says Konstas. "The database sheds light on the crime. It brings in technology to put the pieces together, to help us build criminal enterprise–level investigations."

Better intelligence and better coordination with the prosecutors from the Child Exploitation and Obscenity Section of the DOJ were paying off. Better laws didn't hurt, either. The Adam Walsh Child Protection and Safety Act had created a new federal crime of running a "child exploitation enterprise" and doubled the maximum sentence for sex trafficking convictions from fifteen to thirty years in prison.

Like Knowledge in New Jersey and Stephen Buggs in Texas before him, pimps were finally being treated and punished not as the harmless hustlers they claimed to be but as the human traffickers they were.

• • •

IT WAS a sign of how far things had finally come: what went on largely unnoticed or ignored in the dark alleys, truck stops, and hotel rooms of the nation was at last being talked about openly in the corridors of power in Washington. For a few hours on February 24, 2010, the austere chambers of the U.S. Senate were given over to testimony before the Subcommittee on Human Rights and the Law with the clear and unambiguous title "In our Own Backyard: Child Prostitution and Sex Trafficking in the United States."

Not international trafficking. Not foreign girls from foreign lands. But American girls in America's backyard.

There were the usual platitudes at the Senate hearings. But even platitudes can help shine a light on a neglected problem. Republicans quoted the former president George W. Bush, who declared that "the trade in human beings for any purpose must not be allowed to thrive in our time." Democrats cited President Obama's ringing denunciation of human trafficking as "a debasement of our common humanity."

On a more concrete note, Wisconsin Senator Russ Feingold pointed out that the oft-cited figure of three hundred thousand children are at risk of becoming commercial sex workers underestimated the scale of the problem, "especially when you consider that many children living on the street—runaways, throwaways, and castoffs from the foster care system—remain unaccounted for in America.

"Left to fend for themselves, many of these young girls and boys quickly become vulnerable to abuse and exploitation," he said. "We need to protect child victims of sexual exploitation by ensuring that they are not treated as criminals."

It was, fittingly, the child victims themselves and their advocates who stole the show at the hearings. Shaquana, the young survivor turned GEMS activist who was one of the stars of the *Very Young Girls* documentary, told the Washington audience how at fourteen she had been "manipulated and physically abused to sell my body for a pimp that I hoped would one day love me.

"I was afraid and felt like everything I was suffering was always my fault," she said. "I was living in this big world, but I felt small and alone. I cried myself to sleep many nights."

Her story was far too typical, GEMS leader Rachel Lloyd explained to the politicians. Young trafficking victims in the United States "encounter social workers, cops, nurses in emergency rooms, judges and prosecutors, and community members who either treat them with scorn and disgust or simply look the other way.

"As a nation, we've graded and rated other countries on how they address trafficking within their borders and yet have effectively ignored the sale of our own children within our own borders," Lloyd said. "We've created a dichotomy of acceptable and unacceptable victims, wherein Katya from the Ukraine will be seen as a real victim and provided with services and support, but Keshia from the Bronx will be seen as a 'willing participant,' someone who's out there because she 'likes it' and who is criminalized and thrown in detention or jail."

Lloyd concluded by calling on the politicians to display the same courage the GEMS girls such as Shaquana had shown. "If teenage girls and young women who've experienced heinous violence and exploitation are able to take action and be change agents in fighting against commercial sexual exploitation and domestic trafficking, it begs the question: what are our local, state, and federal legislators and representatives doing?" Lloyd asked.

"I challenge you today to join our young women in ending the sale of children in our country."

In the following months, there were more glimmers of hope that the sale of children for sex in the United States was being addressed, or at least acknowledged. In June 2010, for the first time ever the United States included itself in the State Department's annual report on human trafficking. In August, Attorney General Eric Holder announced a "national strategy" to combat child exploitation, bolstered by the hiring of thirty-eight new assistant federal prosecutors. The nation's top lawman admitted sex crimes, including the prostitution of minors, were sharply increasing.

"Tragically, the only place we've seen a decrease is in the age of the victims," he said.

• • •

IN THE northeast corner of the American prostitution market that was Atlantic City, FBI special agent Dan Garrabrant was doing his best to end the sale of children by going after their sellers and buyers, one bad guy at a time.

By early 2010, he had helped bust yet another juvenile prostitution ring; a thirty-six-year-old man named Kasiem Brown pleaded guilty to sex trafficking: he had seven underage girls and nine adult women making money for him in strip clubs, at sex parties in private homes, and walking various tracks in and around Atlantic City.

The FBI by now had expanded its Innocence Lost initiative to thirty-eight task forces and working groups across the country. In the seven years since the program's inception, the FBI and its partners had rescued over eleven hundred children. The youngest was ten years old.

But the numbers are not what sticks in the mind of Dan Garrabrant. Rather, he sees the faces of the girls he tried to help, and the ones who got away. He remembers walking into a detention center to interview a sixteen-year-old runaway only to find her sucking her thumb. "You have this perception of what these girls are going to be like, and all of a sudden you see this very childlike behavior," he says. "She was just a kid."

Another time he was called out by the local police to meet a young woman working the streets. She was upset, not for herself but for a twelve-year-old who had just been sold to another pimp in Atlanta. "Can you help find her?" she begged him.

Garrabrant knows it is not uncommon for pimps to trade a troublesome girl to a fellow hustler for a few thousand dollars. He figured the girl may have been so young that her pimp feared she would draw too much attention, or she might have been resisting her new life and causing problems. Either way, the pimp who had recruited her did not want to lose on his "investment." Shipping her out of state was an easy solution.

The FBI tried tracking down the twelve-year-old. They had her real name; she had been reported as a runaway to the local police. The Bureau put her name into the National Crime Information Center, a computerized index available to federal, state, and local law enforcement twenty-four hours a day. But without the name of the pimp in

Atlanta or any other leads, there was little hope they would ever find her.

Both the setbacks and successes were what kept Garrabrant going. In the confines of his FBI field office, Garrabrant sifted through more files, typed out more search warrants, and answered more phone calls from local and state police who were always finding yet another juvenile on the street. "Child prostitution is the most overlooked form of child abuse," Garrabrant says. "Our job is to make the invisible visible."

And there would always be that one case, that one scrappy girl who had grown into a determined young woman, who would remain closest to his heart.

"Caught in Between Two Worlds"

Abused in the world of pimps, scorned in the other, Maria felt she was trapped. Long after her pimps had been arrested, convicted, and imprisoned, the girl from New Jersey was still being tugged in all directions. She wanted to escape a life on the streets but couldn't seem to find a way out.

"I was caught in between two worlds," she says.

She had been on the streets since 1999. Arrested in Vegas in 2003. Running for her life from her pimp Knowledge in 2004. "Renegading" in 2005. Stripping in 2006.

"I was at rock bottom," she says. "I was doing coke every single day. I would be working all night as a stripper and sleeping all day. I was looking at my life and saying, 'This isn't one.'"

FBI agent Dan Garrabrant remained her only lifeline. With the case against her pimps closed, there was no longer any official reason for the two of them to keep in touch, but once or twice a month his phone would ring. No longer cop and witness, their relationship had evolved into something deeper. If not a father figure, Garrabrant was a reference point, a center of stability in Maria's still rocky life. "I'm someone who always answers the phone and listens to her," Garrabrant says. "For Maria and for a lot of these young women, there aren't many people beside their pimp that have ever taken the time."

It was not exactly Bureau policy. "But you really have to make it personal," Garrabrant continues. "You can't be judgmental, because that's counterproductive."

For him, it had never been only about putting the bad guys away. He wanted to make a difference in Maria's life, although he was not so naïve to think he or anyone else could "save" her. Only she could make that decision, if and when she was ready. Garrabrant was careful never to get moralistic with her; "no judgments, not at all" was his guiding principle. At the same time he also made it clear he expected better for her.

"You know I worry about you, I'm concerned about you out there," he told her during one typical phone call. "You have got to do what you think you need to do, but you need to be careful."

"I know, I shouldn't be out here," she said. "I'm fucking up, and I don't want to be out here."

"Obviously you don't, because you're calling me," said the FBI man. "Call me if you want me find a program for you. Just let me know. Promise me that no matter what happens you'll stay in contact. Never feel like you can't call me."

■ ■ ■

MARIA WAS living through one of the fundamental rules of rehab: you have to hit bottom before you can begin to climb back up.

And by the summer of 2008, she was about as low as you could get. Broke. On drugs. And still in the sex trade. That was when she discovered she was pregnant; her on-again, off-again boyfriend was no longer around, but she was going to have a child. Alone.

Maybe it was the baby on the way. Maybe it was all those long talks with Garrabrant. Or maybe, at age twenty-two, she was finally ready for a change. Whatever the reason, Maria had begun to realize she needed to turn her life around. Or die.

"There was something different inside of me. I had something to live for," she said when she was three months pregnant. It was enough inspiration to make her stop doing drugs. Just like that. Cold turkey. She knew that her twelve-step recovery program was right there, growing inside her.

But now she had to try to get back what she had lost. Her years on the tracks meant that since age fourteen she had done none of the basic things teenagers and young adults do, like going to school and getting a job. If she was going to be a single mother, she needed to find steady employment. Most prospective employers ran a criminal check or at least asked about her background, and Maria, unfailingly honest, always confessed she had a long arrest record. After several months of job hunting, she landed a telemarketing post but quit after her first day because she was expected to sell phony computer services. "I don't like lying to people," she says, unaware of the irony in her statement, considering how many clients, pimps, and cops she'd had to fool over the years.

Maria had better luck with the next job she landed, at a local toy store. The manager liked her cheerfulness, and she liked the steady work, the first regular job she had held in her life.

When she was thirteen, Maria had been a keen student; now she dreamed of going to a local state college to study business administration. And after that perhaps a bachelor's degree in public relations. "I am good at talking to people," Maria says, then adds, with a teasing glint in her eyes, "I could sell myself, so I'm sure I can sell something else."

So Maria went back to school. While pregnant, she took her GED exam and scored an above average 600 out of 800 in math, sciences, social studies, and reading. But she failed the writing portion of the exam because she was stumped by a short essay assignment that asked students to "define problem solving." Here was a girl who had survived by her wits on the street for nine years, outwitted a powerful pimp, and escaped a deadly kidnapping attempt, and yet she froze when it came to writing about solving problems. "I wasn't going to put *those* examples on paper," she says with a laugh.

But she was serious about getting her GED. She took the writing section of the exam a second time. This time the essay question required her to "describe a person who has influenced your life." That was easy. Maria picked up her pencil and wrote about Dan Garrabrant. She didn't name him as a cop, much less identify herself as the former prostituted child he helped rescue. "I just called him a friend. A helpmate," she says. "A person who got me out of a situation where I thought I would have ended up dead." She passed. At age twenty-two, the young woman who had dropped out of high school as a teenager and ended up being trafficked by pimps now had a diploma. At last she felt she had a chance to make something of herself.

"I like the square world," she says. "Now I just want to be square. I don't want to be a ho."

· · ·

IN LATE April 2009, just two weeks shy of her twenty-third birthday, Maria gave birth to a healthy baby boy. "My son is my saving grace," she says as she cuddles him in a blue blanket, patting the newborn's silky hair. "I don't know where I would be without him."

Becoming a mother also brought Maria close to her own mother. For help with the first few months of child rearing, she moved back in with her parents. On a warm spring afternoon in their living room, her mother and father were busy pampering their daughter and their new grandson. "I've always had a good home," says the onetime runaway. "I think it's always been there, but I lost sight of it."

It was late on a Friday afternoon when special agent Dan Garrabrant dropped by to see the new mother and her child. Maria's parents greeted him as the welcome guest he has become over the years, the man who was always there to talk to them about their wayward daughter, to calm their fears, and to offer them hope.

With the practiced assurance of a father, Garrabrant took the wailing infant from Maria's tired arms. Swathed in his blue blanket and sucking furiously on a pacifier, the two-week-old grabbed on to the FBI agent's large hand with his soft fingers. Garrabrant gently mocked Maria about his magic calming touch as the baby stopped making a sound the minute the agent enveloped the child in his arms.

Then the conversation turned to, of all things, lactose intolerance. It appeared Maria's new baby might need milk substitutes, and one of Garrabrant's children had gone through the same problem. For the next little while they talked about the best price and preferred brand of lactose-free products for babies.

It was a remarkable change from five years earlier, when they sat facing each other for the first time: the tempestuous seventeen-year-old just back from Las Vegas throwing curses at the gruff FBI agent who was about to investigate a pimp named Knowledge. Now they swapped parenting tips. They had traveled far together in a battle that had scarred them both. Through the late-night calls, the arrests, the confrontations with pimps, and the soul-searching, they had come to trust and respect each other.

. . .

BUT MARIA'S past called out to her every day.

There was the lingering fear. She was frightened enough to ask Garrabrant how soon one of her former pimps, Tracy, would be out of prison. Not before 2013 at the earliest, he told her.

"I'm still scared," said Maria.

"Don't be," the FBI agent assured her. "Tracy has plenty of other things to worry about."

And there was the loneliness. When she tried to find new boyfriends, they never stuck around for long. "It sucks to have someone stop calling you and you know why they're not calling," she says. "They must have found out. Someone must have told them what I used to do."

People might respect the strength and courage of an ex-alcoholic or an ex–drug addict who had gone straight, but that admiration did not carry over to ex-prostitutes. Maria felt most people regarded her with disdain—once a whore, always a whore. "Everybody I talk to, when they find out what I used to be, they don't want nothing to do with me," she says. "They look at you like you're dirty."

Money especially remained a problem for a single mother who still dreamed of going to college. She had quit her job at the toy store to care for her baby. She needed to find a decent-paying job, a difficult task at the best of times, never mind in the middle of a recession, for a woman in her early twenties with no job experience and a criminal record.

Maria used to earn more in one hour in prostitution than she made in a week at a minimum-wage job. Her pimp pocketed the money, of course, not her. But the lure is always there. "All the time, I keep thinking I am going to go back to it," she says of her old life. "It would be so much easier if I just went out there and sucked a dick for a quick five hundred or six hundred dollars."

Finally, frustrated and depressed, she made a fateful decision. She would not go back to the tracks, to the world of the pimps, but the "square" world wasn't making life any easier for her and her newborn son. She compromised and went back to stripping.

"It sucks, having to take my clothes off," she told Dan Garrabrant. "I hate this shit, but I've got to feed my son. I have to be there for him."

Garrabrant, forever nonjudgmental, had seen what he called "this roller coaster" before, as young women tried to escape a life on the streets. He took comfort from the fact that Maria was staying away from drugs. "This is not about her, this is about her son," he says. "There's a sense of responsibility."

Maria, too, seemed to know that there was a better life out there for her, that maybe this was just a temporary setback on her road back. You could sense that in her determination to share her life story with other young girls who might be heading down the same path she took. She wanted to find a community group or a women's shelter where she could talk about her experiences with others.

"I would tell them about the times I almost died," she says. "How it feels to have a gun pointed to your head. I would tell them how it feels when you are having sex with a man who has AIDS and he's telling you not to stop and you think your life is over."

She would challenge the illusion the girls cling to that they are "choosing" a life with their pimp. "I'd tell them your choice is gone because you've been brainwashed to think this is the only way," she says. "You can't even make your own choices in life.

"Most girls have it much worse than me. They don't have a family to come home to," she explains. "And if you don't have a place to go home to, what else? That's all you see. Well, you think, *Maybe this guy really is helping me.* But in reality he is not helping you at all. He is only making you suffer."

Most of all, she would try to get the young girls to stop believing the myth their pimps are pushing. "I'd let them know that the man you think loves you doesn't really love you," Maria says. "He loves the money you make. And as soon as the money is gone, he's gone."

■ ■ ■

NOT FAR from the strip club where Maria has struggled to make ends meet, the weekend traffic begins to build up on the Black Horse Pike Highway. The cars speed toward the casinos along the same stretch of road where the bodies of the four prostituted women had been found three years earlier in a ditch.

In the distance, the towers of gambling, sex, and fun along Atlantic City's boardwalk shimmer against the setting sun. Out on the street or in an alley, stepping into a limousine or hanging around in the casino bars, she will be there.

The next Maria.

Another teenage girl who is running from a nightmare or has bought into the dream her pimp is selling.

Another child of the night. Somebody else's daughter.

Acknowledgments

THE BRAVE young women who had the courage and conviction to talk to me about their lives, their struggles, and their dreams were an inspiration. This book is theirs.

My work would not have been possible without the support and help of the staff at GEMS in New York, Breaking Free in St. Paul, and DIGNITY in Phoenix and especially their founders Rachel Lloyd, Vednita Carter, and Kathleen Mitchell, who opened their doors and their hearts to me. I urge you to visit their Web sites and support their work.

Other child rights advocates who assisted me include Lisa Thompson of the Salvation Army; Brad Myles of the Polaris Project; Michelle Collins, Kristen Anderson, and Stacey Urie at the National Center for Missing and Exploited Children; Lisa Goldblatt-Grace of My Life, My Choice; and Cathy Brock and Sam Quattrochi of the Letot Center.

The law enforcement officers named in this book and many others who went unnamed were generous with their time and patience, no matter how many times I kept asking them questions about their work, their frustrations, their triumphs, and their passion. I hope I have captured their dedication

Sue Betz at Chicago Review Press had the vision and compassion to believe in this story. It was her drive that made this book a reality, along with the work of project editor Lisa Reardon and copyeditor Gerilee Hundt. Elisia Bargelletti did many invaluable hours of transcripts.

The idea for this book began in a Washington restaurant when Drew Oosterbaan of the Department of Justice and FBI special agent Emily Vacher, who were both featured in my previous book on child predators, *Caught in the Web*, strongly encouraged me to take the next step and investigate the crime of prostituted children. Sharon Cooper, one of the country's most respected forensic pediatricians and a tireless fighter for the rights of children, prodded me not to give up despite the obstacles. I owe all three a debt of gratitude for their support.

My wife and fellow journalist, Lisa, stood by me as I worked on this project for more than two years. But, more important, she edited, commented, criticized, and cajoled until the manuscript met her high standards. I am blessed to have her as my partner in life.

I always welcome readers' comments and questions. You can contact me through my Web site, where updates to this story, along with interviews and articles, will be posted: www.juliansher.com.

Julian Sher

Resources for Help

To Report Child Prostitution

If you are a victim of commercial sexual exploitation or want to help someone who is, you can contact your local police or one of these national agencies:

**U.S. Department of Health and Human Services
(National Human Trafficking Resource Center)**
(888) 373-7888

**U.S. Department of Justice Trafficking in Persons
and Worker Exploitation Task Force Line**
(888) 428-7581

National Runaway Switchboard
(800) RUNAWAY (786-2929)

**National Center for Missing and Exploited
Children (NCMEC) National Hotline**
(800) THE-LOST (843-5678)

Help in the Community

If you or someone you know is trying to escape from prostitution or needs shelter, food, medical attention, or a sympathetic ear, here are some of the dedicated groups in several cities across the country:

GEMS
New York, NY
(212) 926-8089

Breaking Free
PO Box 4366
St. Paul, MN 55104
(651) 645-6557

DIGNITY
Catholic Charities
   Community Services
4747 North 7th Avenue
Phoenix, AZ 85013
(602) 285-1999

Children of the Night
14530 Sylvan Street
Van Nuys, CA 91411
(800) 551-1300

Sage Project
1275 Mission Street
San Francisco, CA 94103
(415) 905-5050

Veronica's Voice
PO Box 172472
Kansas City, KS 66117-1472
(816) 483-7101

Angela's House
395 Pryor Street, SW
Suite 1025
Atlanta, GA 30312
(404) 224-4415

My Life, My Choice Project
989 Commonwealth Avenue
Boston, MA 02215
(617) 779-2179

The Paul & Lisa Program
PO Box 348
Westbrook, CT 06498
(860) 767-7660

**Chicago Alliance Against
   Sexual Exploitation**
3304 N. Lincoln Avenue, Suite 202
Chicago, IL 60657
(773) 244-2230

Resources on the Web

Most of the community groups listed above have Web pages that not only describe their work but also offer links, educational resources, and ways you can support their efforts:

GEMS
www.gems-girls.org

Breaking Free
www.breakingfree.net

Children of the Night
www.childrenofthenight.org

Excellent research, educational, and academic resources are available from two of the country's leading experts:

Prostitution Research and Education
A nonprofit foundation set up by Dr. Melissa Farley.
www.prostitutionresearch.com

Donna Hughes—Women's Studies Program, University of Rhode Island
www.uri.edu/artsci/wms/hughes/

The following three agencies—the FBI, the Department of Justice, and NCMEC—cooperate to rescue prostituted children and stop the traffickers. Their Web sites provide statistics, legal information, news, and educational resources:

FBI Innocence Lost
www.fbi.gov/innolost/innolost.htm

National Center for Missing and Exploited Children
www.ncmec.org/missingkids/servlet/
  PageServlet?LanguageCountry=en_US&PageId=1501

Department of Justice, Child Exploitation and Obscenity Section
www.justice.gov/criminal/ceos/

In addition, these Web sites offer more information on domestic and international human trafficking:

Coalition Against Trafficking in Women—International
www.catwinternational.org

Polaris Project
www.PolarisProject.org

Global Centurion
www.globalcenturion.org
See especially the Human Trafficking Map at
http://globalcenturion.org/publications/articles/world-demand-hubs-for-
   trafficked-persons/

Salvation Army's Initiative Against Sexual Trafficking
www.iast.net/

ECPAT—End Child Prostitution and Trafficking
www.ecpatusa.org

U.S. State Department—Office to Monitor and Combat Trafficking in Persons
www.state.gov/g/tip/

An updated version of this list, with links, tips for parents, and additional resources, is available on the Internet at the author's Web site, www.juliansher.com/trafficking.

Sources

WHILE THE crime of prostituted children is often either unreported or treated in a sensational and insensitive manner, a handful of journalists across the country have done some excellent writing on this subject. I am indebted to the *Atlanta Journal-Constitution*, the *Chicago Sun-Times*, the *Chicago Tribune*, and Denise Dowling of Salon.com for their coverage of the Players Ball; Brian Hickey of the *Philadelphia City Paper*, Dennis Roddy of the *Pittsburgh Post-Gazette*, and Robin Erb of the *Toledo Blade* for their accounts of the murders of women; Ron Sylvester of the *Wichita Eagle* and Alex Tresniowski of *People* magazine for their reporting on the FBI's Stormy Nights operation; David Rosen of *CounterPunch* for his history and analysis of legislation and politics; Joseph Markman of the *L.A. Times* on the lack of beds for prostituted children; Mark Morris of the *Kansas City Star* on antitrafficking prosecutions; at the *New York Times*, Brad Stone for his coverage of Craigslist and Ian Urbina for a powerful series on runaways and follow-up reports on changing legislation; Sam Skolnik of the *Las Vegas Sun* and Bob Herbert of the *New York Times* for their columns on the city and its mayor; Jim Galloway of the *Atlanta Journal-Constitution* for his analysis of Georgia state senator Renee Unterman's battles; and Steve Peoples and the staff of the *Providence Journal* for their coverage of the battle to change Rhode Island's prostitution laws. Melanie Shapiro's senior honors thesis at the University of Rhode Island—"Sex

Trafficking and Decriminalized Prostitution in Rhode Island"—was an excellent guide to the history of laws in that state.

For a general overview of domestic sex trafficking, I relied on the insight and analysis of two of the country's leading researchers on prostitution, Melissa Farley and Donna Hughes. Their Web sites are listed in the Resources section, and readers who want to learn more should consult their work.

For statistics on the commercial sexual exploitation of children in the United States, several sources were useful including the 2009 *National Report on Domestic Minor Sex Trafficking* by Shared Hope International; the *National Incidence Studies of Missing, Abducted Runaway and Throwaway Children*, U.S. Department of Justice, October 2002; the annual surveys of the National Runaway Switchboard; *Female Juvenile Prostitution* by the National Center for Missing & Exploited Children, November 2002; and *The Commercial Sexual Exploitation of Children in the U.S., Canada and Mexico* by Richard J. Estes and Neil Alan Weiner, University of Pennsylvania, September 2001.

Index